DATE DUE

APR 0 1 02			

DEMCO 38-297

For Bob.
For being ahead of your time.
For knowing when to advise.
For knowing when to remain silent.

The Internet and Social Change

by Carla G. Surratt

McFarland & Company, Inc., Publishers
Jefferson, North Carolina, and London

Library of Congress Cataloguing-in-Publication Data

Surratt, Carla G.
    The Internet and social change / by Carla G. Surratt.
        p.   cm.
    Includes bibliographical references and index.
    ISBN 0-7864-1019-1 (softcover : 50# alkaline paper) ∞
    1. Internet—Social aspects. 2. Social change. 3. Social institutions.
    I. Title.
    HM851.S89   2001
    303.48'3—dc21   2001030695
                                                                 CIP

British Library cataloguing data are available

Manufactured in the United States of America

Cover image © 2001 EyeWire

*McFarland & Company, Inc., Publishers
    Box 611, Jefferson, North Carolina 28640
    www.mcfarlandpub.com*

Contents

Introduction

There is no shortage of pundits who will forecast the future of the information society. Much of their writing is based on extrapolation or slogans, neither of which is an effective guide ... [to understanding] how people and social institutions behave in response to current technology developments and what the effects of particular changes might be.... The ongoing computing and communications revolution requires serious social science investigation [National Resource Council 1998, 7].

In the span of approximately 30 years, the Internet has grown from a Department of Defense command-and-control network consisting of several dozen computers to a popular global network consisting of tens of thousands of nodes (linkage points) and spanning more than 200 countries. With a current (late 2000) estimated population of regular participants at around 195 million people, and a projected world population of around 500 million (by 2003), the Internet is becoming a near-ubiquitous presence not only in the military and research institutions where it got its start, but in schools, libraries, businesses and homes.

Starting with only four hosts in 1969, the Internet consisted of over 105 million hosts by the end of 2000. A big part of that growth resulted from the release in 1991 of the World Wide Web. In 1993 the Web consisted of a mere 130 sites; seven years later it boasted more than one billion.

What are all of these people doing on the Web and the Internet? Over half of regular participants use it for education, entertainment, work and shopping. About one third use it for communication. And nearly three quarters use it for personal information gathering and research. How are they doing this? By accessing, from home, workplace, school or library, an almost unlimited array of businesses, schools, libraries, and nonprofit and

1

government organizations. Of the 56 million hosts on line at the end of 1999, over 18 million (33 percent) were businesses. There were over 12 million "net" hosts, 5 million "education" hosts and over 750,000 "organization" hosts online, not to mention over 680,000 government hosts. The fact remains, however, that despite the explosive growth of the Net, particularly within the last ten years, we know surprisingly little about the social implications of computer mediated communications (CMC).[1]

In the early 1800s, what was to eventually become the modern day discipline of sociology was born. Modeled after the physical and biological sciences, sociology was an attempt by intellectuals of the day to use the scientific method to understand vast social upheavals with which they were confronted—the Enlightenment, political revolutions, the Industrial Revolution, and the rise of capitalism and urbanization. As David Karp, Greg Stone and William Yoels (1977) noted, "A profound shift in the basis of social organization attended the growth of cities in Western civilization during the 19th Century, with far-reaching consequences for institutional and personal life. Probably the most important advances in sociological theory have originated from the many different attempts made by social scientists and social philosophers alike to explain this fundamental transformation in the nature of the social bond" (5).

The central social and political theorists of the day, particularly Karl Marx, Max Weber and Emile Durkheim, were preoccupied with this transformation and devoted their lives to understanding its causes and implications. They sought to understand the interconnections among religious, political and economic institutions, and how fundamental changes in those institutions transformed the daily existence of the individual. It is important to note that two of the defining social trends theorized by present day sociologists, rapid technological change and the growth of cities, were largely ignored as agents of social change by the "founding fathers." Despite the fact that, in some form, the telegraph, the daily newspaper, the telephone, motion pictures and even radio (as a point-to-point rather than broadcast system) existed during their lifetimes, these theorists apparently saw little import in their implications for social organization.[2]

Further, though the growth of cities was, as noted above, a defining trend of that period, and though the city would later come to be seen as a discrete entity worthy of scientific study, none of these early theorists argued that the city per se was essential in explaining this transformation of the social bond. While the growth of the city and vast technological change may have been necessary conditions of these transformations, they were certainly not sufficient ones. Instead, these theorists sought broader explanations of these revolutionary changes, and in so doing, created the modern day field of Sociology. In fact, it would not be an exaggeration to state that the discipline as a whole today is predicated on these theorists' attempts to understand the forces of social change and what those changes mean for how we organize ourselves as a society.

Given this historical precedent, the state of research into what may potentially be an equally powerful source of social change, networked computing and the Internet, is curious on two accounts. First, surprisingly few sociologists have devoted themselves to research in this field. Most of what constitutes theory on the subject is derived from the fields of psychology and communications. Second, sociological research that is available focuses precisely on these areas considered irrelevant by the founding fathers: technology as an autonomous change agent and the role of physical organization (or place) in social organization.

As a cursory glance in any bookstore or library reveals, much of what passes for knowledge about the Internet is based on opinion and impression, not on social science theory or empirical investigation. Further, most of the research that is available is small scale, focused on select groups, dispersed across space and time to the point that meaningful synthesis is next to impossible, and constituted by a "media effects" framework for analysis in which the technology itself is imbued with the power to effect change (Ogburn, 1964). We do not have any overarching, macro-level theory simultaneously capable of unifying the knowledge gleaned from small scale studies and according human beings their rightful place as *the* agents of social change. How do human beings actually use this technology to transform the social world? Does the Internet alter our basic social institutions? If so, are these changes a matter of degree only, or do they truly represent a revolution—an overthrow of previous modes of organizing? Which institutions, public and private, are most significantly impacted by the Internet, and in what ways? These sorts of questions remain unasked and unanswered.

Like so many other students of the Internet, I began my investigations with research questions that centered on the nature of human community. What is community? Can community truly be established and maintained through online interaction? Or are there basic elements of such social bonds that only face-to-face interaction can sustain? In that sense, I and many others have begun precisely where Marx, Durkheim and Weber did before us—seeking to understand the social transformations taking place around us. But in so doing we have assumed that the Internet is a "revolutionary technology" and then concentrated our research efforts on understanding the Internet as a specific *type of place*. Its relative position in the larger processes of social change, its role as a medium of communication operating according to its own logic, has been ignored.

As I will discuss in greater detail in Chapters One and Two, this is, by and large, the same path taken by media studies and urban sociology. The discipline of media studies, since its birth in the 1930s, has centered on the "media effects" framework. In this framework, a core set of narratives has been developed to tell the story of technology. Each narrative describes the technology in question as an autonomous agent of social change. Most often, a medium is fashioned as a "revolutionary" tool that re-shapes the user's perceptions of space and time. The question as to how people use media to alter the social world remains unasked and unanswered. Similarly, the focus of urban sociology has leaned toward examining the urban setting as a "space" (as a specific physical place) rather than as a "locality" (as a point within larger social processes), and studies of the Internet to date have done likewise for the same reason. As Flanagan (1993) noted, "... the sociology of the spatial dimension of social organization emerged at a time when 'the city' was the most dramatic and popularly available spatial manifestation of social change" (3). The Internet has now usurped the status of the city in this respect. With connectivity spanning more than 200 countries, the Internet is now the most dramatic spatial manifestation of social change. It has forced us to re-think how we conceptualize a whole host of human institutions, not the least of which is the nature of human community. While it is important that we continue to probe for answers about the nature and meaning of such interaction at the micro level, it is equally important to assess the macro social implications.

These macro social implications are the focus of this work. With a social constructionist perspective on communications technology as a backdrop, this book serves two interrelated purposes. First, it argues against continued research of the Internet as if it were, first and foremost, an *agent* of change (media effects) or a physical place (urban studies). Arguing that the most fruitful means of understanding the impact of networked computing is to place the changes wrought by the Internet into a wider historical context of social change, this book examines the rise of the Internet as the logical extension of the Industrial Revolution and urbanization consistent with the basic tenets of modernity—as an evolutionary strategy of social organization with *perhaps* revolutionary consequences. It explores how the "virtualization" of our social world is accomplished through the adoption of a "media logic" perspective, resulting in an extension of the social change witnessed and theorized by early sociologists.

Second, rather than assuming we have undergone vast social change as a result of networked computing and focusing on the pros and cons of such change, this book offers an alternate framework through which to understand the Internet. It examines the ways in which people utilize a technological (or media) framework for solving problems, and what the adoption of that framework has meant and continues to mean for core social institutions. From the symbolic interactionist theory of media logic (Altheide and Snow, 1979), an overview of which will be provided in the preface to Part Two of this book, I argue that the Internet, like all media, is an institution that operates according to a specific logic. By examining this logic in detail, we can come to a better understanding of the potential implications of this technology for social organization than we can by assuming "revolutionary change" and attempting to use inductive logic (from small scale case studies) to understand the meaning of it all.

In short, this book does not weigh the good points and the bad points of networked computing, nor does it attempt to reach moral conclusions about the impact of the Net on the individual or society. What this book does do is: (1) attempt to answer the fundamental questions upon which other books are based: are people using the Internet to alter our basic social institutions?; if so, are these changes a matter of degree only, or do they truly represent a revolution—an overthrow of previous modes of organizing?; and finally, which institutions are most significantly altered by the Internet and in what ways?; and (2) offer the reader a conceptual framework (media logic), an examination of relevant popular beliefs and social science research findings in light of that framework, and suggestions for further areas of empirical research.

Accordingly, this book is divided into two main sections. Part One looks at the industrial-virtual continuum. It begins with an examination of popular assertions about changes already brought about by the Internet and forecasts of changes yet to come. It continues by providing an overview of the historic forces of social change (mentioned above) and discusses networked computing and "virtualization" as the logical extension of these historic transformations.

More specifically, Chapter One begins with an overview of the collective state of knowledge about networked computing (particularly the Internet) and social change, knowledge gleaned from both popular accounts made by technology pundits and the limited body of social science research that has been conducted on this issue. It continues by placing this knowledge in an historical framework by examining what we believed we "knew" about previous forms of communications technologies (print media, radio, television and so forth). A constructionist sociology of knowledge is used to argue two points. First, forecasts of the future of the "information society" that are based on extrapolation or slogans, much like our forecasts about the impacts of previous communications technologies, are often not borne out in either the lived experiences of individuals in that society or the actual changes in social organization such a society undergoes. Second, contrary to popular belief, the Internet does not constitute a revolutionary technology, either in its technical make-up or in the ways in which it is socially constructed.[3]

The chapter concludes by arguing that what all of these beliefs have in common is the assumption that the Internet is a technology—and *only* a technology. It is this very assumption that leads to the "pro-con" or "media effects" framework as the organizing principle for our knowledge about all communications technologies, a framework that is insufficient for a fuller understanding of what networked computing means for social organization. It suggests that a more meaningful way to understand the Internet is by looking at it and all other communications technologies as socially constructed institutions that offer people a unifying framework through which to solve the problems of collective living.

Chapter Two serves three interrelated purposes. First, it serves as a primer on the field of urban sociology. It provides an overview of the multiple approaches and theoretical frameworks to be found within the discipline (urban ecology, cultural/community studies, urbanization and world systems theory, and so forth) and offers a rationale for the selection of the framework used here. It then explains this comparative, historical approach of Emile Durkheim, Karl Marx and, most importantly, Max Weber, in detail. In so doing, it provides overviews of the work of these early sociologists and their perspective on the connections between industrialization as a means of social organization and various city/urban forms in history. Finally, this chapter concludes by arguing that the Internet is yet another "city" or urban form—one brought about through "virtualization," and that it is this process of virtualization (the use of media logic as a means of social organization and problem solving), and not the Internet as a physical place, that ultimately has the potential to affect other social institutions.

With the stage thus set, Part Two considers virtualization and social organization, exploring the implications of the Internet for a select set of social institutions. The social institutions covered are broad and multifaceted, and parallel those born in the early stages of modernity. Because this portion of the book is largely theoretical and exploratory, it will likely raise as many questions as it answers. It is my hope that raising new questions within a guiding theoretical framework will ultimately lead to synthesized knowledge based on research rather than supposition. Though this framework is here applied from a Western (specifically a U.S.) perspective, its utility lies in the fact that it may readily be applied in other cultural contexts. In fact, examining the uses of media and their implications for the meaning of the generalized other and changes in social organization would be a great improvement over the blanketing approach of technological determinism, as people of differing cultures adopt different technologies to differing degrees and use them for differing purposes.

Part Two of the book is prefaced with an overview of all those concepts the reader will need to make sense of in the remaining chapters. It will include a short course on the theory of media logic, an explanation of basic sociological concepts (such as "institution" and "social form") and a brief discussion of the division of the remaining chapters into three broad social orders—political, economic and normative.

That said, Chapter Three explores the defining institution of the political order, the nation-state. This chapter begins by providing a brief overview of what the nation-state has meant in terms of social organization, and what many observers see as its future prospects in an era of "globalization." In order to assess the validity of such arguments, the chapter then turns to an examination of the nation-state through the lens of media logic, specifically Internet logic. It assesses the state's ability to adopt the logic of the Internet in relation to another vital actor in the political order—the non-governmental organization—as a means of predicting the extent to which the nation-state will remain the dominant (or even viable) "actor" in the international political arena.

As Chapter Three did with the nation-state, Chapter Four explores the past, present and future roles of the defining organizational form of the economic order—the corporation. It begins with a brief (Weberian) history of the birth of the modern capitalist framework and its interconnections with industrialization, urbanization, bureaucratization and the articulation of a (socioeconomic) class system. It then analyzes how the corporation, as the embodiment of modern capitalism, is faring in its ability to adopt the logic of the Internet. Specifically, so-called new corporate forms (virtual corporations) are compared with "traditional" corporations in order to assess their similarities and differences and the strengths and weaknesses of each. The chapter concludes by addressing the strength of the corporate form relative to the nation-state discussed in the previous chapter.

Chapter Five focuses on what are commonly called primary and secondary groups in the field of Sociology. Such groups fall within the normative order, and for purposes of this research include religion, education and the family. The chapter begins by briefly outlining the histories and functions of these three institutions. It continues by assessing, in turn, the ability of each to adopt the logic of the Internet to further its external significance within the normative order. Specifically, the chapter compares and contrasts the abilities of religious organizations to make use of media logics in the past with their apparent abilities to adopt the logic of the Internet. It then examines the university in much the same manner, comparing and contrasting the capabilities of the traditional university with those of the "virtual university." It concludes with a discussion of the family, how that institution has used media in the past, and how it utilizes the Internet now to sustain its relevance within the normative order of society.

Chapter Six shares the structure of previous chapters. Taking the "post-modern" claim that the self is no longer relevant as its starting point, it traces the idea of "the self" from its beginnings in Classical Greek thought, through modern history and into the virtual world. The self is ultimately argued to be a modern institution and one that makes use of media logic in general to secure its significance in the virtual world. This social institution, though it is central to virtualization, is reserved for final examination because it necessarily incorporates the changes taking place in the institutions discussed in Chapters Three through Five. Thus, this chapter examines the self through the lens of Net logic both directly and indirectly. It both points to direct evidence of the institutionalized self online and posits what that evidence implies about the future of the self. And it revisits key points from previous chapters to assess the ongoing nature of the relationship between the self and the modern institutions of the nation-state, the corporation, the church, the university and the family.

Finally, Chapter Seven wraps up the discussion. It reasserts the key arguments found in detail in preceding chapters, summarizing the problems inherent in relying on an "effects" framework for understanding technology. It highlights the true role of the Internet (and other media) in contemporary society, what that role means for the various social institutions that make up the modern social order, and concludes by arguing that only when the Internet is understood as far more than a mere technology or tool will we be able to fully analyze and comprehend its implications for social organization.

NOTES

1. The year 1969 is taken as the starting point for purposes of this analysis because it marks the birth of the 4-node ARPANET as the precursor of the Internet. All statistics and references to "the Internet" throughout the course of this work are for the Internet only and not the Matrix, which consists of BITNET, UUCP, FIDONET and OSI, in addition to the Internet. The connectivity figure of "over 200" countries for this network is taken from the Matrix Information and Directory Services, Inc. (*www.mids.org*) web page, and population estimates and projections for the network are taken from the NUA Surveys (*www.nua.ie*) web page.

2. Karl Marx (1818–1883) is perhaps the only theorist discussed here to whom this statement does not apply.

3. Though this chapter offers some highlights of the technical development of particular electronic media, a detailed comparison of the technical parameters of the Internet and other media is well beyond its scope. Emphasis is instead placed upon the strong similarities found in the social constructions of these technologies.

Readers who require further evidence of the technical similarities are referred to the following sources:

a. Tom Standage, *The Victorian Internet* (New York: Walker and Company, 1998).

b. Daniel J. Czitrom, *Media and the American Mind: From Morse to McLuhan* (Chapel Hill, NC: University of North Carolina Press, 1982).

c. Melvin L. DeFleur and Sandra Ball-Rokeach, *Theories of Mass Communication* (New York: Longman, 1989).

d. George N. Gordon, *The Communications Revolution: A History of Mass Media in the United States* (New York: Hastings House Publishers, 1977).

e. Irwin Lebow, *Information Highways and Byways* (New York: Institute of Electrical and Electronics Engineers, 1995).

Part I

CHAPTER ONE

Communications Technologies: A Chronicle of Knowledge

It is impossible that old prejudices and hostilities should longer exist, while such an instrument has been created for the exchange of thought between all the nations of the earth [Standage 1998, 83].

This quote from *The Story of the Telegraph* is representative of the euphoria that surrounded the successful completion of the Atlantic cable line. Though the initial idea of the telegraph met with considerable skepticism, by 1858 citizens on both sides of the Atlantic were convinced of its benefits, both economic and humanitarian. Since that time, with the possible exception of the radio, no other means of electronic communication has witnessed the near-unanimous approval garnered by the telegraph. While all have had their supporters, they have also been met with derision by those who were and are concerned with the individual and social effects that such media were and are claimed to engender.

Why should this be the case? Why are communications technologies, originally embraced as the harbingers of world peace, now more often hailed as destructive, even sinister social forces? Are we just getting smarter about the controlling tendencies of these technologies or about their detrimental effects on personal and public life? These are the questions this chapter seeks to answer by examining the historical construction of knowledge claims about the topic.[1] That is, it probes myriad sources—newspapers, books, magazines and the Internet—in order to apprehend the ways in which people construct an ordered, objective reality with regard to assorted technologies of communication. Ironically, in the case of communications technologies, one must, in the end, utilize the very artifacts one seeks to order and objectify to convey the processes by which that task is accomplished.

IMAGINING THE INTERNET: A NARRATIVE HISTORY

Most, if not all, recent knowledge claims about the Internet revolve around the role of networked computing as a force for social change. That is, they revolve around the possible personal and social effects of the Internet. Reasons for this are embedded in the history of social thought about communications technologies in general and are discussed more fully in the next section of this chapter. The end result, however, has been the development of knowledge claims that assume a "media effects" framework. That is, regardless of whether claims are based on "common sense" understandings of the Internet (those based on opinion and impression rather than social science theory or systematic empirical investigation) or on "social scientific" understandings grounded in psychological, sociological or communications theory, they frame the Internet as a "thing" in and of itself, as a technology with a life of its own, as an entity capable of detrimental effects upon the individual psyche and the social order as a whole. As Nye (1997) aptly notes,

> The term "technology" has only been widely used in the twentieth century... It had a positive connotation in writers such as Thorstein Veblen and other advocates of a larger role for engineers in American society. In more recent use, however, the term tends to obscure human action and to represent machines as an abstract force in history. We often read in the newspapers that "technology" causes change ... Machines are not autonomous... Yet if human beings decide which machines to use and how to use them, this does not mean that people collectively know what they are doing. Quite the contrary, the combined choices of inventors, entrepreneurs, workers, and consumers create unanticipated cultural consequences. Because no single individual or institution wills certain changes, they are often mistaken for attributes of the machine itself. And once machines are perceived as active forces in their own right, they become part of narrative [2].

The Internet is no exception. While there is some overlap, its narrative descriptions can be divided into three epochs. The first, and longest, epoch spanned roughly from the birth of the Internet in 1969 through the end of 1991. During this period the narrative was purely technical. This conversation, quite naturally, revolved around simply making the idea of the Internet a technical reality. Initially it was carried on within the confines of that small group of people credited with inventing the Internet; even technical specialists who were not part of this group had little say in the dialogue during the early going. In fact, it was not until around 1981 that a fairly regular stream of articles in computer networking trade journals began to appear.[2]

Only in 1988 did the Internet begin to receive any attention from or coverage by the popular press. In November of that year, Robert T. Morris, then a graduate student at Cornell University, released a "virus" into the Internet that disrupted thousands of connected computers for a short period of time. Several newspapers and magazines, including the *Wall Street Journal, Newsweek, Science* and the *Denver Post,* ran articles about the event that discussed how the virus operated and how it was "cured." Testifying to the public's lack of awareness of the Internet at that time, each of these articles opened with an explanation of what the network was—a series of connected computers used for research and maintained by the Department of Defense.[3]

In 1989 and 1990 a smattering of follow-up articles again appeared in the popular press, this time discussing: the "Morris virus" of 1988 and its effects on the system; an "anti nuclear" virus that affected NASA computers; and plans for an encryption program that would enhance user privacy.[4] Gibson's *Neuromancer* (1984) notwithstanding, this first narrative epoch was little concerned with the topics that would come to dominate the narrative in the third epoch, namely, the social and psychological effects of the Internet.

The year 1991 marked the transition from the first to second epoch. Still technically oriented for the most part, the narrative began to incorporate business and social issues. This change was made possible by a number of developments. First, the National Science Foundation reinterpreted its Acceptable Use Policy to allow for commercial traffic across NSFNET, then the backbone of the Internet. Second, "gopher," the first point-and-click file navigation system, was released by the University of Minnesota. Third, organizations concerned about the future of global computer networking joined together to form the Internet Society, the goals of which were to promote the Net's evolution, to educate users and to provide a forum for user collaboration. Fourth, ECHO (East Coast Hang Out) was established as one of the first publicly available online communities. Taken together, these events marked the beginning of an awareness by a non-technical public that these increasingly "user friendly" technologies might be utilized to achieve personal and social goals—community establishment and outreach, efficiency and decentralization in business management, and so forth.

This second epoch was relatively short lived. Beginning as a trickle of popular press articles in 1992 and ending in a torrent in 1995, discussions about the history, evolution and content of the Internet, the means by which the average user could log on and "surf," and the birth of myriad uses of the Internet (not the least of which were commercial uses and community development) dominated the narrative. Not surprisingly, this popularization manifested itself as a debate among the Internet's "founding fathers" and early users as to what the future of the Net should be. During 1992 and 1993 many of the technical trade journals began to run "cross over" articles—those discussing either the social meaning of the Internet or lay versions of its technical parameters. Further, many of the founding fathers were either interviewed by or wrote their own articles for popular press journals and newspapers. Reporters began logging on regularly and wrote countless articles documenting their personal experiences with both the technology and the other "Netizens" they encountered.

In 1993 America Online, CompuServe and Prodigy began offering access. The World Wide Web navigation software, Mosaic, was offered free of charge. As more and more users logged on, many began to complain of access problems. The Internet was described as "intimate" and declared "a lifeline." Santa Claus could finally be contacted via email. Online advertising was born and the Internet was defined as a "mass market." The Internet was even suggested as a candidate for *Time* magazine's "Man of the Year."

In 1994 and 1995 cybermalls were born, and the idea of virtual communities began to take hold. Constituents of online business and online communities found themselves at odds; myriad articles documenting the perils of online business emerged. It is from the business community's claims, among others, that the idea of the Internet as a "social problem" would eventually emerge. Caught unaware of online social norms and values, pioneers in online business suffered at the hands of computer hackers and jokesters who disabled their systems, canceled their online advertising or otherwise thwarted their attempts at online profit making. Business people were not the only ones who found themselves experiencing "culture shock." Increased ease of access and navigation in 1993 allowed millions of additional new users into the system, not one of whom had the slightest understanding that the Internet, in one form or another, had existed as a *social system* for a relatively limited number of users for some 20 years. Ignorant of the rules of the game, these newcomers began to define the Net as "anarchy." A new narrative epoch was born.

This last epoch, running roughly from late 1995 or early 1996 to the present, is one in which the dominant, but competing, narrative descriptions are "the Internet as a social problem" and "Internet as social solution." Among other things, the Internet has been credited with: reestablishing a sense of community and belonging in a mass society; breaking down the barriers of communications between class levels and ethnic groups; making education more widely available; and increasing the power of the individual over corporations and government institutions. Likewise, it has been accused of: fomenting pornography and the degradation of women; online hate masquerading as free speech; identity theft; a new underclass marked by lack of access to technology; a society of "knowledge workers" who are further alienated from meaningful work; and even a new mental disorder, Internet Addiction Disorder.

Much of this discussion, pro and con, has revolved around the Internet as a "revolutionary technology" that gives rise to a specific type of "place." This place is said to be compressed in both its spatial and temporal features, and such compression is argued to produce unique psychological and social effects. Two points are worth noting about this claim. First, spatial and temporal features have long been used to define that which is "real." Physical proximity has been used (and debated) as possibly the defining hallmark of reality since philosophy and the social sciences began. Second, the elimination of space and time as barriers to interaction was also claimed as a hallmark for all electronic communication technologies that preceded the Internet. Both of these points will be discussed more fully in the pages that follow.

Nevertheless, in support of such claims, many participants with first-hand knowledge of computer-mediated communications attach great meaning to such interactions; some are extremely committed to the reality of "virtual relationships." They claim that the other people they encounter online "speak their language," "feed their soul" and engage in relationships characterized by a very high level of self-disclosure and trust. Some even liken these interactions to "real" interactions physically:

> "It's like a group of people sitting around a big table having coffee and kidding each other" [McCartney and Rigdon 1994, B1].

> "It is a way for homebound people to get out and see friends" [McCartney and Rigdon 1994, B1].

> "There's always another mind there. It's like having a corner bar, complete with old buddies and delightful newcomers ... and fresh graffiti and letters, except instead of putting on my coat, shutting down the computer and walking down to the corner, I just invoke my telecom program and there they are. It's a place" [Rheingold 1993, 24].

In opposition, others claim that participants in CMC are "in denial" about the problems created by the Internet. They define interaction via the Net as a social problem, as a non-real type of interaction that pulls people away from real interaction and leads to a loss of community and identity. They argue that the Internet encourages vicarious, non-real relationships and cultivates psychosis. It lets people have simple relationships in which they can dictate what happens. It can be used as an avoidance of real relationships and as a "cure-all" for isolated people. Further, they argue that the Internet is characterized by a lack of government, anonymity, malicious activities, financial scams, incivility, censorship and intimidation, and thus "brings out the worst" in people.

Social scientific knowledge claims in the field of computer-mediated communications (CMC) parallel those made by lay people. They generally revolve around the assumption that the Net is a revolutionary technology that has resulted in a new form of space-time compressed social place. With this narrative as backdrop, researchers have sought alternatively to document the extent of the realness of this place, its social structure, and its consequences for the individuals involved and the social order as a whole. Research on CMC is thus rooted in the "media effects" framework. This framework has an extensive history, one that will be fleshed out more fully in the following section. But its application to networked computing began in earnest as early as the mid–1970s, when psychologists began conducting experiments on the effects of communication modes on, among other things, group problem solving, risk taking, "social presence," negotiations, learning and de-individuation. Kiesler, Siegel and McGuire's *Social Psychological Aspects of Computer-Mediated Communication* (1984) became the standard-bearer for what came to be called the "cues filtered out" approach to media effects that dominated the field throughout the 1970s and 1980s. In a nutshell, the authors proposed that online communicators suffered from a lack of regulating feedback, dramaturgical weakness, few status and position cues, and social anonymity. As a result, they exhibited social psychological effects such as lowered communication efficiency, more equal and democratic participation among group members, and uninhibited interpersonal behavior. These results, both positive and negative, were attributed to the lack of social cues (body language, dress as a status symbol and so forth) experienced in CMC. The situation was "less real" in this time-space compressed place.

In the 1990s, particularly after 1993 (when the Internet became widely available), this approach was increasingly challenged. For example, Smith (1992) produced an ethnographic account of the production of collective goods in the intentional community of the WELL (Whole Earth 'Lectronic Link). Employing Goffman's (1959) discussion of the creation of the self, network theory and the theory of collective action dilemmas, the author examined the production of social network capital, knowledge capital and communion within the virtual community. In 1993 Hiltz and Turoff also used a "Goffmanesque" approach in explaining both the sociological nature of CMC and its possible impacts on everyday life (81–87). According to the authors, even though participants lose all visual and some audio cues (facial expression, eye contact, body language and so forth) regarding social category or "type" of the other participants due to a "narrowing of the communications channel," they ultimately recover from this situation and proceed to engage in meaningful interaction. As in any social setting, all that is required is that the new participants allow some time to become socialized to the new rules.

Taking their lead from Hiltz and Turoff, researchers from the mid–1990s onward have continued to focus on the possibilities for online community. Narrating the nature of online places, cultures and identities from a post-modernist framework, researchers have continued to emphasize the effects of a supposedly revolutionary reordering of time and space on the meaning of the individual and the social groups to which he or she belongs. For example, Lawley (1995) made an argument for the community nature of online communications by utilizing Bourdieu's sociology of culture and his constructs of field, class, habitus and symbolic capital. She argued that CMC in its entirety constitutes a "field"; that "class" can be defined through one's expertise with CMC and an affiliation with a particular system of relatively "high" or "low" status; and that "habitus" can be seen as the linguistic conventions and system of netiquette, both of which are forms of symbolic capital unique to CMC.

In 1997 and 1998 Jones edited collections of articles that use a largely post-modernist framework to examine "cultural identifiers" in the "social landscape" of the Internet, and how those relate to cybersex, online hate groups, social control in virtual communities and the idea of the Internet as anarchy.[5] Additionally, in 1998 several researchers took up the application of this framework to issues of social justice. Individually, Perelman, Ebo, Loader, and Schon et al. edited collections of articles that examine, among other things, the relationship between the "commodification of information" and class structure; the changing nature of work and job displacement; environmental effects of the "information revolution"; and the role of class, gender and race online.[6]

The framework even spawned the development of a journal dedicated to understanding the nature of the unique social space that is the Internet. *The Journal of Computer-Mediated Communication*, begun in 1995 and sponsored by the University of Southern California's Annenberg School for Communication, is perhaps the defining journal in the field. It has continued the post-modernist approach to understanding the nature and implications of online community, and has even expanded the analysis into topics such as collaborative universities and CMC's role in higher education; the nature and functioning of the virtual organization and electronic commerce; and the nature of work and play in online worlds.

Though all but the most ardent proponents and critics willingly note that the Internet can be both a "social" and an "antisocial" force, the underlying framework in this narrative epoch is that the Internet (and technology in general) advances at a pace that cannot be matched by society's moral and ethical judgments. The result is Ogburn's (1964) "cultural lag"—a condition marked by humankind's inability to control the technologies it creates. Humankind is thus tasked with developing strategies to "deal with" computerized communications in a manner that promotes our own ends (as opposed to those of the technology itself). We must get technology back under control. These analyses, lay and academic, view the Internet as a "thing," as a technology that impinges, for better or worse, on our way of life from the outside. Since 1994, when the Internet really began to take off as a communications technology available to large numbers of people, hundreds of books have been published that deal with its social aspects.[7] Similarly, popular press coverage of Net-related issues has grown from a handful of articles in the late 1980s to a torrent of articles too numerous to count. At the turn of the century the Internet is fodder for both daily coverage in newspapers and dozens of periodicals devoted exclusively to the subject.

Regardless of whether the authors of these articles and books are technical experts, social scientists or lay participants in and observers of the Internet, and regardless of the specific topic under discussion, the narrative description contained therein is almost universal. It is a narrative of technological determinism in which the Internet, though it may be a force for social good, has the potential to significantly alter, in an undesirable way, all that we hold dear about interpersonal communication and cherished cultural practices. According to this narrative, the Internet has taken on a life of its own. It has been infused with autonomy, identity, culture, personality and even power. It is a force to be reckoned with, and one over which humankind must gain control if we are to coax from it its potential for economic growth, community building, personal enrichment and education. All of this must be done carefully, lest individuals forfeit their autonomy, identity and well-being to the service of machines.

This approach to understanding communications technology, to imbuing it with meaning, has been around for quite some time. It has been the dominant approach since Plato had Socrates opine that books are inferior to discussion and that (the technology of) writing "weakens the mind." Regarding *electronic* communications technologies, the overarching determinist narrative has been the "rearrangement of time and space" through the development and use of "revolutionary technology." What are the defining elements of this narrative? Does the Internet represent a revolutionary technology in this respect? It is to these questions that we now turn.

Conceptualizing Communication: Narratives of Effects

As noted earlier, the 20th century has witnessed the objectification of technology and its incorporation into our constructions of social order. That is, people collectively have developed a number of stories about the nature of technology and its role in social change. As Nye (1997, 179) notes, these narratives include:

1. Technology as "natural" outgrowth of society
2. Technology as agent of social amelioration
3. Technology as means of social control
4. Technology as re-shaper of perceptions of space and time
5. Technology as agent of unexpected outcomes (satire)
6. Technology as agent of doom

Note that while these claims are discussed as "narratives" or "stories," this does not imply that there are not elements of truth in each one. Certainly, through the agglomeration of individual choices, many technologies have yielded unexpected outcomes. Likewise, it is true that nuclear bombs, if detonated, are capable of destroying the earth—of dooming at least human life to extinction. Further, technologies such as the telephone and the television have allowed for communications at a faster pace than was possible before those technologies existed.

However, the narrative forms commonly used to express those facts—those outlined above—present the technologies in question as deterministic forces. They are used to frame technology as "autonomous." They ignore the fact that human beings are the real agents of social change, and that the technologies they create, adopt, adapt and discard are expressions of cultural preferences, value systems, beliefs and social norms. Further, they ignore that it is these preferences, values, beliefs and norms that result in: the individual choices leading to unexpected outcomes; the decision of whether to detonate the nuclear bomb; and the decision as to how speedier systems of communications should be used and to what end.

Nowhere is this more true than in the narrative descriptions of communications technologies. At different times, to different degrees and for varying purposes, all of the narratives listed above have been pressed into service. As we shall see in the pages that follow, the overarching narrative has been "technology as re-shaper of perceptions of space and time." Arguing from technical change to social-psychological effects, this narrative has been selectively combined with others in the list to produce the desired story. Combined with "technology as agent of social amelioration," as was indicated in the quote that opened this chapter, the story of the telegraph began. Combined with "technology as agent of doom," as the discussion below will highlight, the story of television is told. Regardless of whether the outcome is happy, the underlying theme is that the *technology itself* affects us.

There are any number of questions one might ask about communications technologies, particularly those defined as "mass media." Among them are, "How does mass communication take place?" "What is the impact of a society on its mass media?" That is, does mass communication differ from interpersonal communication? If so, in what ways? Is it in principle or only in form? Why are mass media configured as they are? What cultural, political and economic factors lead to those configurations? What cultural parameters determine the acceptance or rejection of a particular type of medium, and how do they impact how any given medium will be used by the public? The ultimate use of any given communication technology has never been clear from the outset. Rather, the use to which a technology is put is determined as we go; over time, these uses become routinized. How can we better understand the factors involved in determining and even directing such use? To what extent do the technical parameters of any given medium actually define its use?

Interesting as these and other questions about media are, comparatively little research has been conducted that might serve to illuminate the answers. Because the accepted framework of truth is centered on the idea of "cause and effect," and because we choose to accord entities other than people (technology, corporations, institutions) causative power, the vast majority of research conducted in the arena has focused on the following question: "What does exposure to mass communication do to people?" Whether the paradigm employed is structural-functionalism, social conflict theory, symbolic interactionism, behaviorism, psychoanalysis or cognitive modeling, the underlying assumption is (almost always) that media "exposure" affects people individually and, ultimately, collectively, and usually in undesirable ways. As a result, most knowledge claims regarding communications technologies assume this "media effects" framework. The narrative they tell is "what media do to us" and not "what we do with media."

Though the term "mass media" did not gain widespread usage until the 1940s (and only then in the U.S.), the effects approach to understanding and narrating media, including the Internet, began with the invention of the telegraph. Upon its completion in 1858, the Atlantic Telegraph line was dubbed by *Scientific American* the "instantaneous highway of thought between the Old and New Worlds" that annihilated space and time.[8] (Note the similarity between this description and that of the Internet as the "information superhighway," also a technology purported to "annihilate" space and time.) Initial narratives of the telegraph utilized the "technology as an agent of social amelioration" approach. It was believed that such a re-ordering of space and time would herald world peace: "What can be more likely to effect peace than a constant and complete intercourse between all nations and individuals in the world." The telegraph was lauded as "the nerve of international life, transmitting knowledge of events, removing causes of misunderstanding, and promoting peace and harmony through-out the world" (Standage 1998, 90–91). At that moment it was inconceiv-able that shared experience could lead to anything other than shared understanding. Similarly, Dertouzos (1997) argued for the prospect of a computer-aided peace, and suggested that digital networks are capable of establishing "electronic bonds" that may help prevent ethnic hatred. And Cairncross (1997, 279) proclaimed, "Free to explore different points of view on the Internet... people will become less susceptible to propaganda from politicians who seek to stir up conflicts. Bonded together by the invis-ible strands of global communications, humanity may find that peace and prosperity are fostered by the death of distance."[9]

But the telegraph, like the Internet, was used by a wide variety of peo-ple for a wide variety of purposes. While most conducted routine business over the wires, others with less than honorable intentions used the tele-graph for financial fraud and deceit (for example, placing gambling bets and manipulating stock prices). Interestingly, people also used the tele-graph to develop and advance personal relationships and "online" com-munities with shared culture in much the same way people use the Internet today:

> Telegraph operators were members of a closed, exclusive community. They had their own customs and vocabulary, and a strict pecking order, based on the speed at which they could send and receive messages... Col-lectively, the world's telegraphers represented an online community encompassing thousands of people, very few of whom ever met face to face. And despite the apparently impersonal nature of communicating by wire, it was in fact an extremely subtle and intimate means of communi-cation. Experienced operators could even recognize their friends merely from the style of their Morse code—something that was, apparently, as rec-ognizable as an individual human voice. Each operator on a particular telegraph line also had a two-letter signature, or "sig," with which to iden-tify themselves online... [Standage 1998, 129–130].

With its ability to send messages electronically, rather than by train, boat or horseback, the telegraph marks the first separation between com-munications and transportation, the first "annihilation" of space and time.

Though many claimed that the world would become "one neighborhood" as a result, that technology exhibited many of the same problems associated with the Internet, including message accuracy, secrecy and privacy, mechanical breakdowns, vandalism and abuse of trust. The completion of the Atlantic line in 1858 marked the peak of intellectual and popular exultation for the telegraph. The narrative that started with optimism for world peace ended with pessimism. Curiously, though, this pessimism did not result from the fact that some people used the technology for fraudulent purposes. Nor did it result from a skepticism about online communities, the impacts the technology might have on important social institutions, or even the technology's failure to bring about world peace and understanding. These critiques of media would come later. Rather, it resulted from the disenchantment of intellectual and social elites of the day with the rising popularity of the penny press—that form of "mass" communication *made possible by* the telegraph.

The birth of the daily newspaper in American society marks the point at which social scientists and social critics began to try to assess the "effects" of media, both good and bad, on the individual and society. Such attempts at assessment were, in the beginning, marked by ambivalence. Theorists saw the potential for both positive and negative effects of media, and the narratives they employed vacillated between technology as an agent of amelioration and technology as an agent of doom. In particular, early theorists such as Charles Horton Cooley and Robert Park argued that mass communications would restore broad moral and political consensus destroyed by industrialization, immigration and urbanization. The dominant form of social organization would return from gesellschaft to gemeinschaft.[10]

Cooley (1909) in particular seemed to equate modern communication with democracy. He argued that the newspaper was more efficient and effective than any prior forms of communication in terms of "expressiveness" (ability to cover a broad range of ideas and feelings), permanence of record (ability to overcome time), swiftness (ability to overcome space) and diffusion (access to information for all social classes):

> The general character of this change is well expressed by the two words "enlargement" and "animation." Social contacts are extended in space and quickened in time, and in the same degree the mental unity they imply becomes wider and more alert. The individual is broadened by coming into relation with a larger and more various life [63].

However, Cooley was not completely convinced by his narrative of social amelioration. He simultaneously argued that modern media created an "environment of strain and anxiety" through the rapid flow of personal images, sentiments and impulses, the effect of which was to "break down character": "[because of the newspaper] he is kept stirred up, sometimes to excess, by the multitude of changing suggestions which this life brings to him" (Czitrom 1982, 100). It was this side of Cooley's analysis, with its language of "pathology," that would eventually give rise to the behavioristic model of media effects, with its focus on manipulation and negative outcomes for the individual psyche. That model would dominate theory and research from the 1930s through the 1960s (Czitrom 1982).

Robert Park, himself a journalist before becoming a sociologist, engaged in a more systematic analysis of media than did Cooley. Among other approaches, Park analyzed "the news" as a form of knowledge and theorized its ability to unite people in times of crisis; its contributions to history, sociology and folklore; and its role in the formation and legitimation of public opinion. He further suggested that the medium of the newspaper represented a "referential" type of communication; it communicated ideas and facts. In contrast, motion pictures as a medium represented "expressive" communication, a form that communicates sentiments, attitudes and emotions. Park argued that the newspaper, by fulfilling its "referential" role, would serve as an integrating and socializing entity—it would promote increased intimacy and understanding. Conversely, Park criticized movies and even periodic fiction as "demoralizing forces" that undermined traditional social controls. They were "subversive cultural influences" that emphasized the expressive side of communication: "This restlessness and thirst for adventure is, for the most part, barren and illusory because it is uncreative ... It is in the improvident use of our leisure, I suspect, that the greatest wastes in American life occur."[11]

Others were less enthusiastic about the newspaper form brought about by the telegraph. In 1889 the London *Spectator* opined:

> [Through newspapers] the recording of every event, and especially every crime, everywhere without perceptible interval of time–the world is for purposes of intelligence reduced to a village... All men are compelled to think of all things, at the same time, on imperfect information, and with too little interval for reflection... The constant diffusion of statements in snippets, the constant excitements of feeling unjustified by fact, the constant formation of hasty or erroneous opinions, must in the end, one would think, deteriorate the intelligence of all to whom the telegraph appeals... This unnatural excitement, this perpetual dissipation of the mind [Czitrom 1982, 19].

The loss of old-style journalism, in which a newspaper was founded on the opinions and personality of its owner, was also bemoaned by the *Atlantic Monthly*:

> [The telegraph] transformed journalism from what it once was, the peri-
> odic expression of the thought of the time, the opportune record of the
> questions and answers of contemporary life, into an agency for collecting,
> condensing, and assimilating the trivialities of the entire human existence.
> In this chase for the days' accidents we still keep the lead, as in the conse-
> quent neglect and oversight of what is permanent and therefore vital in its
> importance to the intellectual character [Czitrom 1982, 19].

Implicit in these narratives of the new newspaper form is the claim
that the post–Civil War newspaper no longer fulfilled its "referential" role.
Rather, with an emphasis placed on the "human interest" story, newspapers became more like motion pictures. They fulfilled an "expressive" role
by focusing on sensational, attention grabbing stories. This new style,
termed "newspaperism," was claimed to be a decadence-producing "poi-
son."

Not surprisingly, similar claims have been made regarding much Internet content. Internet Relay Chat rooms are said to consist of mindless con-
versations on trivial topics. Usenet news group postings are not to be
trusted, as they often contain erroneous claims made by anonymous participants. Routine Web searches return insurmountable numbers of "hits,"
most of which are of only marginal interest and some of which direct the
user to "deviant" online sites, such as hate groups and pornographic cybersex areas. Also not surprisingly, these are precisely the topics that newspapers continue to focus on when running stories about the Internet—the
sensational, attention grabbing stories.

Turning now to a brief history of the telephone, it is interesting to note
that many similar claims were made with respect to its effects. However,
it appears that the first systematic empirical study of its uses and "effects"
did not occur until 1981. In the 1870s, as Brooks (1975) noted,

> The telephone was technically near, but philosophically far... Human
> speech, as opposed to dot-and-dash code [transmitted by the telegraph],
> was considered sacred, a gift of God beyond man's contrivance through
> science. Public reactions to the very idea of telephony in the 1860s and
> 1870s wavered between fear of the supernatural and ridicule of the
> impractical. People were made uneasy by the very notion. Hearing voices
> when there was no one there was looked upon as a manifestation of either
> mystical communion or insanity. [12]

Nevertheless, by the early 1900s the telephone was widely adopted (in
the U.S.) as a substitution for and expansion of face-to-face communication in personal and business dealings. In his 1981 *Social Functions of the
Telephone*, Singer is the first to empirically examine the phone's role in
social organization, family life, emergencies, scheduling and coordination.

Noting that "literature treating the telephone is scattered, often anecdotal, and frequently found in the popular press," he perhaps inadvertently offers evidence of the role of the popular press in knowledge claims about the telephone; a review of his extensive bibliography reveals, from a total of 153 sources, that 123 are from popular press articles in newspapers and magazines (Singer 1981, 6).

As was the case with other technologies, its adoption begot any number of criticisms from contemporary social commentators. Many of the narratives in these sources depict the telephone as an agent of social deviance. Not surprisingly, the social problems "caused" by the telephone parallel those of the telegraph before it and the Internet now. For example, as early as 1907, critics were warning that the telephone was being used to communicate illegal bets, provide racing results and solicit the services of prostitutes (or "call girls"). Today critics decry the existence of online gambling and virtual sex. Later the phone was also used by pranksters to make "crank calls" and for the promotion of "deviant ideologies," as when non-mainstream political groups record irresponsible or offensive messages that could be heard by dialing a given number. Today the phone is used for telemarketing, and the Internet is used to send "junk" email and to promote the views of assorted hate groups. Telephone party lines, which were common (particularly in rural areas) when the telephone first gained popularity, were also similar to the Net in that they were notoriously lacking in personal privacy. Human operators commonly listened in on calls, as did neighbors sharing the line.

In order to deal with these and other problems, a number of people produced "telephone etiquette" guides that informed users how to deal with operators, how to answer the telephone correctly, what to do in the case of a wrong number, what sorts of subjects could be appropriately discussed over the phone, and so forth. Today these guides have their counterparts in online Netiquette guides that explain to the new Internet user how to "surf," how to behave in various online groups and how to convey social cues that go beyond words on the screen (Stern and Gwathmey 1994; Singer 1981).

It is interesting to note that, like other technologies before it, when the phone first became widespread, many people felt it would be the "great equalizer" because users would not be able to evaluate one another on the basis of appearance, status and ability (Singer 1981). This is precisely the same argument one often finds in research about the Internet, as noted earlier in this chapter. Similarly, what later came to be called the "cues filtered out" approach to media effects (see above) was used to explain problematic telephone interaction in much the same way as it has been for the Internet. This was despite the fact that, at the time, the telephone was seen as a vast improvement over the telegraph because of the relative *abundance* of cues it transmitted. Unlike the telegraph, which only transmitted "the facts," the telephone was seen as transmitting the *identity* and *state of mind* of the speaker. As a result, it was considered a *uniquely personal* form of communication that could be used as a substitute for travel (Lebow 1995).

This pairing of the "re-ordering perceptions of space and time" narrative with either the "technology as agent of amelioration" or "technology as agent of doom" narrative continued as motion pictures, radio and television were invented, adopted and altered. With the assumptions of the "media effects" paradigm firmly in place, the only thing that changed was the superficial theory engaged to prove the assumptions involved. From the 1930s through the 1960s, researchers employed a behaviorist model, and the volume of empirical research into media effects exploded in four main areas: propaganda analysis (following World War I), public opinion research, social psychological effects of media (usually movies) on children, and market research.

The underlying assumption was that "mass media" were (or could be) agents of social control, and the dominant approach was the "four question" model: "Who says what to whom and with what effect?" (Note that the question "why?" is not asked; this points to the emphasis on the practical application of the answers received.) In Lasswell's work on propaganda, for example, the issue was the extent to which truth could be managed and manipulated through media stories, rumors, reports and pictures. Lippman's work on public opinion shared the concern that people, rather than acting on their own knowledge of the world, were acting on "pseudo environments" constructed through modern media. Studies sponsored in the early 1930s by the Payne Fund sought to understand the impact of movies on children's sleep, health, emotional well-being and interpersonal behavior. Finally, Lazarsfeld's pioneering work in the field of market research sought to explain the effects of advertising on individual behavior and the extent to which the individual could be manipulated, or even controlled, by advertising (Czitrom 1982; Davis and Baran 1981).

Despite the fact that these studies consistently found that the media "effects" were not as significant as anticipated (it was found to be quite difficult to ascribe direct behavioral effects to media exposure), these types of studies and their underlying assumptions continue to be popular today. Social critics continue to claim direct correlations between movie or television violence and violent behavior seen in children—repeated, frequent exposure to violence on the screen *causes* children to be violent. Psychologists claim that people are becoming "addicted" to the Internet—they cannot stop themselves from logging on. From this perspective, electronically mediated communication is seen as a social problem. It "locates the cause of media effects in the text itself, establishes the agent of action in the individual responding to the text and finds the effect in the behavioral acts attributed to the individual acting under the influence of the text" (Anderson and Meyer 1988, 311).

In the case of motion pictures, the causal agent is not only the "text" of the medium, but the physical surroundings in which one views it. As reported in the early 1900s in the Journal of the American Medical Association and by the National Board of Censorship, respectively:[13]

> [Movies create] intense ocular and cerebral weariness, a sort of dazed good for nothing feeling, lack of energy, or appetite.

> It is evil pure and simple, destructive of social interchange, and of artistic effect.

It is likely that early movies drew such ire from critics for three interrelated reasons. First, movies were born in and popularized by the often dingy, grimy nickelodeons found in the newly formed immigrant areas of cities. These places, and the entertainment they provided, were perceived as a threat to "culture," one inseparable from urbanization, immigration and the rise of the factory system of labor. Second, they were seen as "commercialized leisure." That is, they altered peoples' patterns of leisure and created a new "pop" art form. Finally, because the motion picture represented a new "conquest of space and time" with the ability to transmit images in addition to sound, it appeared to be a medium that touched the everyday life of the viewer more immediately than had the telegraph or even the telephone.

Today, with most movie theaters being rather posh environments in which to pass time, and with the general acceptance (if not approval) of "popular" culture as a legitimate form of expression, narrative descriptions of the motion picture focus on the third concern—the movie's ability to directly affect everyday life in an immediate way. Most commonly, the narrative expresses concern over the violent content of movies, and claims that children and teenagers, exposed to enough of this content, believe that violence is without consequence and therefore will mimic what they see on the big screen. Similar arguments are made about video games and the Internet. Children exposed to video game violence believe all violence is fantasy and without consequence, and so they imitate the video game in real life. Similarly, the Internet affords the participant an environment in which behavior is supposedly without consequence, due to anonymity, and thereby encourages violent, or at least antisocial, behaviors.

In the case of the radio, the narrative description again wavered between the ameliorative and social control attributes of media. As the first means of instantaneous, collective communication (in its ultimate, broadcast configuration), the radio represented yet another "conquest of time and space"—the ability to penetrate simultaneously and directly into the home of every individual. As a result, the radio became more than a mere technological fad (as it had been when only the technological tinkerers known as "hams" were involved with radio broadcasting). The radio, like the telegraph before it, became the technology upon which hopes for a brighter future were placed. It was hailed as a powerful force for world peace, a savior of democracy and a force for educational, religious and cultural advances. M. H. Aylesworth, then president of the National Broadcasting Corporation, proclaimed, "People in all countries of the civilized world, hearing the same programs—music, speeches, sermons and so on—cannot fail to have a more friendly feeling for each other" (Rhodes 1999, 70).

Such beliefs were, to a certain degree, supported by the rapid rise in popularity of the radio and by its ability, at least in the early going, to bring families together and to transmit news of importance and "high culture." In their 1929 study of culture in a Midwestern town, the Lynds discuss the place of the radio:

> Though less widely diffused as yet than automobile owning or movie attendance, the radio nevertheless is rapidly crowding its way in among the necessities in the family standard of living. Not the least remarkable feature of this new invention is its accessibility. Here skill and ingenuity can in part offset money as an open sesame to swift sharing of the enjoyments of the wealthy. With but little equipment one can call the life of the rest of the world from the air...Far from being simply one more means of passive enjoyment, the radio has given rise to much ingenious manipulative activity...
>
> As this new tool is rolling back the horizons of Middletown for the bank clerk or the mechanic sitting at home and listening to a Philharmonic concert or a sermon by Dr. Fosdick, or to President Coolidge bidding his father good night on the eve of the election... readjustments naturally occur [269].

The Lynds go on to note that residents of Middletown listened to the radio instead of reading, going to the movies and driving around town. They also state,

> Doubtless it will continue to play a mighty role in lifting Middletown out of the humdrum of every day; it is beginning to take over that function of the great political rallies or the trips by the trainload to the state capital to hear a noted speaker or to see a monument dedicated that a generation ago helped to set the average man in a wide place [271].

As the structure of radio continued to shift from independent "ham" operators who served as both transmitters and receivers of radio programming to a corporate structure in which media conglomerates served as transmitters for the general public, concern over the role that advertising would play abounded. Many, citing the lofty goals of radio outlined above, thought it inconceivable that "so great a possibility for service, news, entertainment, education and vital commercial purposes" be allowed to "drown" in advertising "chatter" (Czitrom 1982, 76). By the mid–1930s, it had been declared that:

> In point of fact the radio has been extremely timid about permitting the broadcasting of anything that contravenes the established order. Its influence has gone towards stabilization rather than change. The best broadcasting stations everywhere are owned by large corporations... it objects to that which provokes and stimulates independent thinking as "too controversial" [Czitrom 1982, 81].

While the details of the technical developments of the radio and the Internet are beyond the scope of this chapter, it is intriguing to note that interest in both of these technologies initially lay with amateur, technical tinkerers. For radio, this group consisted of the "ham" operators who were sophisticated enough to operate the crude equipment:

> Indeed, a critical new factor entered the wireless scene in the early 1900s: the amateur wireless operator. All over the nation thousands of amateurs, many of them schoolboys, constructed wireless receivers and transmitters, mastered telegraphic codes, and claimed the ether for themselves. The discovery that several types of crystals would serve as cheap, easy-to-make detectors of radio waves launched the amateur boom around 1907. By 1917 over 8500 amateurs operated transmitting stations, and between two and three hundred thousand had receiving sets... amateur wireless sets provided an invaluable training ground for future researchers and broadcasters, and these "hams" formed the first audience for the earliest radio broadcasts [Czitrom 1982, 67].

Similarly, the early users of the Internet were computer tinkerers. Before the advent of "plug and play" hardware and software and "point and click" navigation, these individuals had to be skilled at installing IP (Internet Protocol) stacks into their computer systems, using acoustic coupled modems (as it was illegal to connect electrical equipment to the phone system), acquiring PIP or SLIP account access to the online world, installing Ethernet cards into the operating system, and using an arcane set of commands and programs to gain access to chat rooms and news groups, transfer files and "telnet" into other computer systems.

As each of these mediums became more "user friendly," the population of users exploded. And in each case, this popularization was viewed by industry as a means of increasing profits. Debate raged over both technologies about the extent to which commercialization should be allowed, and, in the end, each adopted roughly the same financial structure: free content for the listener/user supported by advertising dollars. As a result, both radio broadcasting and the Internet have been criticized as degrading, rather than enhancing, the quality of news, cultural and educational materials they transmit. In particular, the form known as "talk radio" has engendered comparisons to the Internet in the form of the "technology as agent of doom" narrative:

> Internet sessions can be like talk radio, with participants making strident or even subversive arguments just to get heard. The comments can be anonymous, and their accuracy hard to verify. These discussions are no-holds-barred gripe sessions. This is a problem because people play on human fears and a willingness to believe everything that passes over electronic networks [Ziegler and Sandberg 1994, B1].

Finally, we come to the case of television as a medium, one that has been criticized on all of the grounds used for other media—and then some. For example, Van der Haag (1968) stated that television, like other "mass media," "alienates people from personal experience and, though appearing to offset it, intensifies their moral isolation from each other, from reality and from themselves. One may turn to mass media when lonely or bored. But mass media, once they become a habit, impair the capacity for meaningful experience" (5). Similarly, MacDonald (1968) claimed that television viewers become 'passive consumers' who lose their human identity because they are no longer related as members of a community. According to this critique, people lose their sense of self and must look to television for a confirmation of self-image. Ultimately, the television is a tool of political domination, of tyranny.

In 1971 Rosenberg declared that "Television is an hallucinogen ... the masses are victims of a merciless technological invasion that threatens to destroy their humanity...it anesthetizes people and they are tricked into believing everything they see on television" (4–6). Continuing the narrative of television as an agent of doom and social control, Ellul (1991) stated that "Only technicians use the mass media, and it is out of the question to penetrate their domain. The amateur has only his hobby. He is more eager to accept the information, because he feels he is taking part in the big game. The belief that anyone can send information is only a wish and a myth; not reality... the proliferation of media seems to be fundamentally anti-democratic" (353).

These narrative descriptions of television as an "agent of doom" closely parallel those of the motion picture and the Internet. Rather than offering programming of a "high culture" sort, television panders to the least common denominator in terms of taste. Like a sort of combination between the radio and the movie, it has the power to penetrate simultaneously and directly into peoples' homes with visual imagery so compelling that people, exposed to that imagery repeatedly, will begin to imitate it. Through this narrative, television is seen as the technology with the greatest impact on everyday life.

Many of these same causative factors have been attributed to the Internet as well. People are said to be "addicted" to surfing the Web, following news group discussions and engaging in real time chats. The Net consumes vast quantities of time, time that would be better spent with "real" friends and "real" community or doing constructive work. The Net is imbued with a power to "entice" users to log on, after which they are said to indiscriminately believe everything they read and "hear" simply because the information has passed through the medium of the computer.

To summarize, contemporaries understood each of the communications technologies described above in terms of a narrative in which media "conquer space and time." Then, given their assumptions about the way a given medium operates, the narrative was fleshed out in either a positive or negative manner. Hopes were initially high for the ameliorative abilities of the telegraph, the telephone and the radio. But over time, the "effects" of these media were seen as primarily negative rather than positive. For movies and television, the narrative of "media as agents of social control" (and in some cases, of doom) has been predominant throughout history. For the newspaper and the Internet, the narrative has been a mix of positive and negative. The ultimate determinants of the direction taken by the newspaper were thought to be form and content. Newspapers fulfilling the "referential" role had the potential to produce democracy, "unity of mind" and intellectual ability. Those fulfilling more of an "expressive" role were doomed to degrade the individual. Similar claims have been made about the Internet since the medium was popularized in 1995. Some held and continue to hold great hope that the Internet will break down ethnic, national, class and other boundaries, unite people in a bid for world peace, enhance economic growth and foster universal education. Others contend that the Internet is nothing more than an artificial environment that will, like television, continue to pull people further and further away from real community and personal understanding and fulfillment.

Two key, interrelated questions are ignored in these assessments, both having to do with the role that individuals play as agents of social change. The first is, "Why do the particular technologies we have get invented in the first place?" The second is, "How are the technologies that have been invented variously adopted and adapted until they reach the configurations we are familiar with today?" Present narratives of communications technologies, steeped as they are in the media effects framework, are simply incapable of telling a story that answers the questions "why" and "how." In order to accomplish this, one needs to talk about human beings, not machines, as agents of social change. And while it is true that people collectively may not "know what they are doing" in terms of guiding technological development and use, it is equally true that individuals have goals and engage in motivated behavior. Machines do not. Ultimately, the question that needs to be addressed is not "what are media doing to us?" but "what are we doing with media?"

MEDIA: A CONSTRUCTIONIST NARRATIVE

The invention of the printing press coincided with the Protestant Reformation. The printing press allowed Protestants to break the monopoly held on scribes by the Catholic Church in order to spread their views of religious order and meaning. Likewise, the Reformation created a need for a machine such as the printing press. Each institution enabled the other. Once the relationship was established, the literacy rate began to grow, urban population growth spawned bureaucracy, capitalism began to flourish, and the Renaissance marked a rebirth of interest in things cultural, all of which resulted in an increase in secular literature.

Similarly, the adoption of the telegraph required more than its mere invention. Independently, Morse and Cooke toiled in obscurity for years in order to build working prototypes, only to be met with skepticism about the machine's usefulness on the part of government and private industry. The first telegraph line in the U.S., from Baltimore to Washington, D.C., was not inaugurated until 1844, 12 years after Morse began his experiments. Still, the invention was considered a "novelty":

> Morse and his associates faced apathy. Even though the use of the experimental Washington-Baltimore telegraph was free, members of the public were quite content just to come and see it, and watch chess games played between the leading players of each town over the wires. But the telegraph wasn't regarded as being useful in day-to-day life. "They would not say a word or stir and didn't care whether they understood or not, only they wanted to say they had seen it" [Standage 1998, 52].

Time and again, Morse had to return to Congress with arguments for the benefits of the telegraph in an effort to secure funding for additional research and construction. Eventually he turned to private industry for funding, and formed a company to extend line construction. Business communications, rather than the governmental or personal communications envisioned at the outset, became the target market. Once business people "discovered the merits" of using the telegraph for communications, line construction and usage soared:

> But the public had thus far shown very little interest in benefitting from the telegraph and the Congress demurred at further involvement with such an economic white elephant... In the USA, the transmission of intelligence was to be neither necessarily nor exclusively a government function. Others, the press and business, could also be involved. After that crucial hesitancy in the first year, stock speculators began to see the utility of the telegraph and the beginnings of that process which today allows global simultaneous participation in a multitude of international money and commodity markets to be demonstrated for the first time. Newspapers became avid consumers of telegrams, which had a considerable effect on their contents [Winston 1998, 27–28].

The same sort of nexus appeared in America between the mass newspaper and the rise of industry. Precursors to the modern day newspaper existed in classical Rome in the form of publicly posted news sheets. These sheets were posted in the public square so that the educated elite of Roman society could have access to all of the most important information. Similarly, in Colonial America there were small audiences, consisting of the educated "middle class," who were hungry for the latest commercial and political news, essays and literature. But it was not until the 1830s that the strategies of private ownership and freedom of the press would combine with a system of statewide public school systems and advances in printing and paper technology to set the stage for a "mass" publication. Only when these social and political strategies combined with the telegraph in the 1840s and the creation of the "reporter" did the modern newspaper form emerge:

> The mass newspaper, like the other media that followed it, was an invention that occurred only after a complex set of cultural elements had appeared and accumulated within the society. Like almost all inventions, it represented a combination of these elements in a social setting that permitted the acceptance and widespread adoption of the newspaper as a culture complex. As a technical device, it was consistent with, and perhaps even required by, other cultural institutions of the day. The relevant institutional structure of the society in terms of economic, political, and educational processes, as well as demographic and ecological patterns, provided a setting within which the particular combination of elements represented by the penny press could emerge and flourish [DeFleur and Ball-Rokeach 1989, 24].

In the case of the telephone, forerunners existed as early as the 1600s in the form of ear trumpets, speaking tubes and string phones. And the first electromagnetic device capable of converting electrical waves into sound was invented in 1837 in Massachusetts (Winston 1998, 33). But it was not until 1876 that Bell patented his version of what we now accept as the modern day phone. In those intervening years, social and even religious ideology effectively limited inventors willingness to press ahead:

> The notion of electrically based voice communication was, from the 1840s on, regarded as chimerical—a sort of term of reproach—and an indication, in any searching for it, of a measure of mental disturbance... The telephone sacrificed its respectability as an object of proper scientific inquiry ... because of the long tradition of subterfuge associated with remote-controlled speaking figures going back, perhaps, to the oracles of the ancient world. In such a tradition, "assertions of ventriloquism" continued to find their mark. This factor certainly affected Bell, who was inhibited by fear of ridicule... "Fearing ridicule would be attached to the idea of transmitting vocal sounds telephonically, especially by those unacquainted with Helmholtz's experiments, I said little or nothing of this plan" [Winston 1998, 38].

As was the case with the telegraph, the telephone rose in popularity only after its business uses were clearly defined. As Winston goes on to note, "The single major factor impacting ... telephony was the legal creation of the modern corporation... These refined commercial operations necessitated the modern office and the building to house it (skyscrapers)... This in turn accelerated the introduction of the ... passenger elevator, the typewriter, the desk calculator and the telephone" (51). The corporate use of the phone dominated for many decades. Only when the phone became more "user friendly" and physically attractive did its installation in the home spread.

The birth of the modern day movie also resulted not only from the combination of several different inventions, but from the rise of the city, the development of the factory system of production and the growth of immigration. Until the mid 1890s, movies did not have "audiences." Rather, viewing a movie was a solitary exercise in which one looked *into* a projector to see the film. Only in 1895, when the Lumiere brothers invented a single machine that served as both camera and projector, did projecting movies onto a screen in a theater become feasible. Further, despite its potential as a news document, the film was adopted largely for entertainment. These developments were no more "inevitable" than were the eventual configurations of the telegraph, the newspaper or the phone. As Gordon (1977) observed,

Edison had resisted this development, probably envisioning his Kineto-scope as a sister or brother of his phonograph... What Edison foresaw was probably a home-sized Kinetoscope in every home parlor in the country next to the phonograph... Edison's vision was not to come true, because the cinema was not going to be domesticated in the same manner as his photograph and electric light. It was, instead, to find its home in the world of the theater... Curiously, also, despite what the Lumieres had demonstrated about the capacity of film to capture real history in the making ... the numerous journalists who must have seen this new invention at work did not appear to recognize in it any deep relationship between the movies and the publication of the daily news [82–83].

Further, the motion picture, like the telephone, encountered ideological resistance from those concerned about its potential effects. With its ability to transmit visual imagery, the movie represented an entirely new "pop" art form—one that challenged conventional definitions of culture. Only when entrepreneurs, recognizing the success of short films in vaudeville theaters, opened hundreds of nickelodeon theaters was the movie able to stand on its own as a form of entertainment. In so doing, it withstood (and continues to withstand) the critiques of cultural traditionalists.

As for the radio, it was invented at the dawn of the 20th century as a system of point-to-point communication that elaborated on the telegraph and telephone. As Czitrom (1982) notes, "The point-to-point model of the wireless stemmed from the military implications that many saw in it. As early as 1897, Marconi himself had pointed out the military potential of wireless telegraphy for exploding gunpowder and the magazines of ships from a distance; he clearly had military uses in mind when discussing the urgency of improved tuning. Others noted the prospects for steering torpedoes, firing mines, and blowing up forts with 'radio waves'" (67).

"Hams," the first amateur radio operators, were both the transmitters of and audiences for communication via radio waves; many believed that this model would persist and that eventually everyone would own both a transmitter and a receiver. It was not until after World War I that the technology of the broadcast system was developed in combination with Federal regulation of the medium. This was a change that no one really expected. But, as with the movie, the public's fascination with the novelty of the technology sent it in unanticipated directions. After KDKA's successful broadcasts in Pittsburgh, hundreds of broadcasters entered the field. Listeners were attracted to the radio's ability to transmit music and voice and various cultural events, not to mention the latest news.

Finally, the television as a medium was also born of, impeded by and ultimately popularized within its own set of economic, political and social environments. In a sense, the television's path was lubricated by the radio;

it adopted radio's financial basis (as listeners were already used to the idea of commercials), the FCC's regulations for its corporate structure, and the tradition of networks and network affiliation popularized by radio. With social acceptance in hand, the only impediments to adoption were World War II and a brief FCC freeze on new broadcasting permits. Electronics manufacturing facilities were converted to war-time production for the duration of World War II. Once the war ended, there were so many broadcasting permit requests that the FCC feared chaos resembling the early days of radio would erupt. Accordingly, the agency imposed a freeze from 1948 to 1952 while it mapped out a nationwide strategy to allocate channels properly. Once these problems were overcome, the medium of television spread rapidly.

Though we are quite accustomed to present-day critiques of media as "inevitable" structures impinging on the individual from the outside, forcing him or her to conform to the "inferior" tastes and intellect of a "mass society," this is clearly not the case. Not only was the acceptance and eventual use of these technologies contingent on a whole host of social, economic and political factors, it was only in the first half of the 19th century that newly developing print technologies (relatively cheap cloth bindings, the steam-operated printing press, the mass production of paper, longer lasting inks, and the associated transportation and distribution systems) allowed for the label of "mass" communications. In fact, the very idea of "mass" society as it is currently understood was born around World War I, at a time when other developments in communications technologies (magazines, photography, motion pictures and the radio), combined with the mechanized factory system of the Industrial Revolution, made possible the production and consumption of tangible goods in great quantities (Gordon 1977). As Greer (1962) points out, the narrative of "mass society," upon which so many other forms of social critique have been based, was constructed out of a strong anti-urban bias based upon a distortion of the works of early sociologists and readily accepted without question. By and large, critiques of "mass media" and "mass society" go hand-in-hand.

Though this anti-urban bias will be discussed in detail in the next chapter, it is important to note here that there is a fundamental problem with the popular conception of "mass society." From a sociological perspective, a society can be said to exist only insofar as it consists of an accepted set of definitions of social reality and the problem-solving strategies that are in keeping with and required by that strategy. A society, above all else, is a mental construct created through an ongoing social process in which its members act *toward it* and in so doing constitute it as an *object*. This process of construction requires that individuals align their actions and interpretations of their social surroundings in order to fashion an ordered, stable reality. If one accepts this idea of society as a social construction, as an "imagined community," then there is no such thing as (and in point of fact there cannot be) a "mass society." As Herbert Blumer noted, a mass "lacks self-awareness and self-identity and it is incapable of acting together in an organized way to secure objectives" (McQuail 1994, 38). A group cannot simultaneously be a society and a mass; the two definitions are mutually exclusive. This conclusion has important implications for our understanding of communications technologies. That is, these technologies are not "mass" media as traditionally understood, but are, instead, social institutions. They are collective strategies that operate according to a specific logic that people use for explaining and understanding social reality.

People do with these technologies what they do with any other sort of institution. They reject, adopt and adapt them to suit their purposes and, in so doing, use them to create an objective, ordered meaning for the social world. As Nye (1997) observed,

> Machines are social constructions which Americans long have built into both their narratives and their sense of place... Americans have appropriated and developed machines in their own way, and woven them into landscapes, social relations and a sense of history... People use technologies to reshape and re-imagine their material context, and their experience of any space is a complex, mediated encounter. Machines do not simply appear. People invent and shape them within a larger context, which includes visual practices and narrative strategies [1–2].

In this sense, communications technologies are socially constructed institutions, just as are governments, educational systems, family structures, self-help and charitable organizations, and so forth. That is, the various forms of media we are familiar with today were invented, adopted and adapted, as are all institutions, in conjunction with the simultaneous development of political, social and economic needs for them. Further, as do other social institutions, media operate according to a certain logic. That is, media, like all other institutions, offer a framework, or lens, through which people may interpret the world around them:

> As logic they [media] involve an implicit trust that we can communicate the events of our daily lives through the various formats of media. People take for granted that information can be transmitted, ideas presented, moods of joy and sadness expressed, major decisions made, and business conducted through media... Media logic consists of a form of communication; the process through which media present and transmit information. Elements of this form include the various media and the formats used by these media. Format consists, in part, of how material is organized, the

style in which it is presented, the focus or emphasis on particular characteristics of behavior, and the grammar of media communication. Format
becomes a framework or a perspective that is used to present as well as
interpret phenomena... In contemporary society, the logic of media provides the form for shared "normalized" social life [Altheide and Snow
1979, 9, 10, 12].

Clearly, this notion of "institution" as a strategy for defining, understanding and controlling the social world, particularly when applied to the
case of technology, flies in the face of most taken-for-granted understandings about what an institution *is* (not to mention what a technology
is). But if we expect to more fully understand the social implications of
the Internet, we must first understand what we mean by "institution." Traditionally, people assume that institutions are somehow "separate" from
individuals in society. Institutions are seen as the major spheres of social
life that somehow "emerge" and take on lives of their own. As the narratives of media throughout this chapter claim, and as the following definition
suggests, institutions are "its":

An institution is a type of action, interaction or organization that is especially important to society. It is a pattern that acts as a guide, an important
norm that tells all of us how things are to be done in society. It is a central
value, and we feel obligated to defend it, even fight for it. It is also an
important truth to us, since most of us most of the time regard it as the
only right way to do things in society [Charon 1993, 115].

What definitions of this sort fail to account for is human agency. Somehow, these actions, interactions, organizations, patterns, norms, values and
truths simply appear. The end result is a system of narrative descriptions
that assume the "effects" framework discussed above; institutions, acting
from the outside, exert their power over the individual. However, if "society" is a social construction, then the institutions of which it consists cannot be objective social facts. These, too, exist only insofar as people act
toward them. As a result, the concept of "institution" is better understood
as a relational pattern manifested by a group. Groups are organized sets
of inter-human behaviors; institutions are the relations displayed therein:

Groups are systems or patterns of social behavior which arise when pluralities pursue their individual and collective aims in common... Groups
are not something different from social behavior; they are merely special
semi-established regularities of social behavior. Institutions are defined as
the standardized solutions to the problems of collective life... A group is a
strategy of interhuman behavior, that is, a plan of action intended to
achieve common objectives.... A group is a concrete system of activities;

a group institution is the solution to the problems of social life [Martindale 1966, 39–46].

The conceptualization of groups as concrete patterns of interaction and institutions as solutions to the problems of social life has, as its analytical starting point, human activity. Nothing happens unless and until people act. Further, these actions are not determined by external rules, structures or technologies. Rather, individuals appropriate rules and technologies selectively and in so doing, design narrative descriptions that give meaning to their choices. According to DeFleur and Ball-Rokeach (1989), this appropriation has evolved through five distinct stages: signaling, speaking, writing, printing and mass media (7–8). For the authors, each of these stages represents an advance in human ability to "exchange, record, recover and disseminate information." For example, the shift from signaling to speaking arguably led to the ability to reason, plan and conceptualize. The acquisition of writing, particularly phonetic writing on paper as opposed to stone, further increased abstract thought and the efficiency of information transfer and storage. Ideas could be stored and accumulated for future generations. Print and mass media continued the trend by further eroding the barriers of time and space. Over time, communications patterns (who communicates with who) depended less and less on proximity, similarity (in beliefs and interests) and group membership.

More important than advancing the human ability to exchange, record, recover and disseminate information, each stage in the human communication process represents a change in the human ability to conceptualize the *generalized other* and, therefore, the nature of the *self*. In his *Mind, Self and Society*, Mead (1934) theorized the process of socialization as one in which the individual simultaneously acquires definitions of the self and the generalized other. For Mead, this generalized other refers to the organized community or social group which gives to the individual his or her sense of self. It is that to which the individual responds in all his or her behavior. Through interaction, one develops a sense of the generalized other and of the self within a particular scene or frame. That is, the self and the social order are simultaneously framed through the symbol system of language. Through the use of language, itself a technology, individuals create their selves and their reality; they indicate to themselves and each other what their responses to objects will be, and thus what the meanings of those objects are. Language brings meaning to the self and to the world because there is no ultimately "real" world; the world and the self are "real" insofar as they are known through language.

By extension, each new communication technology offers up a different logic by which one may interpret, define and respond to the generalized other. Each affords new possibilities for bringing meaning to the self and the other because each medium utilizes a different logic in its re-presentation of the world. The Internet, then, with its ability to compress time and space, represents not a revolutionary technology but one in a long line of modifications that enables the individual to alter his or her conceptions with respect to the nature of the social self and the surrounding world. Propinquity, defined by so many as the "revolutionary" aspect of CMC, dissolved with the printed word and the telegraph. Likewise with "similarity in interests and beliefs" and "group membership." People have been incorporating others from far away places with differing belief systems into the generalized other for quite some time now.

Consequently, the Internet is unique not because it "conquers space and time," but because it is the first strategy that operates according to a many-to-many (one-to-one) communications pattern or logic. If the means of social organization can be found in a society's communications patterns, it follows that institutional arrangements themselves are the embodiment of such patterns and differ only in content. These forms and their contents may or may not adhere to and support overarching meanings and definitions of society, as systems of communication can serve many different threads of social interaction. The more open the access, the more diverse these interactions *may* be. In contemporary urban society, "mass" media represent the defining communications patterns. As such, they collectively represent the logic to which other institutions adhere. Each medium has served as the cultural mainstream in this regard, but increasingly the Internet is coming to hold this position of prominence. Thus, regarding the Internet, the task at hand is to understand the ways in which its "logic," or lens, alters (or upholds) dominant institutional arrangements by expanding the possibilities for many-to-many (one-to-one) interactions. As McQuail (1984) noted, art, religion, politics, philosophy and science are interpretive activities. They provide frameworks within which meaning can be made of diversity and discontinuity, choices made, and objectives chosen. They are institutions (as are media) because they provide lenses through which we can make sense of the world around us. So the question is, "Does the Internet operate according to a revolutionary framework, or logic, through which entirely new meanings and objectives can be chosen, or does it serve (as do other media) largely to support the already accepted core meanings and objectives?"

In 1929 Hertzler argued that, "Institutions are first and foremost psychic phenomena. The institution has primarily a conceptual and abstract, rather than a perceptual and concrete existence. Their essence is ideas and other concepts, interests, attitudes, traditions. In a very real sense, institutions are only in our heads; they are common and reciprocating attitudes"

(35). He noted, however, that institutions are also "societal structures," secondarily, in the sense that various social groups with norms of behavior and *physical extensions* utilize these psychic phenomena to create and justify systems of social organization. It is precisely on this point that the Internet has been misinterpreted. To the extent that available research assumes a media effects framework and concentrates on the physical manifestations of the Internet (as a series of chat rooms, virtual classrooms, news groups, websites, and even as a physical link for electronic business), primacy has been accorded to what Hertzler rightly argued was of only secondary importance about institutions. The Internet, incorrectly assumed to be nothing more than a "societal structure," has been disregarded as a psychic phenomenon, as a communications logic. Before turning (in Part Two) to an examination of the Internet as a "psychic phenomenon" and the implications of its logic for various social institutions, we turn to Chapter Two, in which we shall see that this focus on the physical manifestations of social change harkens back to the earliest debates in the social sciences about urbanization, the nature of community, and the role of "place" in explaining the social order.

NOTES

1. This chapter does not probe as deeply as it might using what Ritzer described as Foucault's "archaeology of knowledge": an ultimate set of rules that determine the parameters of all that might be said on a given topic at a particular time. See George Ritzer, *Contemporary Sociological Theory,* 3rd ed. (New York: McGraw Hill, 1992) for details.

2. At this time, some banking trade journals also featured technical networking articles. There was also an occasional mention, in somewhat less technical terms, of uses of networking in higher education. This, of course, was the logical result of a system originally designed for military and university research. The term "Internet" was not used until 1982.

3. For the full text of these articles, see:

a. "FBI to Consider Charging Computer Buff for 'Virus,'" *Wall Street Journal*, 9 November 1988, p. 1.

b. Eliot Marshall, "Worm Invades Computer Networks," *Science* 242, no. 4880 (11 November 1988): 855.

c. "Clever, Nasty and Definitely Antisocial," *Newsweek* 112, no. 20 (14 November 1988): 24.

d. Michael J. Ruhl, "Computers Cured After Virus Removed," *Denver Post* 97, no. 96 (5 November 1988), p. D1.

4. For the full text of these articles, see:

a. Bob Davis and Paul B. Carroll, "Virus Hits NASA Computer Network, 100 University Centers Face Infection," *Wall Street Journal*, 18 October 1989, p. 1.

b. Vin McLellan, "Data Network to Use Code to Insure Privacy," *New York Times*, 21 March 1989, p. D5.

c. Mark Lewyn, "Hacker May Face Charges Next Week," *USA Today*, 21 July 1989, p. B2.

d. Katie Hafner, "Morris Code," *The New Republic* 202, no. 8 (19 February 1990): 15.

e. "Hacker Gets Probation, $10,000 Fine for Unleashing 'Worm' on U.S. Computers," *The Atlanta Journal and Constitution*, 5 May 1990, p. A5.

5. The interested reader is referred to:

a. Steven G. Jones, ed., *Virtual Culture: Identity and Communication in Cybersociety* (Beverly Hills, CA: Sage Publications, 1997).

b. Steven G. Jones, ed., *CyberSociety 2.0: Revisiting Computer-Mediated Communication and Community* (Beverly Hills, CA: Sage Publications, 1998).

6. The interested reader is referred to:

a. Michael Perelman, *Class Warfare in the Information Age* (New York: St. Martin's Press, 1998).

b. Bosah Ebo, ed., *Cyberghetto or Cybertopia?: Race, Class and Gender on the Internet* (New York: Praeger Press, 1998).

c. Brian D. Loader, ed., *Cyberspace Divide: Equality, Agency and Policy in the Information Society* (New York: Routledge, 1998).

d. Donald A. Schon, Bish Sanyal and William J. Mitchell, eds., *High Technology and Low Income Communities: Prospects for the Positive Use of Advanced Information Technology* (Cambridge, MA: MIT Press, 1999).

7. This is a continuation of a trend: Before the popularization of the Internet, scores of books were published on the social and ethical dimensions of computers and computerization in general. See, for example, Murray Laver, *Computers and Social Change* (New York: Cambridge University Press,1980), in which the author outlines possible consequences of widespread computer use on the economy, employment, education and leisure, privacy, crime and war, and democracy; and James R. Beniger, *The Control Revolution: Technological and Economic Origins of the Information Society* (Cambridge, MA: Harvard University Press, 1986), in which the author discusses the rise of information as a commodity and the origins of the "information society" by assuming that "society" is a living, biologic organism engaged in purposive conduct and evolution through the development of information processing techniques.

8. Tom Standage, *The Victorian Internet* (New York: Walker and Company, 1998), 74, citing *Scientific American* (1858).

9. Note that Cairncross also attributes this effect to the "thousands of television and radio channels that will eventually be available." In earlier times, these were precisely the technologies *blamed* for instigating conflict via propaganda.

10. The terms *gesellschaft* and *gemeinschaft* were coined by Ferdinand Tonnies in 1887 in an attempt to describe the rapidly changing nature of social organization. Tonnies defined *gemeinschaft* as "community," as a type of social organization in which people are bound closely together by kinship and tradition—any social setting in which people form what amounts to a single primary group. He contrasted *gemeinschaft* with the idea of *gesellschaft*, meaning "association." Associations are types of social organizations in which people typically have weak

social ties and a great deal of self-interest. People are motivated by their own needs and desires rather than a desire to advance the well-being of everyone. In this context, modernization is equated with the progressive loss of human community, which provided personal ties, a sense of group membership and loyalty within small communities. The social world of the community was circumscribed in space as well as in its way of life; modernity erodes such possibilities. The significance of these concepts for the Internet is discussed more fully in Chapter Two.

11. Robert Park, "Community Organization and the Romantic Temper," *Social Forces* 3 (May 1925): 675, quoted in Daniel J. Czitrom, *Media and the American Mind: From Morse to McLuhan* (Chapel Hill, NC: University of North Carolina Press, 1982), 119.

12. Ellen Stern and Emily Gwathmey, *Once Upon a Telephone: An Illustrated Social History* (New York: Harcourt Brace & Company, 1994), 8, citing John Brooks, *Telephone: The First Hundred Years* (New York: Harper & Row, 1975).

13. Daniel J. Czitrom, *Media and the American Mind: From Morse to McLuhan*, 44, citing Dr. George M. Gould, in the *Journal of the American Medical Association*, quoted in *Health*, "Survey 29" (15 February 1913): 677; and John Collier, *The Problem of Motion Pictures* (New York: National Board of Censorship, 1910): 5.

CHAPTER TWO

Netropolis: The Internet as City in Virtual Society

As noted in the introduction, the two key definitions of the Internet are "Internet as revolutionary technology that annihilates space and time" and, correspondingly, "Internet as unique, physical place." By outlining the narrative epochs of the Net, placing them into an historical comparison to narratives spawned by older communications technologies, and arguing for the idea that all communications technologies are socially constructed institutional strategies for collectively defining and interpreting the social world, the previous chapter dispensed with the notion of the Internet as a revolutionary "annihilator of space and time." Not only do the technical aspects of networked computing bear strong resemblance to the technologies that preceded them, the narrative descriptions—the ways in which these technologies have been imagined—are strikingly similar. Each was hailed, in its own way, as annihilator of space and time, and each was alternately argued to be an agent of social amelioration or social control.

The previous chapter also alluded to two other important points. First, it suggested that the "places" created via networked computing are of only secondary importance relative to the psychic phenomenon of the Internet and its meaning for social organization. Second, it suggested that the "place-oriented" research now dominating the field is a continuation of the place-centered (and often negative) research in the field of urban sociology. Thus, the tasks of this chapter are to explore these claims in greater detail and dispense with the belief that primacy should be accorded to online *spaces* and their so-called effects.

Because the problem of social order is paramount in Sociology, and the role of the sociologist is to describe, explain and predict patterns and regularity in social life, according primacy to the physical extensions of institutions has a long history in the field. Specifically, for the urban

46

sociologist the task has been to order the diversity found in the socially heterogeneous environment of the city—to make sense of the city in a broader socio-historical context. In this attempt, present-day theorists have tended to focus on the city as a physical presence. However, this was not the approach taken by the "founding fathers" in the field. The transformation of research in this field parallels that found in media studies, and understanding this transformation will lead to a better understanding of why much current research on the Internet is relatively small in scope. What follows is an overview of the multiple theoretical frameworks and methodological approaches to be found in this field, a more in-depth examination of the approach taken by these "founding fathers," and, finally, an argument for the linkage between the urban settlements they studied, modernization (meaning a combination of industrialization and capitalism) as a defining aspect of social change, and their logical present-day extensions—the Internet and virtualization.

A BRIEF HISTORY OF URBAN SOCIOLOGY

Given the long history of the discipline, one would imagine that the sociological scope of urbanization, industrialization and "the city" would by now be consensual, if not self-evident. However, this is hardly the case. Though the sub-field of urban sociology is nearly as old as the discipline itself, there remains little agreement about the precise meaning and relevance of these core terms. In fact, the passage of time has served largely to exacerbate the problem. As once discrete "urban" physical spaces continue to expand, as "sprawl" continues to merge one metropolitan area to another, how can one know precisely where "the city" begins and ends? Similarly, how can one assess the degree to which social problems, modes of interaction, and belief systems and attitudes are city-related or society-wide? Is the distinction between urban and non-urban even a relevant one? What is the nature of the interaction between city form and larger social change? Over time, these have been some of the core questions in the field of urban sociology.

In their attempts to answer these and other questions, urban sociologists have, since the early 1900s, vacillated between two contrasting theoretical approaches: the "impact of the city" (on the experience of the individual inhabitant, on the behavioral patterns and thought process of groups of people, on the modes of interaction among groups) and "the city impacted" (by global economic restructuring, by changing political currents, and so forth). In between these points on the continuum are approaches that see the city as both cause and consequence of social change—it is an incubator of social problems and a battlefield for economic struggles that simultaneously affect the experience of the individual and evolve according to larger political and economic forces they helped to create. This strain between focusing on the urban setting as a "space" (as a specific physical place) or as a "locality" (as a point within larger social processes) is "...an historical artifact, a product of the fact that the sociology of the spatial dimension of social organization emerged at a time when 'the city' was the most dramatic and popularly available spatial manifestation of social change" (Flanagan 1993, 3). Consequently, as the table below depicts, there are multiple urban sociologies, each utilizing a set of assumptions and each attempting to explore and explain particular aspects of "the urban."

Clearly there is some overlap among the various approaches to urban sociology in terms of the aspects of "the urban" each attempts to explore, as well as the assumptions made. This is particularly true among the "conceptual," "cultural" and "ecological" frameworks. As is often the case in social analysis, the theorists of the day drew from their predecessors, interpreting their methodologies, intentions and findings along the way, and adding their own assumptions and conclusions. A brief examination of these frameworks will highlight the connections among them, illuminate the rationale for focusing on the "conceptualist" approach in this work, and lay the foundation for arguing that the Internet is but another urban form or physical extension, the importance of which is subsumed by the larger "psychic phenomenon" of virtualization.

URBAN SOCIOLOGIES

Framework	Theorists	Issues Explored	Key Arguments
Urban Conceptualism (Comparative-Historical)	Spencer, Maine, Tonnies, Marx, Durkheim, Weber	—Changing basis of social organization —Core institutions —Relevance of territory	—Aggregation of heterogenous peoples in densely settled area affects the nature of social organization —Medieval urban systems are the only city form worthy of analysis as discrete units.
Culturalism (Community v. Society)	Tonnies, Durkheim, Simmel, Wirth	—Impact of urbanization on social organization —Impact of urban setting on psychological experience and behavior of individual	—Aggregation of heterogenous peoples in densely settled area affects the nature of social organization —A distinctive (negative) cultural system emerges from a particular social form (the city)

Framework	Theorists	Issues Explored	Key Arguments
Urban Ecology (Subset of Human Ecology)	Spencer, Park, Burgess, Wirth, Hawley, Sjoberg	—Interdependencies of inhabitants of the city and their changes over time —Process of adaptation by inhabitants to the urban environment —Regularized patterns of social relationships	—Equilibrium is at the heart of social order—the city is a social organism —A distinctive cultural system emerges from a particular ecological form (the city)
Urban Political Economy/ World Systems Theory	Marx, Wallerstein, King, Harvey, Castells, Saunders	—The impact on urban centers (First World) of economic restructuring —Role of colonial expansion and domination in the urbanization process	—Local change is not local in origin —International capitalism is preeminent agent of social change —Conflict is at heart of social order

I begin with a discussion of the Culturalist approach, as this was the first that dealt specifically with "the urban" as a discrete unit of analysis.[1] At the heart of the Culturalist framework is the now age-old "community" versus "society" argument; what constitutes "community" or "society," and are the two qualitatively different from one another? Defining "community" has always been a difficult task. Even for individuals who specialize in the study of community, a clear, meaningful and lasting definition has proved elusive. The term is one which is complex and abstract; research on the subject mainly consists of case studies of particular settings that researchers assume to be communities, because the basic question "what is a community?" is a question with many possible answers.

One possible definition of community is a people who interact within a limited territory and who share a culture. Or it might be defined as the largest social organization whose patterns make a significant difference to the individual's actions—the social organization within which all other social organizations exist. But exactly what constitutes territory and interaction, and how can one determine which social organization is the largest one that makes a "significant" difference to the individual? With the advent of the telephone, the television, the computer, the multinational corporation and so forth, is any system of social relations bound by a geographic limit other than a global one? According to Bell and Newby (1974), "...out of community studies, there has never developed a theory of community, nor even a satisfactory definition of what a community is. The concept of community has been the concern of sociologists for more than two hundred years, but even a satisfactory definition of it in sociological terms appears as remote as ever" (xliii).

This dilemma regarding which social groupings may legitimately be called communities has its roots in the work of Ferdinand Tonnies (1887). Tonnies, like other Conceptualists discussed below, examined the changing modes of social relations accompanying the emergence of capitalism. He defined pre-capitalist community, *gemeinschaft*, as a type of social organization in which people are bound closely together by kinship and tradition—any social setting in which people form what amounts to a single primary group. In *gemeinschaft*, people are bound together by shared values and sacred traditions; social solidarity arises from common identity and kinship. He contrasted *gemeinschaft* with the idea of *gesellschaft*, meaning "association." Associations are types of social organizations in which people typically have weak social ties and a great deal of self-interest. People are motivated by their own needs and desires rather than a desire to advance the well-being of everyone. In *gesellschaft*, one finds a heterogeneity of values and traditions; individual differences reduce social solidarity and individualism is paramount. *Gesellschaft* is thus an elaborate superstructure erected against what Hobbes called a "war of all against all." Associations are contractual, and thus none have value in and of themselves. They are therefore characterized by instability.

Gemeinschaft and *gesellschaft* were set against one another, as two ideal types[2] on opposite ends of a continuum of social relations. Modernization (urbanization, capitalism and industrialization) was equated with the progressive loss of human community, which provided personal ties, a sense of group membership and loyalty. However, even Tonnies argued that "natural will" (the basis of *gemeinschaft*) and "rational will" (the basis of *gesellschaft*) are inextricably linked. There is a tendency rooted in individual will for every instance of *gemeinschaft* to become *gesellschaft*, and vice versa. Thus, rather than being a one-way, evolutionary path, the continuum of social organization flows both ways.

Nevertheless, Tonnies' contrasting of "community" with "society" infused the urban sociology of the Culturalists with a focus on physical place, moral undertones and a romanticism for the past. Combine this with the fact that many of these later theorists ignored the qualifiers and conditions the classical theorists placed on their ideal types, and it is easy to see how they could argue that "the city" represented *pure gesellschaft*.[3] Further, the Culturalists then used these classical frameworks to differentiate the *quality* of the character of urban life from rural life and to "detect" the social consequences of urbanization. Ultimately, this led to a preoccupation with the "disorganizing, alienating and individualizing" influences of urbanism in the works of the more influential Culturalists such as Simmel and Wirth.

The most significant work by Simmel in this area was his *Metropolis and Mental Life* (1903). This work, which would later serve as a link between the intellectual framework of the Conceptualists and the observations of the still-to-come Chicago School of urban ecology, centered on "how the personality accommodates itself in the adjustment to external forces" (reprint 1971, 325). To understand this process, Simmel separated form from content. That is, he abstracted the *forms* of human interaction from "real world" interaction and developed several ideal types of his own, such as exchange, conflict, cooperation, sociability, intimacy, distance, domination, submission and so forth. In so doing, it was his belief that society is a "web of patterned interactions," and that, by concentrating on the generalized patterns of behavior that underlie different social contexts, the sociologist could make sense of the social world. He could grasp that "man [sic] is not partially social and partially individual; rather his existence is shaped by his fundamental unity with society around him" (Coser 1977, 184).

Accordingly, Simmel argued that "the city" was a social form (in opposition to "the rural"). That is, the city consists of patterns of behavior—institutional strategies—that underlie its large scale, dense population, and highly diverse social groups and activities. Contrasting pre-modern and modern social arrangements, he argued that "Medieval organizational forms occupied the whole man. They did not only serve an objectively determined purpose, but were rather a form of unification englobing the total person of those who had gathered together in pursuit of that purpose" (Coser 1977, 189). By way of contrast, associations in modern society are functionally specific. Each individual is a member of multiple groups rather than one all-encompassing group. As a result, the individual's "personality" is transformed.

In this regard, his ultimate argument was that the city is both the basis of personal freedom and the basis for social disorganization. While its vast array of stimuli promotes the intellectuality and individuality of those exposed to it, it also promotes emotional reserve and a "blase attitude" as the principle adaptive mechanisms of the individual to life in the metropolis. In contrast to the small town, in which the mental life is emotional, in the city, life is intellectual. Because the individual's emotional life is "intensified" due to swift and continuous exposure to external stimuli, the personality becomes "metropolitan"—it responds rationally, rather than emotionally, as a mechanism for self-preservation. As a result, one can witness the development of a specific metropolitan "type" (again in the ideal type sense) of personality.

Other theorists utilized Simmel's idea of social forms and types and, ignoring his claim that they are never "pure" (for example, there is no "pure conflict" relationship) and capitalizing on his ultimate disenchantment with urban life, claimed that the city ultimately represented a mode of life in which people come together out of self interest and are devoid of any loyalty to family or community. Wirth's *Urbanism as a Way of Life* (1938) is perhaps the most influential example of this. It is an extension and modification of Simmel's work on social forms, combined with the urban ecology focus on "density" and "dominance" (discussed below). His was an attempt to account for the (mostly negative) ecological, organizational and social-psychological elements of urbanism by synthesizing Park's human ecology and Simmel's forms of association into a theory of urban personality.

In a nutshell, Wirth argued that size, density and heterogeneity of population were the causes of urban characteristics, and from those he asserted the "characteristics" of the city in a deductive manner:

> The central problem of the sociologist of the city is to discover the forms of social action and organization that typically emerge in relatively permanent, compact settlements of large numbers of heterogeneous individuals. We must also infer that urbanism will assume its most characteristic and extreme form in the measure in which the conditions with which it is congruent are present. Thus the larger, the more densely populated, and the more heterogeneous a community, the more accentuated the characteristics associated with urbanism will be [Reiss, 1964, 68].

Beginning with these ecological characteristics, he derived the following social-psychological consequences: the city increases individual variation; the segregation of population groupings by common characteristics; the segmentalization of personal life; the depersonalization of human association; sophistication and rationality; the substitution of formal for informal social controls; social stratification; and the probability of collective behavior. Interestingly, though he demonstrates a sound understanding of Park's (1936) conception of human ecology, claims it as the basis for his conclusions, and states that common sense notions of Tonnies' ideal type "community" have been erroneously incorporated into the field, in the end his assertions regarding the social-psychological consequences of city life appear to rest largely on that common sense understanding. He argues that sociological definitions of the city, urbanism and urbanization must be improved, yet he adds nothing to them. He states that, "All of these phenomena (weakening bonds of kinship, declining social significance of the family, disappearance of the neighborhood, and so forth) can be substantially verified through objective indices," yet he provides no references (Reiss 1964, 80). His argument relies, for the most part, on reasserting the claims of Tonnies, Weber and Simmel, all of whom clearly argued that their notions of the city form were ideal types. His claim that the idea of urbanism as a way of life is grounded in human ecology (the branch of urban sociology to which we now turn) is tenuous at best.

Urban ecologists, as one might have already guessed, combined the works of these Culturalists with contemporary theories of ecology. They (and other "classifiers" of cities, such as Sjoberg) sought, with varying degrees of attention to theory, to identify patterns of similarity among events that would otherwise seem unrelated (Reissman 1970, 93–121). While some categorized cities according to common, abstract indices based upon the urban-rural continuum of the Culturalists (population size, economic function, occupational distribution, moral integration and so forth), others used empirical data gathered from firsthand observation. It is to these practitioners that the term urban ecologist most appropriately applies. They were analysts of urban patterns who combined theory with empirical data and thus, in contrast to the Culturalists, were able to develop what many in the field considered to be the closest approximation of a *systematic theory* of the city to date (Reissman, 1970).

The application of ecological theory and methods to the study of the city got its start in the early 1900s at the University of Chicago. At that time the city was seen as a social organism; theories of natural ecology were used to develop theories of urban structure, urban process and urban psychology. The basic idea was that in the city, as in nature, there are both direct and indirect interdependencies among inhabitants of an area, and each adapts its behavior to the other and to the natural world. Thus, the environment (natural or urban) is impelled toward an equilibrium in which each living thing tries to move toward a "harmonious balance." The goal of the urban ecologist was to trace these lines of interdependence and track the changes that occurred; to discover the regular patterns of social relationships and how populations adapt collectively and unconsciously to one another and to their environments.

Robert Park's *The City: A Spatial Pattern and a Moral Order* (1926) was a defining work in this field. Like Simmel, Park believed that society was a product of interactions among individuals. These interactions were simultaneously constituted by and constitutive of the body of norms and traditions that ultimately bound a society together. Accordingly, Park's main interest lay in understanding mechanisms of social control—mechanisms such as competition, conflict, accommodation and assimilation—through which individuals organize, contain and channel their behavior.

Applying this basic framework to the study of the city, he utilized the ecology analogy to its fullest. He argued that the city, like any other ecological space, contained "natural areas," such as the neighborhood and the region, and that the city strove for equilibrium through the natural processes of competition, adaptation, dominance, symbiosis, invasion and succession.

These "natural areas" and "natural processes" were similar to Simmel's social forms. That is, they represented ideal type constructs by which a systematic theory of city organization and evolution could be developed and tested through empirical research. These areas and processes were dynamic; equilibrium was never achieved—in the sense that city evolution never stagnated—and ultimate social control was never achieved.

Park viewed the city as the central phenomenon of modern life and believed its subject matter to be constituted by the number, position and mobility of its dwellers. In this he shared the assumption of the Culturalists before him that a specific spatial aggregation (the city) yielded distinct, and relatively unpleasant, forms of life. He sought to study its "biotic order," which he defined as "a population, territorially organized, more or less completely rooted in the soil it occupies, the individual units of which are mutually interdependent," in order to understand its "social" or "moral" order (Coser 1977, 363). He sought to understand the substitution of law for custom, and the divergences in the mores of the diverse social groups found in the city (which he largely attributed to migration), by studying the "natural history" of the urban environment.

This urban ecological framework, combined with elements of the Culturalist approach, dominated the field of urban sociology throughout the early and mid–1900s. However, after the post-war decades, in which both the city as a unit of analysis and the qualitative research methods of the ecologists were superceded by Parsons' structural-functionalism (grand theory) and its accompanying quantitative approaches to research, the 1970s and 1980s witnessed the rise of urban political economy and World Systems theory. This transition marked a paradigm shift in relation to urban ecology by asserting that conflict, not equilibrium, is at the heart of urban social order (Flanagan 1993). With a focus on the role of a global capitalist economic order, proponents challenged the relatively functionalist approach of urban ecology by asserting that the contemporary economic restructuring concentrated the wealth in the hands of ever-fewer numbers of people, resulting in localized urban political unrest and economic strife among social classes. According to Walton (King 1990, 5), the key characteristics of this approach are as follows:

1. Urbanism and urbanization could not simply be taken for granted but required definition and explanation; they must assume the status of "theoretical objects" in the sense that they arise and take different forms under various modes of social and economic organization and political control.

2. The approach is concerned with the interplay between relations of production, consumption, exchange and the structure of power manifest in the state.

3. Actual or concrete urban processes, for example, ecological patterns, community organization, economic activities, class and ethnic politics, must be understood in terms of their structural bases or how they are conditioned by the larger economic, political and socio-cultural milieu.

4. The approach is essentially connected with social change and sees this as growing out of conflicts among classes and status groups. Changes in the economy are socially and politically generated as well as mediated.

5. The perspective is tied to the concerns of normative theory—concerned with both drawing out the ideological and distributional implications of alternative positions but also being critically aware of its own premises.

The ultimate claim is that local urban problems and social change are neither local in origin nor ultimately harmonious in outcome. For Wallerstein (1979), the interconnections among societies that cause this local change and unrest are of two basic forms—world empires and a world economy. World empires, created through military conquest and the extraction of valuable labor and resources, were built around strong states and represented the dominant form of connection before the 1400s. The world economy, by contrast, evolved after the capitalist revolution. It is founded upon multiple "core" states, all relatively equal in military power, which compete with one another for trade privileges with "periphery" states, through which they may legitimately continue to extract valuable resources and cheap labor. It is this world economy, consisting of "core," "periphery" and "semi periphery" states, that dominates today's world system.

King (1990) elaborates on this notion of world economy and its relation to urban form, unrest and change in the form of both "world" and "colonial" cities. He accepts Friedmann and Wolff's (1982) definition of both: "...the world economy is defined by a linked set of markets and production units, organized and controlled by transnational capital; world cities are the material manifestation of this control, occurring exclusively in core and semi-peripheral regions where they serve as banking and financial centers, administrative headquarters, centers of ideological control and so forth" (12–13). Among the many important characteristics of these world cities, they contain a disproportionate number of the headquarters facilities of the world's 500 largest multinational corporations and international banks; experience a rapid rise in the number of highly paid "international elite"; serve as centers of global transportation, communication and production of news, information and culture; are centers of international investment; and witness expansion of the service sector and a polarization of high and low paying jobs.

By contrast, "colonial cities" (their size, functions and social, cultural and spatial forms) can only be understood in relation to these world cities. They exist because they are the means by which the colonial periphery was and continues to be incorporated into the urban core:

> For each of the main colonial powers, a colonial urban system was established, from the metropolitan capital and port cities, through a network of colonial port cities, colonial capitals, regional and district centers, down to the outlying stations of the colonial bureaucracy and system of military control. All were linked by transport, communications, and subsequently, electronic and other media... At each link in this urban chain, there was an ongoing process of economic and political, as well as social, cognitive, cultural, and environmental transformation [King 1990, 34–35].

Thus, for the first time since Durkheim, Marx and Weber examined the changing nature of cities, the urban political economists asserted that urban sociology may, in fact, not be a legitimate sub-field of inquiry. Committed to the concept of "the global" as the ultimate unit of analysis, they asked, "Is the city a discrete structure, worthy of specialized study?" They argued, as did Marx, Durkheim and Weber, that what had historically been thought of as "urban" cultural phenomena were now "mass society" phenomena manifested by industrial capitalism.

Interestingly, it can be argued that the urban ecologists and the urban political economists, though they disagreed on the nature of social order, could agree on two key points with respect to urban sociology. First, it seems they could agree on a definition of the city as a physical and spatial expression of economic arrangements and conditions. Where the urban political economy approach assumed that international capitalism is the dominant agent of social change, the urban ecology approach assumed that local economic (natural) forces of competition, invasion and succession were the agents of change. Thus, the only difference is the scale (local versus global) of the approach. Second, though they arrived at this conclusion from different angles, both schools of thought agreed that "the urban" ultimately *is* an analytically distinct framework worthy of special study. For the ecologists (as well as the Culturalists) this was true because the city represented a specific ecological form that yielded unique cultural traits. For the political economists it was true because the city consisted of distinctive spatial features: "The urban is a distinctive spatial aggregation of the economic arrangements of wider society, and the modern city is the physical expression of capitalism in particular" (Flanagan 1993, 110).

Similarly, the World Systems approach to the urban argues that the city retains its importance as an object of theory and empirical research. This time, however, it is not because of its "unique cultural forms" or "distinctive spatial aggregations." Rather, it is because the cities of the world now comprise a single urban system that transcends national boundaries. National boundaries dissolve, and towns, cities and large "functional urban regions" are once again the chief physical features of the world map. In the World Systems approach, as noted above, cities and the process of urbanization are conceptualized in terms of colonial expansion and domination; the framework offers a global, structural analysis of how cities grow and change. Urban systems, not the nation-state, are the ultimate unit of analysis because they do not stop at national boundaries (Flanagan 1993).

Just as communications technologies share a core set of narrative descriptions constituted by and constitutive of the "media effects" framework of analysis, the urban and the rural as distinctive social spaces share a narrative. In this story, the spatial arrangement and physical features of a space are the causative factors. In a sense, the description of both media and the city is the same; both annihilate space and time and thereby reorder the individual's perception of these parameters. The end result is often deemed detrimental to both the individual psyche and the social order.

CONCEPTUALIZING THE URBAN: CITY FORM AND RELEVANCE

What of the urban Conceptualists, the "founding fathers" of Sociology whose works were the basis, often inadvertently, of the many forms of urban sociology that followed? Interestingly, though their research and writings dealt with the city to a large extent (Marx's and Weber's more so than Durkheim's), they did so primarily in terms of the relationship between the city and the development of capitalism and industrialism—modernity. According to most subsequent interpretations of their works, all three argued that a distinctive urban sociology cannot be developed in the context of advanced capitalist societies. After the Medieval period, they claim (and urban political economists would agree) cities are nothing more and nothing less than concrete examples of the development and consequences of capitalism. Because they focused on the changing basis of social relations brought about by capitalism, the Conceptualists tended to examine the city in two ways: 1) as an historically important object of analysis in the context of the transition from feudalism to capitalism, and 2) as a secondary influence on the development of and fundamental processes generated within capitalist societies. In the narrative of Karl Marx, Emile Durkheim and Max Weber, the city is not a cause, but a significant condition of certain social changes. And interestingly, though their methodologies and beliefs were different, each reached this same conclusion about the city (Saunders 1981).

Central to this conclusion was their argument that the history of the city is not one of continuous development and evolution. On the contrary, the Ancient city, the Medieval city and the Industrial city are very different social phenomena, characterized by differing bases of social organization and degrees of relevance of various social institutions.[4] In the Ancient World, "the urban" and "the rural" represented distinct forms of social organization, each with its own set of institutional arrangements; while rural peasants continued to live in self-sufficient tribal communities in much the same way as inhabitants of pre-class tribal organizations before them, urban inhabitants constituted the beginnings of a new form of social organization in which primary loyalty was owed to the city rather than to a specific clan or tribe. In contrast to pre-class society, which was characterized by a minimal division of labor, communal property, a migratory existence, and the importance of kinship and religious institutions, Ancient society was a city-based form of organization with the first definitive divisions of labor and social class (Giddens 1971).

Ancient cities, which often resulted from the union of several tribes into a city, "either by agreement or by conquest," were city-states governed by priest-kings (Giddens 1971, 27). Subjects, while afforded the protection of the city and the opportunity to participate in trade and other activities, were required to obey city laws, pay taxes, worship city gods and protect the city from outside intruders. Further, they were economically dependent on both the free labor of the city (the new merchant class) and the slave-based agricultural system in the countryside. It is perhaps this dependency on a slave-based rural economy that best characterizes the Ancient city and ultimately explains its downfall. Though free craftsmen lived in the city and produced for the urban market, they ultimately represented a small proportion of the economy. Slave-based agricultural production in the countryside dominated in Antiquity because limited technological developments made agricultural production very labor intensive, and because the continuous wars in which successful Ancient cities engaged provided an almost unlimited supply of new slaves. In turn, this ready supply of labor suppressed the competitive capabilities of the free craftsmen and entrepreneurs of the city and any labor-saving devices they might have developed (Zeitlin 1990).

Cities of Medieval Europe, on the other hand, were marked by the rise of feudalism and serfdom over slavery as the "mode of production." As the ready supply of slaves began to dwindle (due in some measure to both an inability of the ever expanding city-states to retain control over vast expanses of territory through warfare, and a "barracks" system of housing that prevented slaves from having families that would replenish the labor supply), estates in the countryside converted slaves into serfs. The resulting disintegration of Ancient cities, particularly the Roman Empire, gave rise to a period of urban decline and stagnation that lasted about 600 years, during which time "retinues" were born and increased in power. Retinues consisted of military leaders with groups of followers who engaged in raids and wars, as members of professional armies had done for the city-states. Recruited for their military prowess from diverse clans and tribes, members of "retinues" were loyal only to their military leader and were allowed to keep the booty from these raids for themselves. These retinues eventually became established institutions, constituting feudal nobility as powers of the ruler were deemed hereditary, and tribal or clan ownership of land was replaced by seignorial ownership.

Feudal society reflected the power of these lords; peasants, who were increasingly tied to their economic function, paid dues to the feudal lords for protection. Initially, the feudal economy was characterized by this small-scale peasant agriculture, supplemented by handicraft production in towns. It was largely a rural system, as the towns' populations were limited by food supplies (due to poor food transportation, preservation and storage capabilities). But by the end of these "dark ages," the Medieval city was the center for handicraft production and various political, religious and educational functions (Sjoberg 1973). As these cities continued to grow, they gained administrative autonomy from feudal kingdoms, largely through the "municipal movement" of the 12th century. And, as was the case in Antiquity, this growth of towns corresponded with the formation of a new merchant class and a monetary system. The continuing development of urban centers into wealthy commercial and manufacturing centers, in turn, led the feudal system to its ultimate collapse as serfs poured into the cities to bolster the new urban middle class (the bourgeoisie) and continued to stimulate the ever-widening use of money (Giddens 1971; Zeitlin 1990).

Ultimately, modern capitalism developed out of these late Medieval cities. The rise of the new middle class ultimately spelled the demise of the guild system that dominated production in the 14th and 15th centuries. In place of these older forms of what Weber called "political capitalism" arose "modern industrial" or "bourgeois" capitalism. The defining element of industrial capitalism was the establishment of a *mode of production* based on free labor and fixed plants, operated by the plant owner at his own risk to produce in a competitive market for the anonymous consumer. (This shift in the type of capitalistic production marks a transition from what the world systems theorists called "world empire" to "world economy.") And central to its operation were the "rational organization of labor" (meaning that the wage earner was separated from ownership of the means of production), and "bureaucracy" as an administrative tool. (We will return to a discussion of Weber's description of this modern form, the corporation, in Chapter Four.)

Overlapping the rise of modern industrial capitalism was the rise of industrialism, which is characterized by "the use of inanimate sources of material power in the production of goods, coupled to the central role of machinery in the production process. Industrialism presupposes the regularized social organization of production in order to coordinate human activity, machines and the inputs and outputs of raw materials and goods" (Giddens 1990, 56). In such an environment the industrial city loses all of the unique features that Marx, Durkheim and Weber argued were necessary for their classification as discrete sociological entities. No longer the economic seat of trade and commerce, the political and economic fortress or garrison, the administrative court district or the oath-bound confederation, the industrial city, with its technical/ scientific/ factory base, melted into the nation-state system. Given these sweeping changes in city form, it is not surprising that the founders of sociology argued that the Medieval city alone was worthy of a distinctly "urban" sociology. But how did they reach this conclusion, given their disparate theoretical and philosophical assumptions and research methods? It is to a brief analysis of their arguments that we now turn.

Marx was concerned, first and foremost, with the material conditions of existence—the relations of the worker to the means of production—and how the technical and social processes of production changed over time. In his work on cities, Marx examined the relationship between the town, the country and the capitalist mode of production. He argued that, in the Ancient city, because slavery was the dominant mode of production and the wealth of the ruling class was founded on the ownership of agricultural land, the mode of production remained rural or "tribal." Accordingly, the town-country relationship was entirely a political one; the city was the administrative center superimposed on the slave-agriculture mode of production.

However, in the Middle Ages this relationship changed. The growth of the merchant class led to an increase in the number of trade links, which lead to an increase in the division of labor between towns, and a corresponding growth of new industries. Capitalist manufacturing begins in the countryside where the labor power still resides, and towns grow up around these productive areas. Feudalism reflects the conflict between the town and country and *conflicting modes of production*. It is at this point—in the Medieval City—that the city itself is important as a subject. Gradually, as new productive forces undermined feudalism and commerce, and the cities continued to grow, peasants who had come to the city to escape their feudal lords became what Marx termed the "new capitalist class" or "bourgeoisie." As their wealth continued to grow, they essentially overthrew the landed nobility, and the capitalist mode of production spread; the town and the country were no longer in conflict. For Marx, "urbanism" is an "ideological" concept we use to make sense of everyday life (in the sense of urban problems), not a discrete scientific concept to analyze or explain (Saunders 1981; Macionis 1993).

For his part, Durkheim examined the relationship between the city, the division of labor and the moral basis (form of social solidarity) of different forms of human settlements. The nature and transformation of the social bond over time were his key concerns. Following the lead of Tonnies, he developed the concepts of *mechanical* and *organic* solidarity. According to Durkheim (1893), these forms of social solidarity are largely a function of the relative degree of homo- or heterogeneity of the population and the resulting level of the social division of labor. As one might expect, *mechanical solidarity* occurs in the equivalent of Tonnies' *gemeinschaft* through the development of what Durkheim called the "collective conscience." This collective conscience, demonstrated through the existence of repressive law, represents a commonly held morality that prevails where individual differences are minimized and the members of society are very much alike in their devotion to commonly held values and beliefs.

In contrast, *organic solidarity* is signified by the existence of restitutive law, and parallels the conditions of *gesellschaft*; community members hold a variety of beliefs rather than sharing a common, unifying morality, and are held together by an interdependence that results from a complex division of labor. According to Durkheim's principles (though he was never explicit on this point), the Medieval European city is the only instance in history in which "the urban" is uniquely characterized by organic solidarity, while "the rural" remains characterized by mechanical solidarity. How did this occur? Durkheim implicitly defined "urbanization" in terms of the following: 1) "dynamic" or "moral" density—the rate of communication between members; 2) "material density"—the number of individuals in contact per unit of space; and 3) "volume"—the geographical space defining the physical boundaries of a particular society (Karp, Stone and Yoels 1977, 21). The city of Medieval Europe gave rise to increases in both dynamic and material density. It put more heterogenous groups of people into contact with one another in a given geographical space and allowed for a far greater frequency and intensity of social contact among them. This urbanization of the population caused a more complex social division of labor; a population thus concentrated, he argued, can only survive through differentiation of its members' functions (Saunders 1981).

However, an increase in dynamic and moral density is only a necessary, not sufficient, condition for the division of labor. One must also have a weakened collective conscience. The Medieval European city, with what Weber noted as its "rational codification of law," signified this weakened collective conscience with its emphasis on restitutive rather than repressive law. These increases in dynamic and material density, combined with the rise of restitutive law and an urban population that grew primarily through immigration of the peasant population rather than natural birth, undermined traditional social controls, even though the city may have still contained small moral communities within it. It is the Medieval city that eventually extends its influence over the surrounding countryside and "urbanizes" society as a whole, after which there is no longer any significant distinction to be made between "the urban" and "the rural" in terms of forms of social solidarity.

Weber had yet another perspective, but reached the same conclusion. Focusing on economic and political organization (rather than size, population density and diversity, and so forth), he examined the city and its relationship to the growth of bureaucracy and rationality. According to Weber (1958), cities are appropriately defined by the existence of an established market system and at least partial political autonomy. That is, they survive off of trade and commerce rather than agriculture, and are politically and militarily independent from other cities and larger social systems. Only settlements that meet those qualifications might appropriately be defined as distinct human settlements worthy of independent study. As a result, the late Medieval city, after the overthrow of the feudal manor and before the rise of the nation-state, is the only urban form that can be meaningfully distinguished from its surrounding environment: "The city of the Medieval Occident was economically a seat of trade and commerce, politically and economically a fortress and garrison, administratively a court district and socially an oath-bound confederation" (111). Cities prior to this period (and even Medieval cities outside Western Europe) are disqualified because the dominant form of human association was still kinship. The later Industrial city does not qualify on the grounds that it is not politically or militarily separate from larger social systems; the power of cities of the Industrial Age was superceded by that of the nation-state system (Saunders 1981; Karp, Stone and Yoels 1977).

Ultimately, though his focus was not the political or economic tyranny of the system or the specific nature of the division of labor, Weber agreed with Marx and Durkheim that the city in the Middle Ages was highly significant, as it represented a break with feudalism and laid the foundation for the development of capitalism. Guilds of the Medieval city were the basis for the development of economic rationality, and while the city itself did not spawn capitalist industry, it did create the ideological and institutional legacy that formed the urban population of Medieval Europe into a ready-made audience for the doctrines of the Protestant Reformation (Saunders 1981). Politically, the Medieval city gave rise to administrative officials and rational codification of law, which ultimately undermined the authority of nobility and fortified democracy. Only in the Medieval city do we find that the city itself was the basis of human (political) association. Before the Medieval city, kinship was the basis; afterwards, the nation-state.

Each of the urban Conceptualists discussed here ultimately argued that, after the Medieval European city passed, there was no longer a useful distinction to be made between "the city" and society in general. As Saunders (1981) argued (and I agree), attempts at a systematic urban theory since the Conceptualists bear this out. He suggests that a continuing problem for the field of urban sociology has been the attempt to "fuse a theory of specific social processes with an analysis of spatial forms" (Saunders 1981, 9). Claiming that these two questions are distinct and mutually exclusive, he says we must abandon space as a theoretical concern. We must forgo the effort to define "urban sociology" in terms of a specific concern with spatial forms.

This is not to say that urban ecology, urban political economy and world systems theory have not proved useful in understanding "the city." To the extent that they abandon concerns with spatial considerations and focus instead on the city as a framework for human interaction, whether those interactions are at the level of the individual or the nation-state, they have served to illuminate the patterns and problems that recur in human social life. For their part, urban ecologists continue to contribute to the quality of life in cities, either by assisting urban planners or by examining so-called "urban" problems. Similarly, urban political economists have enlightened us about the extent to which our individual lives are impacted by larger structures and events in a global system. However, both camps have accomplished these goals largely by abandoning the insistence on physical space as a defining factor of "urbanization" and "urbanism." While both schools argue that the city is worthy of specialized study, they do so because they ultimately concluded that the city is a "process," or social form, or pattern of interaction constituted by and constitutive of other social institutions.

Interestingly, if one examines the research that has been conducted to date on networked computing and the Internet, one finds that it corresponds with the early research done on cities. As noted in the previous chapters, myriad case studies (mine included) in the Culturalist tradition of debate over "community" versus "society" dominate the research. And while it remains to be seen whether this research will eventually evolve to encompass the computer-mediated equivalent of urban political economy, one thing is certain: We have bypassed the equivalent of the urban Conceptualists. We have assumed that the Internet, like the city, is a discrete space worthy of sociological analysis, and have neglected the examination of "virtual" worlds as psychic phenomena.

In the final section of this chapter, I make the case for examining this very possibility—for doing away with the assumption that the Internet represents a discrete social entity, and for understanding it, instead, as nothing more and nothing less than the physical manifestation of a wider social process of virtualization. While one could argue, given its relative youth, that the Internet today is the equivalent of the Medieval city (in that it represents a unique social form distinct from the society that surrounds it), I argue that this is not the case. I argue that seeing the Internet as *nothing more and nothing less* than a physical manifestation of the phenomenon of virtualization is far more fruitful.

NETROPOLIS AND THE INDUSTRIAL-VIRTUAL CONTINUUM

As I noted at the outset of this chapter, the long and prolific history of urban sociology has not witnessed any consensus as to the precise meaning of "the city," urbanization, or industrialization. However, what is generally agreed upon is that each concept is inextricably linked to the other, and each constitutes an aspect of modernity. Consider first conceptions of the city. Alternatively seen as bazaar, jungle, organism and machine (Langer 1984), conceptualizing the city means conceptualizing the modern. For example, Redfield (1930, 1941), in his examination of forms of human settlements in Mexico, articulated a "folk-urban" continuum and stated that "the city" is not so much a specific place or community as it is a "setting in which new states of mind could come into being" (84). For Redfield, this "setting" was distinctly modern in that it employed Tonnies' *gesellschaft* or Durkheim's organic solidarity as a means of social organization.

Similarly, Greer (1962) stated:

> [The city is] a division of labor distributed over space, associated with a division of rewards that, in the form of residence, is also spatially distributed, coordinated through organizational structures that produce and depend upon the flow of messages, persons and goods. The integration of the city is only a particular case of the integration of any social system; it is based upon a network of interdependence and a resulting mutual modification of behavior extending over space and through time [40].

This social system that manifests itself in the political and economic organization of the city is society in general:

[Society is] the bounded network of interdependence resulting in mutual control of behavior: as the scale of organizational networks increase, there is an increase in the size of meaningfully defined "society" [40].

This definition clearly implies "the city" as a modern concept in keeping with the ideas of Marx, Durkheim and Weber. It is a division of labor and, as such, is the physical manifestation of bourgeois capitalism, rationalization and bureaucracy, and organic solidarity. It is the *social form* commonly associated with modernity in that it consists of a set of institutions (industrialism, capitalism and mediated communications) through which its members meet the challenges of the modern era.

Likewise, conceptions of urbanization, industrialization and capitalism also revolve around "the modern." As a process, urbanization includes not only the growth of cities in population size and density, but the articulation of a class system, the conversion of the city's "institutional values and structures" to a national scale, and industrialization. Industrialization and capitalism include the creation of an open market, the rational pursuit of profit, the development of corporate forms, the expansion of bureaucracies, the increased use of energy and an increase in productivity. These ultimately result in a shift in the economic center from the land to the market and factory; an increase in the division of labor; a decrease in rigid social divisions; an increase in mobility in the class system; and corresponding rises in democratic ideals, constitutional guarantees, and the political ideologies of nationalism and imperialism that legitimate the economic expansion.[5]

Nisbet (1966) argued that these "themes of industrialism"—the transformation of property and the conditions of labor, and the rise of technology and the factory system—overlap and have a common center in the development of the industrial city form. That is, it is in the industrial city form that we witness: 1) the rise of a heterogeneous and formless working class not bound to larger society either by tradition or by property ownership; 2) the development of new forms of property, such as industrial and financial capital, that brings about an urban middle class through a rapid accumulation of wealth independent of ownership of real estate; and 3) the rise of a factory system that leads to the separation of home and work (Karp, Stone and Yoels 1977, 24).

The industrial city is constituted by and constitutive of these elements of social organization; it is a necessary, but not sufficient, condition of the development of *modern* society. As the table below depicts, the social form of the industrial city is but one element in the transition from pre-modernism to modernism. More important was the transition in the logic used to define, interpret and respond to the generalized other. As the explanatory power of science overtook that of religion in defining the "other," and was subsequently enhanced by media logic, other social institutions were restructured in order to solve the new problems that these changes in meaning brought about. Technological change was part and parcel of these transitions; technology itself became an institution, a strategy designed to meet particular problems recognized by the community. Through narrative, technology and technological change were woven into the fabric of the modern community form.

TRANSITION TO MODERNITY

	Pre-Modernity	*Modernity*	*High Modernity*
Basis of Definition of Generalized Other	—Religion —"Information" not Significant	—Science —"Information" Significant (One-to-Many Global Information Dissemination)	—Media —"Information" Significant (Many-to-Many/ One-to-One Global Information Dissemination) —Rapid Increases in "Dynamic" and "Moral" Density
Political Order	—Feudal System (Fief-Holding and Vassalage) —Non-Bureaucratic —Rural, Homogeneous Population	—Nation-State System (Citizenship and Rights) —Bureaucratic and Rational-Legal —Urban, Heterogeneous Population	—Nation-State System (Human Rights) —Bureaucratic and Rational-Legal —Networked, Heterogeneous Population —New Forms of "Actors": NGO, Transnational Governmental Organization
Economic Order	—Political Capitalism —Rural, Slave-based Means of Production (Non-Regularized Production, Unity of Work and Family) —Pre-Class System —Form of Capital: Real Estate —Source of Production Power: Animate	—Rational Capitalism (Private Ownership of Capital, Propertyless Wage Earner, Competitve Markets) —The Corporation (Regularized Production in Large Scale Industry with Increased Specialization, Technological Division of Labor, Instrumental Attitude Toward Work, Separation of Work from Family) —Class System: Working Class	—Rational Capitalism (Private Ownership of Capital, Propertied Wage Earner, Competitive Markets) —The Corporation (Regularized Production in Dispersed Organizations, Continued Division of Labor, Personal Fulfillment Attitude Toward Work, Less Separation of Work and Family) —Class System: Working Class (Wage/Service Labor), Middle Class (Knowledge Worker) —New Forms of Capital (Intellectual Property) —Source of Production

	Pre-Modernity	Modernity	High Modernity
		(Wage/Factory Labor), Middle Class (Merchant) —New Forms of Capital (Industrial, Financial) —Source of Production Power: Inanimate	Power: Animate (Mind) and Inanimate (Networks, Computers)
Normative Order	—Religion of Great Importance —Collective Conscience from Gemeinschaft —No Mass Education —Family/Clan/ Tribe Fundamental Unit of Organization	—Religion Less Important —Collective Conscience from Gesellschaft —Beginnings of Free, Public Education —Individual is Fundamental Unit of Organization (Spread of Property and Individual Rights, Nationalism and Constitutional Government) —Family Functions as Agent of Socialization	—Religion Less Important —Collective Conscience from Gesellschaft —Increases in Levels of Education and Specialized Continue —Individual is Fundamental Unit of Organization (Continued Spread of Property and Individual Rights) —Family Functions as Source of Support and Validation of Individual
Self	—Subsumed Within Family/ Clan/Tribal Affiliation —Understood as "Soul"	—Institutionalized as "Individualism" —Foundation for Other Modern Institutions —Understood as Synonymous with Identity	—Incorporated as "A Life" with a Life Course —Foundation for Other Modern Institutions —Understood as Collection of Identities

Interestingly, while all agree that rapid technological developments—the transition from a handicraft to a machine technique, from a tool economy to a machine economy—were instrumental in the development of the Modern, many have also suggested that these developments did not represent a complete break with previous types of knowledge and forms of social organization. On the contrary, they were founded on earlier advances in the natural and applied sciences, and were in keeping with the "rational manipulation of the environment" posited by the Catholic Church and the Protestant Reformation (Becker 1961; Turner 1975). Further, some argue that traditional societies were (and continue to be) actively selective regarding the industrialization process. For those societies not imbued with Weber's "spirit of capitalism," modernism does not intrude on the traditional order as a unitary, structured force that pushes aside or displaces the traditional order wholesale. On the contrary, as Blumer (1973) argued, there are at least five ways in which traditional social orders respond to the industrial:

1. Rejective: the traditional order may reject all or part of the industrial process.

2. Disjunctive: the industrializing process, though not rejected, operates detached from traditional life.

3. Assimilative: the traditional society absorbs all or parts of industrialization without disrupting the regular patterns of social life.

4. Supportive: industrialization strengthens or reinforces the traditional order or significant parts of it, as individuals use it to pursue traditional group interests and to maintain traditional social positions.

5. Disruptive: the traditional view of the effects of industrialization, in which the traditional order capitulates to a modern order [99–104].

The importance of these claims for present purposes is twofold. First, they point to the significance of the interconnections between the social bases of organization and meaning, technology and technological change, and the physical manifestations of social order. Second, they point to the fact that, contrary to what we may choose to believe about our relative "helplessness" in the face of such change, people actively use technology as a problem solving strategy in conjunction with a system of values and beliefs to define and interpret social reality. It is in this sense that the invention of networked computing in general, and its physical manifestation in the form of the Internet in particular, represents an evolution of a technological strategy with *perhaps* revolutionary consequences. For, while the degree of change between pre-modern and Modern (industrial) society does not represent a complete break with the past, it did result in changes in the nature of social reality—roles and institutions that, I argue, are sufficient to constitute a transformation that leans toward the "revolutionary" point on an "evolution-revolution" continuum.

Conversely, the shift from Modernity to "high" Modernity is *currently* more in keeping with change on an evolutionary scale. This is not to suggest that people have not been witness to notable changes in social institutions such as work, family, community and so forth. On the contrary, the second part of this book is devoted to an examination of these types of institutions and the changes that may occur in the future. What I am arguing is that the *defining aspects* of Modernity—the belief in science as truth-teller (via "mass" media), progress as the ultimate social goal, and the worth of the individual as an "inherent, natural reality"—remain unchallenged.

In many respects, these defining aspects are heightened, taken to the "next level," such that what we are left with as a social system is not "post-modernism" but "high modernism."

What are the characteristics of this highly modernist society? A brief overview here will serve to set the stage for a more detailed exploration of this social form and the nature of its various institutions in the remainder of this book. Chiefly, a highly modernist society is a virtual society. Webster's (1983) informs us that "virtual" means "being in essence or effect, not in fact; not actual, but equivalent so far as effect is concerned" (2042). As such, virtual society is, quite simply, one that exists for its members *in effect*, if not in "fact." How is such a society accomplished? I argue from the theoretical standpoint of symbolic interactionism that it is accomplished in precisely the same manner as every other society before it— through interaction.

In Chapter One, I discussed a symbolic interactionist perspective on the nature of the generalized other and the self. Generally, symbolic interaction is the study of the making of meaningful behavior. Symbolic interactionists assert that meaning emerges from consensus among actors and is established in interaction. That is, meaning is not inherent, it is created and therefore unstable and problematic (Brissett and Edgley, 1975). Within this context, one explored in greater detail in Chapter Seven, the self is defined as the meaning of the human organism; a meaning which is highly situational (Stone and Farberman 1970). The self is established by its activity and by the activity of others towards it. It is not inherent in the individual because the "individual" is a shared, interactive phenomenon; self is an outcome, not an antecedent of behavior. What one does establishes who one is, not vice versa; there is no useful distinction to be made between actor and action. Further, interactionists argue that human beings are primarily symbol users; the meaning of the self and all other subsequent meanings, including that of the generalized other, are constructed through symbols, which are the primary cultural resource (E. Becker 1962).

Another way of phrasing the statements above is to say that society *is* symbolic interaction (Blumer 1969). That is, all human interaction is mediated by the use and interpretation of symbols. And, in order for such interaction to occur and be meaningful, each participant in that interaction must be able to take the role of the other through the use of the sign system, or technology, of language. An important consequence of this use of language to bring meaning to the self and the world is that there is no ultimately "real" world; the world and the self are "real" insofar as they are known through language, and they expand to the *extent* and *depth* that communication will practically allow (E. Becker 1962).

In the early 1900s, when W. I. Thomas was conducting a study of

Polish peasants in Europe and America, he asked a Polish peasant about the extent of a neighborhood. The peasant replied, "It reaches as far as the report of a man reaches—as far as the man is talked about" (Cappetti 1993, 77). It is through communications technologies that the "report of a man" is extended and deepened, that role-taking is extended to the global level and society accordingly virtualized. In essence, to "virtualize" society means to use media logic to render irrelevant the physical aspects of human social existence in the construction of meaning and social reality. Virtuality is a social form, specifically a form for organizing interaction without regard for the physical aspects (limitations) of that interaction. Communications technologies have long operated according to a logic that afforded individuals the opportunity to disregard space, time, physical and geographical place, the physical body, co-presence and perhaps even age, ethnicity and gender—to the extent that they choose in favor of a focus on the "textual" aspects of reality construction. Networked computing, unlike previous communications technologies, operates according to a logic that alters interaction patterns specifically because it utilizes a many-to-many (one-to-one) format, in contrast with the one-to-many or so-called mass format of previous technologies.

The Internet is a virtual human settlement (real in effect)—the physical manifestation of virtualization. But virtualization began in earnest as a *psychic phenomenon* with the telegraph. To correctly interpret the role of networked computing is to understand it as an extension of a phenomenon that started with the invention of the telegraph and continued through the advent of the television. The entire history of communications technologies is one of virtualization. Meaning emerges through interaction. While all interaction has historically been mediated by language, in contemporary society interaction is mediated by communications technologies. To understand the process of virtualization and its resulting form of social organization, one must understand the logic by which those technologies operate. Ultimately, it is a matter of understanding that the *form* by which we communicate is at least as important as the content of that which is communicated. Note that this claim is not synonymous with the saying, "the medium is the message" (McLuhan 1967), because the form encompasses more than the technological hardware and because people are active agents in shaping, adopting and rejecting the form.

Each medium operates according to its own logic, and the Internet is no different. With its capacity for an infinite array of many-to-many interactions, the Internet seems to have an enormous potential to further problematize the construction of meaning, particularly overarching meaning on any scale other than one-to-one. Because the self is also a meaning constructed in interaction, virtualization via the Net expands the situational possibilities through which identity may be legitimately constructed, thus further problematizing the self. As a result, defining the self and the generalized other in a meaningful way becomes one of the key problems of social order in the highly modern world. Institutional frameworks of the past must be reworked, to varying degrees, in order to meet this new challenge. To what degree do those institutions change, and what do those changes imply for the generalized other and the self? It is to those questions that we now turn.

NOTES

1. The conceptualists, though they contributed what I will argue are the most profound insights on the nature of urbanization, industrialization and social change, ultimately concluded that the physical entity of "the city" was, with the exception of the Medieval city, less important to social organization than other larger social processes.

2. The term "ideal type" is most appropriately attributed to Max Weber. According to Coser (1977), an ideal type is "an analytical construct that serves the investigator as a measuring rod to ascertain similarities as well as deviations in concrete cases. An ideal-type is formed by the one-sided accentuation of one or more points of view and by the synthesis of a great many diffuse, discrete, more or less present and occasionally absent concrete individual phenomena, which are arranged according to those one-sidedly emphasized viewpoints into a unified analytical construct. It does not refer to moral ideals" (223). While Tonnies did not coin this phrase, and while his discussion of the contrasts between *gemeinschaft* and *gesellschaft* were decidedly ideological, he did note that he "did not know of any condition ... in which elements of *gemeinschaft* and *gesellschaft* are not simultaneously present... Pure *gesellschaft* is something imagined rather than real" (Szacki 1979, 345).

3. Unlike Tonnies, Durkheim did not agree that *gesellschaft* represented an artificial superstructure. He claimed that, as a form of solidarity, it was just as natural as *gemeinschaft*; restitutive laws (those focused on repayment and the restoration of normality and that serve as the foundation of organic solidarity) could not be viewed as discrete associations of otherwise unrelated people together momentarily for the sake of a contract. On the contrary, contracts can only be built from the implicit social foundations found in mechanical solidarity. David A. Karp, Gregory P. Stone and William C. Yoels, *Being Urban: A Social-Psychological View of City Life* (Lexington, MA: D. C. Heath & Company, 1977).

4. In their research, Marx, Durkheim and Weber were particularly concerned with city forms of the West. Weber in particular sought to understand the specific cultural differences between Occidental and Oriental city forms, and ultimately argued that, based upon the criteria he believed defined "the city," none of the city forms outside the West qualified as being worthy of discrete sociological analysis. Similarly, most contemporary writers, when tracing the evolution of the city, refer most substantially to those cities that emerged in Western culture within these

three time periods. As a result, the analysis in this chapter is likewise confined. John Sirjamaki, *The Sociology of Cities* (New York: Random House, 1964).

5. Some theorists, such as Reissman and Nisbet, approach industrialization and capitalism as a unitary process. Others, such as Giddens, view each as a specific, individual aspect of modernity. Regardless, many of the same features and consequences are emphasized. See, for example, Leonard Reissman, *The Urban Process: Cities in Industrial Society* (New York: The Free Press, 1970) and Anthony Giddens, *The Consequences of Modernity* (Stanford, CA: Stanford University Press, 1990).

Part II

Preface to Part II

Before delving into the analysis of specific institutions and the ways in which they may be altered via networked computing, it is necessary to outline the parameters of the arguments to follow. Four points should be made. First, these chapters are designed to analyze contemporary social institutions. Accordingly, to the extent that each chapter involves historical examination of a subject, it will be limited to the realm of Modernity and deal only with what I described in Part I as the transition from modernism to "high modernism."

The second parameter is as follows. In an effort to manage the examination of a transition that is so obviously enormous in scope, I have chosen to partition the discussion into three large scale but commonly accepted divisions of social order—political order, economic order and normative (ideological) order (Poggi 1990). Accordingly, the chapters that follow serve as overviews of the transformation of these spheres by probing the relationship between the logic of the Internet and the status of the core institutions within those orders—the nation-state (political order), the corporation (economic order), and the church, university and family (normative order). Discussion concludes with an examination of the modern self as it is constituted by and constitutive of those institutions.

Third, since we are dealing with an analysis of institutional change, it would be prudent to reiterate exactly what institutions *are* in the sociological sense. To put it plainly, institutions are, first and foremost, psychic phenomena. They are problem-solving strategies—the standardized solutions to the problems of collective life (Martindale 1966). Taken together, a collection of these strategies make up what Simmel (1950) termed a "social form." According to Simmel, society is nothing more and nothing less than a complex web of interactions among individuals, and a "social form" is best understood as a process, or framework, through which people render reality intelligible. It consists of and operates as a set of strategies

75

and rules (institutions) to deal with some phenomenon, some problem of living. In his broadest application, Simmel used the idea of form to explain the fact that humankind chose "association" as the general, defining principle of life. Because humans as a species could just as easily have selected to be unsocial, as do many other animals, "association" itself must be understood as the most general social form. Taking the explanation down a level, a "social form" is a form of association that consists of institutions designed to solve the problems of collective life. Most social scientists argue that these social forms are of three general types—hierarchy, network and market—the details of which will become more clear in the chapters that follow.

As I pointed out in Part I, the focus of research into social forms and institutions has historically centered on their physical manifestations. This has served largely to detract from the development of clear understandings of the role of media in contemporary society. However, if we allow the conceptions of form and institution outlined above to inform our thinking, the waters are a bit less muddy. We can compare and contrast previous and current social forms with their attendant institutional frameworks to better anticipate where we may be headed. Accordingly, the remainder of this book takes as its starting point the notion that Modernity is a social form. It consists of a set of institutional strategies designed to solve the problems of human association. Within this broad framework we are witnessing a transition to "high" modernism that is both cause and consequence of the change in patterns of human association brought about (most recently) by networked computing. This "virtuality," if you will, is the result of applying media logic (most recently Internet logic) to the problems of collective life. It is the result of organizing interaction without regard for the physical aspects (limitations) of that interaction. This change in patterns of interaction creates new problems for social order and identity, and the continued viability of various social institutions depends upon the ability of each to alter its internal workings in order to meet those problems.

This brings us to the fourth and final parameter—the examination of core institutions of high modernism through the lens of media logic. It has been argued, as I noted in Chapter One, that all media operate according to a "logic" or framework:

> In general terms, media logic consists of a form of communication; the process through which media present and transmit information. Elements of this form include the various media and the formats used by these media. Format consists, in part, of how material is organized, the style in which it is presented, the focus or emphasis on particular characteristics of behavior, and the grammar of media communication. Format becomes a

framework or a perspective that is used to present as well as interpret phenomena... The present-day dominance of media has been achieved
through a process in which the general form and specific formats of media
have become adopted throughout society so that cultural content is basi-
cally organized and defined in terms of media logic ... an interaction
between organized institutional behavior and media [Altheide and Snow
1979, 10, 15].

In the chapters that follow I examine the challenges to and potential adap-
tations of various institutions through just such a framework. I apply the
idea of "media logic" as a *communication form*—as a framework through
which information is presented and transmitted, through which social reality is constructed and interpreted, and through which social action occurs—
to the specific instance of networked computing. Taking my lead from
Altheide and Snow (1979), I argue that the Internet, like other modern
forms of media, is a technology and as such carries

...a connotation of rationality. Consequently, both communicator and
audience are oriented toward a rational means-end type of communication—rapid dissemination of vital information at relatively low cost. This
practical approach to communication is a logic in itself. An audience also
expects the information received to be accurate and current. In turn,
media producers strive to at least give the impression of being accurate
and topical. This rational/practical character of media logic further leads
to dependability—in other words, audiences want information that is relevant to their desires. In total, these characteristics become a form of communication that is consistent with the modern scientific manner in which
contemporary society operates [15].

But media logic as a communication form is more than "consistent
with" modern, contemporary society—it defines it. Prior to the 20th century, media reflected the form of and reality defined by the dominant institution. That is, media served to enhance the collective consciousness
inspired first by religion and then by science. Today, however, according
to the media logic perspective, media are the dominant force to which other
institutions conform. The result of this shift is what Snow (1983) termed
"media culture"—the condition in which the characteristics of institutions
and the content of culture develop through the use of media to define and
interpret reality. "When a media logic is employed to present and interpret
institutional phenomena, the form and content of those institutions are
altered.... In contemporary society, every major institution has become
part of media culture. Changes have occurred in every major institution
that are a result of the adoption of media logic in presenting and interpreting
activity in those institutions" (11). In media culture, institutions follow

media logic in the definition and solution of problems. Media legitimate institutional strategies, as they are used by interactants to define relevant subject matter, create "experts" on those subjects, and guard and influence "official" (and unofficial) information. In so doing, media serve to affect both the internal workings and external significance of other institutions.

Like other media, the Internet contributes to media culture. It employs a number of formats (frameworks to present and interpret social phenomena), each of which consists of: (1) Grammar (which includes the organization and scheduling of content [syntax], the rhythm and tempo of content presentation [inflection] and any special features of language or gestures [vocabulary]); and (2) Perspective (the viewpoint/strategy employed to define and interpret content). Taken together, the grammar and perspective of each Internet format combine to constitute an overall communication logic that people employ as means of understanding reality.

While details of these formats emerge more meaningfully in the context of specific institutional frameworks, a brief overview here serves to set the stage. If the newspaper is the "daily institution," the novel the "medium of dreams," the magazine the "medium of subcultures," the radio the "companion medium," the film the "emotion medium" and television the "cultural mainstream," then the Internet is "all of the above" (Snow 1983). The many formats of the Internet, including World Wide Web pages, file transfer protocol (FTP), gopher, real time chats (e.g. Internet Relay Chat) and asynchronous discussions (e.g. Usenet, Fidonet and listservs), are capable of adopting all of these approaches, with their attendant grammars and perspectives, and in certain instances may create entirely new grammars and perspectives. Taken together, the Internet is, above all else, the *interaction* medium. These interactions are founded on the "network" as a social form, meaning that interaction occurs and reality is constructed in a pattern of interaction characterized by voluntary association, reciprocal exchange and horizontal communication patterns. Thus, in order to understand the institutional transformations underway, it is necessary to understand the operational logic, or strategy, of the distinctly interaction-oriented, network-based (as opposed to "mass") communications medium that is the Internet. This means analyzing the overall logic of the Internet, the various formats it offers to convey information and define/interpret reality, and the degree of coincidence, or "fit," between those formats and the institutions in question. It is to this analysis that we now turn.

CHAPTER THREE

The Nation-State in the Virtual World

As Becher (1998) noted, the predominant subjects of and sources of information on the nature of political order have changed over time. As the geographic scope of thinking has grown from regional to transcontinental to global, the key subject has likewise shifted from the "will of the ruler" to the "power of the sovereign state" to the "management of interdependence." More interesting is the fact that the dominant communications technologies used to define, analyze and contest the political order have evolved in corresponding fashion from print media to television and increasingly the Internet. This chapter is concerned precisely with this transition in subject matter from "sovereign state" to "interdependence," and information source from older technologies to the Internet.

Despite the fact that it has long been accepted as the key "actor" in the political order (and still is by many who concern themselves with such matters), the nation-state remains an elusive concept. Debate abounds about the nature and evolution of nations and their connections to "the state," the meaning of political power, and the future of a state apparatus that supposedly rests on the continued viability of territorial sovereignty in an age of globalization. Though deliberations over the birth and forms of nationhood and nationalism continue, it is generally accepted that "the nation," as a form of community, is created through interaction and communication. It is a "self aware" associational form that encompasses ethnic, religious, linguistic and institutional legacies to varying degrees. It is a shared imagining.

Beyond this general definition, however, the concept becomes more problematic. For the nation is not any sort of imagined community. It is one which ensconces its members in a sense of shared history and destiny; it serves as a backdrop of shared assumptions about the past and visions of the future. Fundamentally, its self-awareness rests on the belief that it is intrinsically linked to a territory over which it has the right to claim sovereignty. Though nations may be held together by this sense of shared character and destiny, and not by the authority of the state, it is "the state" as a legal, internationally recognized entity operating within a nation-state system that helps to secure this territorial sovereignty. It is the state, an "abstraction capable of existing in perpetuity," that is "the most massive and significant modern manifestation of political power" (Poggi 1990, 18). It is the physical manifestation of the nation in that the state and *only* the state may legitimately use force to control both its borders and its citizens:

> Two features of the state ... the state's sovereignty and its territoriality, jointly produce a most significant consequence: the political environment in which each state exists is by necessity one which it shares with a plurality of states similar in nature to itself. Each state is one unity lying next to others within a wider entity, the states system. But it is important to see that these units do not consider themselves, and do not conduct themselves in relation to one another, as organs of that wider entity, as they would if the latter had established and empowered them and were in a position authoritatively to regulate their conduct. Sovereignty entails that all states are [to an abstractly equal extent] primary, self-positing, self-sufficient entities; it is not the states system which brings them into being, but on the contrary their independent existences which generate the system.... Thus the relations between states are not structured, monitored and sanctioned by a higher power, for no such power exists: the state is the highest level locus of power present in the modern political environment [Poggi 1990, 23–24].

It is because the nation, a tenuous, complex and imagined community form, is wedded to the state, a precisely defined (if still abstract) legal entity, that students of it have long debated its continued viability. Particularly problematic are the notions of "political power" and "territorial sovereignty" emphasized above. It is the attempt to impose the precision of these ideas on an associational form that is by definition abstract that has contributed to confusion over the present status of the nation-state as a means of social organization. In recent decades, such confusion has been ignited by the concept of "globalization."

Some who are more cautious about the prospect of burying the nation-state maintain that, because the idea of the "nation" has been imagined on different premises and under different circumstances, its viability as a social form and as a basis for individual identity may remain—despite "globalization." As Smith (1981) notes,

> Nationalism has proved to be an extraordinarily potent force, and it also appears to be highly malleable in its formation and expression.... A

national appeal attracts the widest possible following, cutting across social divisions and inviting expressions of popular participation ... nationalism is primarily a quest for unity, not for rationality based on equal rights.... One of the strengths of the modern state has been to harness nationalism to its cause, and that is true irrespective of the nature of the regime or the level of development reached by a society ... we should be wary of assuming that nationalism is a spent force or that the "outmoded" state can be readily supplanted by even more rational forms of political organization [198–199].

Others add that, though some functions of states—especially those related to economic development and monetary policy—have been altered by "globalization" since the 1970s, other roles have been enhanced, and still others have been newly adopted. States still control education, health, welfare and taxation (within limits set by, and in spite of, external pressures). They still maintain exclusive rights to the legitimate use of force, both within their own borders and internationally. For this reason alone, they remain the key "actors" in international relations. In general, the state has continued to grow in both the size and diversity of institutions that make it up, and in the active involvement in an expanded range of activities. The activities of the state have expanded as people increasingly reconstruct private troubles as social issues. More and more, groups ask the state to either intervene in their behalf or alter its policies in their favor. In so doing, individual citizens, multinational corporations, non-governmental organizations (local and transnational), terrorist groups and the like continue to act, positively or negatively, *toward the state* and thereby continue to constitute its legitimacy.

Despite the validity of these arguments, many students of the nation-state system have adopted what Anderson and O'Dowd (1999) term a "strong" globalization perspective, which accentuates,

...the novelty of recent forms of globalization, with the 1970s typically seen as the watershed. They stress the development of a "borderless" global economy, the dominance of new communications and information technology, and the intensification of transnational cultural and governance networks, with signs of an emerging global consciousness. The more extreme variants see the "end of the state-centric world of territoriality and borders," and the "end of the nation state"; the "end of ideology"; and even the "end of geography" [597].

The astounding growth of the Internet has fueled this perspective. As of the year 2000 there were an estimated 250 million regular users of the Internet—a population that is expected to double by 2003 and triple by 2005. While over half of those users are in North America, 62 million are in Europe, 42 million are in Asia, and the online populations of South America, the Middle East and Africa (currently totaling around 11 million) are steadily climbing.[1] Equally compelling is the fact that the World Wide Web consists in part of around 19 million commercial (.com) domains, over 12 million network (.net) domains and over 800,000 non-profit (.org) domains.[2] The 19 million ".com" domains represent private enterprises that, though they may not fit the traditional definition of a "multi-national corporation," are nevertheless capable of behaving as if they do via networked computing. Further, some of the 12 million ".net" domains and many of the 800,000 ".org" domains represent non-governmental organizations of activists that, while scattered around the globe, are capable of acting in concert via networked computing.

Proponents of "strong" globalization have argued that these figures portend great changes for the defining political form of the Modern world, the nation-state. Though opinions within this perspective range from claims that the nation-state is already "dead" to more modest claims that it is "in serious decline," most appear to be in agreement that the Internet is rapidly becoming the most significant contributor to the phenomenon of "globalization," and that multinational corporations and transnational, non-governmental organizations are in a position to usurp the authority of the nation-state, break down its physical boundaries, and raise serious doubt about the notion of sovereignty:

> In the rapidly growing literatures on globalization, many authors have emphasized the apparent disembedding of social, economic and political relations from their local-territorial preconditions. It is argued, for instance, that the "space of flows" is superseding the "space of places"; that territoriality and even geography itself are being dissolved; that national borders have become irrelevant, redundant or obsolete; that nationally organized politico-cultural identities are being "deterritorialized"; and that "supraterritorial" spaces based upon "distanceless, borderless interactions" are decentering the role of territorial and place-based socioinstitutional forms. Whatever their differences of emphasis, research object and interpretation, common to these diverse analyses of globalization is a focus on the accelerated circulation of people, commodities, capital, money, identities and images through global space. These accelerated, globally circulating flows are said to embody processes of deterritorialization through which social relations are being increasingly detached and disembedded from places and territories on sub-global geographical scales [Brenner 1999, 431].

Given the historical focus on physical territory as a defining hallmark of all human communities, the focus on the territorial sovereignty of the nation-state comes as no surprise. As noted in Chapter Two, since the dawn of the city as a social form, theorists of community have been preoccupied with the spatial manifestations of associational forms. Generally, this preoccupation has evidenced itself in the overarching theme of "community." This term invokes a specific form of social organization in which people are bound closely together by kinship and custom. Community is a social setting in which people derive social solidarity from common identity and tradition. Interestingly, though Tonnies originally intended this term as a descriptor of pre-capitalist spatial forms, it has since been used to describe myriad spatial arrangements. As noted above, "community" is commonly used to describe the national-state system. Increasingly it is used to describe the emerging "global civil society" as well.

Because forms of social organization are first and foremost psychic phenomena, and because humankind is capable of imagining "community" in any spatial arrangement suitable to its purposes, it is arguable that current attempts to understand "what is going on" with the nation-state by focusing on territorial sovereignty and traditional ideas of political power are misplaced. Underlying this focus is the assumption that, "It is probable that the three powers (or rather, the groups which have built up one or the other of them as a facility for the pursuit of their own interests) will contend with one another. Their contest will have two overlapping aspects. On the one hand, each power will seek to restrict the autonomous sway of the others, diminishing their autonomous impact upon that ultimate object (the activities of citizens). On the other hand, each will seek to enhance itself by establishing a hold upon as great as possible a quantum of the others, by converting itself to some extent into them" (Poggi 1990, 8).

This chapter suggests that attempting to assess "who will win" the competition among the powers (political, economic and normative) in a "zero-sum" game is not the most salient goal. The question is not whether the state can maintain sovereignty in the face of "globalization." Rather, given the media culture in which institutions currently operate, the question is to what extent can any institution, the nation-state included, adapt to and utilize new media logic. Specifically, can the nation-state take advantage of the "interaction medium" of the Internet and the "network" as the social form upon which that medium is based in order to secure its internal stability and external significance? The traditional and often "gut-level" response to this question is "no." The state is argued to be, by definition, centralized, bureaucratized and hierarchical at its core, and is therefore not only antithetical to the "network" as a form, but internally incapable of discarding "hierarchy" as a form and adopting "network" in its place. Because the network form is seen as the newest, most rational, most efficient and therefore most effective form, it is argued that other forms of organization are in jeopardy.

How accurate is this assessment? It may well be too soon to tell. Certainly the state has been slower to adopt an interaction, or network, strategy than private enterprise and non-governmental organizations (NGOs). But, let us not forget that states, like nations, are imagined and operated according to different normative parameters. It is not enough to declare the nation-state a form in opposition to the network and globalization and therefore obsolete. After all, for better or worse, the political process has historically proved capable of conforming to other media formats (Altheide and Snow 1979). So in order to assess the possibilities for its continued survival we need to set aside this fundamental assumption about the uniform and unchanging nature of the state. We need to think about whether it is the network form *alone* that affords political power, or whether that form is simply more conducive to utilizing a new media logic through which power is obtainable. We need to compare and contrast instances in which the network form has come into conflict with the state, been adopted by the state and successfully rejected by the state in order to determine the extent to which the nation-state remains capable of providing solutions to the problems of collective living. Only then are we able to accurately assess its status in the political order.

NET(WORK) LOGIC AND THE POLITICAL ORDER

Perhaps the best way to explore the problems of and possibilities for the nation-state vis-à-vis the network form is to compare it to the institutional strategy that appears to inherently conform to that framework—the non-governmental organization (NGO). (While many argue that the multinational corporation is the more dominant force to be reckoned with, I suspect that the MNC is confronted by its own set of problems due to globalization/virtualization. This argument is left for the following chapter.) NGOs are argued by many to be the "up and coming" actors in the political order precisely because they adopt a network form and are thus capable of taking advantage of the possibilities for the increased speed, depth and breadth of circulation of information afforded by the Internet. The arguments of Keck and Sikkink (1998) on this point are possibly the most compelling. In *Activists Beyond Borders*, the authors examine the rise of a specific type of NGO—transnational advocacy networks—and how those organizations seek to exercise power and change the behavior of the state (and other international organizations) through the "production, exchange and strategic use of information" (Keck and Sikkink 1998, X). In so doing, NGOs are claimed to serve as sources of new and alternative visions, ideas, norms and identities.

These networks are based on shared beliefs and values, as are many types of organizations. Further, like most organizations, they seek to "frame" issues in a given light in order to make them comprehensible to target audiences, attract attention and encourage action. What makes NGOs unique is their network form; they are characterized by voluntary, reciprocal and horizontal patterns of communication and exchange. Populated by committed, knowledgeable actors working in specialized issue areas, the source of their power is the ability to generate information quickly and accurately and deploy it effectively. In a world characterized by media culture, in which information circulates instantly and institutions and individuals adopt a media logic for interpreting that information, speed and flexibility in framing a situation within the parameters of media formats are said to accord the network form an inherent source of power. For this reason, NGOs are uniquely suited to adopt their frames to the logic of the Internet.

As the interaction medium, the Internet affords NGOs leverage previously unavailable. As Keck and Sikkink note, NGOs typically engage in four types of tactics: information politics (timely and credible generation of usable information that can be positioned for political impact); symbolic politics (definition of a situation for a faraway audience through the use of symbols and stories); leverage politics (engagement of powerful actors to affect a situation when weaker network members are unlikely to have influence); and accountability politics (attempt to hold powerful actors to their previously stated policies and principles). The Internet appears to enhance the NGO's capability in these areas in three related ways.

First, it greatly increases the speed and reduces the cost of circulating information, two former barriers to NGO success, particularly in information politics. Second, and more importantly, the increased speed and reduced cost enable the NGO to transmit more and *more engaging* information. That is, through the use of sophisticated web pages, newsgroups and real time chats, NGOs have access to multiple venues through which an issue may be meaningfully framed or defined for the distant audience. Discussion areas, whether real time or asynchronous, afford possibilities for "testimonial" evidence—"real life" accounts of a situation as experienced by persons on the scene. Increasingly sophisticated video technologies make possible the distribution of visual information about the situation, both through high quality still photography and streaming video. No longer forced to rely on the relatively static and "mass" forms of communication (such as newsprint and television), NGOs have the ability via the Internet to frame situations themselves and to actively engage the "audience" in the discussion of and solution to the problem so defined.

Finally, and perhaps most importantly, this many-to-many form alters the pattern of interaction around a situation and holds out the possibility for a redefinition of the generalized other. The pool of interactants around a given situation or event is potentially expanded beyond those who are immediately (physically) involved to those living at great distances who become psychically involved due to the engagement format. The more distant the audience, the more it relies on media to frame and interpret information. The fact that the Internet allows participants to actively engage in that framing process does not negate the possibility that many interactants may accept the frame uncritically. Nor does it negate the fact that, even given active, critical participation, users remain bound by the technological parameters of the medium in their ability to perceive and understand the situation at hand. In fact, it is the interactive format of the Internet that lends credibility to the information therein. *Interactivity turns information into knowledge.* This increased possibility for the distant audience to actively effect change, combined with the framework of *engagement* at the grass roots level integral to the NGO form and supported by the logic of the Internet, make an understanding of the Net's grammars and perspectives (logic) vital.

One approach to understanding these grammars and perspectives relative to the political order is to examine cases in which Net formats have been employed by transnational NGOs, with varying degrees of success, to in some way alter the behavior of other international "actors." For our purposes here, we shall briefly examine the Free Burma Coalition (FBC), the International Federation for East Timor (IFET) and the Zapatista network. Each of these networks was created out of a desire to right perceived wrongs done to a portion of a state's internal population by that state. The Free Burma Coalition was formed in response to the refusal by SPDC (State Peace and Development Council), formerly known as SLORC (State Law and Order Restoration Council), to honor the results of the democratic election of the NLD (National League for Democracy) party and its leader, Daw Aung San Suu Kyi, in 1990. The International Federation for East Timor was formed around the same time as an effort to coordinate the decolonization process and uphold human rights in East Timor as it sought (and continues to seek) independence from Indonesia. Finally, the Zapatista network, which represents a much looser coalition of organizations and groups, was organized later (1994) in an effort to garner support for the EZLN (Zapatista National Liberation Army) and its leader, Subcommandante Marcos, in the peasant uprisings in the Mexican state of Chiapas. Though these networks have in common this general organizing principle, the degree to which they have been able to alter the actions of other "international actors" has varied depending on their ability to conform to and make use of the grammars and perspectives of the Internet.

On this score, the Free Burma Coalition (FBC) and the International Federation for East Timor (IFET) have been more successful than the Zapatista network. Examination of the grammars and perspectives (logic) of their respective networks of web pages and interactive areas (chat rooms, listservs and newsgroups) provides insight as to why this is the case.

Consider first the Free Burma Coalition (*www.freeburmacoalition. org*). It combines a remarkably complex grammar (including syntax, inflection and vocabulary) with an elementary "ideal norms" perspective for solving problems. Regarding grammar, its syntax (organization and scheduling) can be described as "centralized" and "current but ambiguous," respectively. That is, the FBC web page serves as the central location for access to the most complete and up-to-date information about Burma. The importance of this fact should not be overlooked, because such an organization facilitates the network's ability to draw new members into the fold. A centralized starting point makes it easier for the web surfer to find and believe in the frame that the network uses to define the situation. Additionally, it gives the participant a sense that he or she fully understands the issues (i.e. there is no extraneous, possibly contradictory, information floating about) and can therefore appropriately *identify with* the network's stated goals. Similarly, the current but ambiguous scheduling of information in a centralized location allows and requires participants to remain active in the network. That is, anyone who is concerned with democracy in Burma expects the FBC website and related interactive areas to provide him or her with the most up to date information and insights possible. In the age of networked computing, up to date means instantaneous. However, unlike the scheduling of information in other media, in which updates are anticipated only at—and precisely at—certain times of day (e.g. the morning edition of the newspaper, the 6:00 P.M. television news broadcast and so forth), the scheduling of information via the Internet is ambiguous. One never knows when "updates" and "urgent action alerts" will be posted to the web page, nor does one know when new insight will be added to a newsgroup or when one might "get mail" from a listserv. This ambiguity heightens the participant's sense of belonging to the group and its cause, because ongoing interaction that is not solely at the discretion of the individual serves to remind him that the struggle of his group is continual.

More striking than its use of centralized organization and ambiguous scheduling of information is the FBC's remarkable array of inflection devices. New possibilities for inflection, the rhythm and tempo of content presentation (particularly combinations of inflection devices), is what really separates Net logic from other media formats. On the Internet, organizations can combine newspaper, magazine, photography, radio and television formats with asynchronous and real time interactions in a way that enables a highly orchestrated frame. On the FBC web page, inflection devices range from font type, font size and color choice, to the extensive use of exclamation points, to blinking and flashing icons, to the "question and answer" format, to strategically positioned hypertext links. Each of these devices serves to draw the viewer's eye to the information deemed most critical. "Action Alerts" (Your Involvement and Support are Critical Now!!) are emblazoned in large, red lettering. Updated information is marked with flashing logos. The page is dominated by the central question, "What can YOU do to help end the atrocities in Burma?" which is followed by a list of four simple actions the reader can take to contribute to the solution.

But most important is the site's strategic positioning and use of hypertext links. In terms of rhythm and tempo, there are plenty of links, but not too many; the time required to reach each new link is very low; and old, out of date links are practically non-existent. These link attributes are vital to maintaining what Csikszentmihalyi (1990) termed "flow," a condition of "optimal experience" in which one participates in a goal-directed, non self-conscious activity that requires intense concentration and yields a sense of control. Fast links to striking, meaningful and internally consistent content are the sum and substance of Internet rhythm and tempo. They enable the participant to become fully engaged in the story that a particular website has to tell. Nothing on the Internet is more disruptive to flow, and consequently to the NGO's desired frame, than slow or dead links.

Beyond successful link positioning and speed, the FBC site offers highly engaging interactive link content. From a central location one can follow links to FBC press statements and releases, daily news items, weekly news summaries (from BurmaNet and other sources), current FBC campaigns in which individuals may become involved, campaign victories (success stories), lists of additional activities for the individual who wishes to work toward a solution, the FBC official manual (including its list of tools and resources for lobbying, organizing demonstrations, contacting and working with various media, writing press releases, contacting expert speakers and acquiring human rights documentaries, videos, films and readings), refugee news from the UNHCR (United Nations High Commissioner for Refugees) and, most importantly, lists of affiliated individuals, organizations, asynchronous newsgroups and real time chat rooms. It is this obvious but vital function of links that provide access, not just to additional information but additional *organizations*, that enables NGO networks to use the grammar and perspectives of the Net to their best advantage.

Taken together, linked content that combines as many media strategies as possible is capable of presenting and engaging the individual user in a unified and seemingly inevitable definition of the situation. In other words, the more links to affiliated organizations offered, and the more media formats used across those links, the more "self evident," all-encompassing and effective the network's overarching perspective for presenting, defining and interpreting the situation. We will return to the idea of "perspective" momentarily. But in order to understand how the FBC (and other NGOs) achieves success with its perspective, one must understand a bit more about its use of these linked inflection devices (media formats).

From the FBC web page one can gain access to myriad additional sites. Perhaps the most relevant to this discussion is the "freeburma.org" page, which consists entirely of links to still other sites. Divided into four categories (information, action, interactive and cultural), this page offers links to anything from insights into the culture and people of Burma to activists groups around the world to real time interaction (in Free Burma Live Chat) to sources of visual and audio current events. "Action" links are those described above. They highlight steps that can be taken by the individual to solve problems in Burma, and range from online activism (letter writing) to organizing boycotts to sponsoring refugees. The page even offers the "Burma Benefit Button," which, when clicked on, takes the user to Amazon.com where any purchases will result in a donation to the FBC. Beyond these individual actions, "interactive" links serve to solidify one's identity within the Burma activist community. One can participate in live Burma Chat or an asynchronous forum (soc.culture.burma) to discuss recent events in Burma, thoughts, feelings and possibilities for action. Or one can subscribe to the BurmaNet News listserv and receive regular news updates. In terms of media formats, this listserv functions as a newspaper. That is, it adheres to the event-centered grammar of the newspaper. But, unlike traditional papers, it employs the strategy of "advocacy journalism" rather than "objective journalism." Generally speaking, the stories contained therein follow a specific rhythm—an urgent, eye-catching and dramatic opening, followed by a lengthy background section which uses dreadful detail to draw the reader further into the story, and ending, interestingly, with an air of upbeat uncertainty. The overall theme of these sorts of stories (both those in listservs and those on web pages) is slow but steady progress. This is a point we will return to in the discussion of "perspective."

Of all "information" links, the most compelling are those that revolve around audio and visual information. With the RealPlayer program installed, the computer is capable of serving the same function traditionally reserved for the radio. RealPlayer enables access to Voice of America Burmese Service, the Democratic Voice of Burma Radio and Radio Free Burma. While all of these programs are in Burmese and thus arguably do more to support "Burmese" as a national identity (a point discussed in more detail later in the chapter) than to increase membership in the network, in so doing they serve the traditional purposes of radio—companionship and identity formation. As Snow (1983) noted, the organization and scheduling of radio content follow the listener's daily routine and serve to compartmentalize activities within that routine. Thus, radio is a companion. Further, the content of these radio programs (which includes news, speeches, songs by request, satire, poetry, perspectives, book reviews and so forth) is important to and for listener identity. Because the content of the programs noted above is consistent with that of related web pages, chat rooms and asynchronous newsgroups, RealPlayer audio programming serves to further legitimate identification with that organizational perspective. The ultimate result is the feeling that one is a part of something larger, that one has the power to contribute, to affect change on an enormous scale.

Additionally, some Free Burma pages make use of visual information, usually in the form of still photography but occasionally in the form of video. Video information is of two types—speeches by NLD leader Aung San Suu Kyi or "documentary" style tapes of trips made into the region by freelance reporters and human rights workers. The videotaped speeches bear some resemblance to the television news magazine or one-on-one talk show format in that they revolve around a specific question. Though never shown or heard from, one gets the impression, seeing Aung San Suu Kyi seated at a table, that the interviewer is just across the table from her, listening intently to her answer. Naturally, because she is the leader of a democratically elected (if exiled) political party, the tapes lend the goals and perspective of the FBC tremendous authority. Combine this type of visual information with that presented in videos of reporters and human rights workers "on the scene" in documentary style (as they carry their own cameras and narrate the scene as they go), and one gets an impression of the situation that is difficult, if not impossible, to disbelieve.

Not to be overlooked as a critical inflection device is the use of still photography. Generally, still photography is found in two places within a website. First, individual photos that are defined as "capturing the moment" often accompany leading news stories and "action alerts." Strategic use of individual photos in these locations immediately draws the eye of the viewer to the story and serves as evidence that what the text says is, in fact, true. Beyond this, however, photography is used more extensively to provide background on the situation. These photographs are usually found deeper within a given website and are grouped together in "galleries" that revolve around a specific theme or occurrence. Most often, graphic and, frankly, demoralizing photo galleries of massacres and torture are juxtaposed with galleries of more serene photos, such as landscapes and culturally significant gatherings and festivals. The clear objective behind such organization is to compare the unacceptability of the present condition with what would otherwise be. The use of still photography in this manner is perhaps the most successful inflection device. Its defining attribute, like the motion picture, is that of emotion (Snow 1983, 169–209); it creates visual knowledge that is both highly believable and nearly impossible to ignore.

A brief note about vocabulary, the final component of grammar, is in order. Two points should be made. First, with respect to the FBC and affiliated sites, the vocabulary is relatively sophisticated. It references fairly complex political issues and the complex connections among them. Second, the main sites discussed above, in fact almost all affiliated sites, are written in English. Both these traits indicate a specific target audience for the perspective contained therein.

Taken together, these cultural, actionable, interactive and information links, along with their attendant and complementary grammars, serve to legitimize overarching perspectives. For the Free Burma Coalition, these perspectives are "journalism" and "ideal norms" (Snow 1983). Traditionally, journalism as a perspective has relied on the notion of objectivity. News consists of a bundling together of "the facts" as obtained through detached reporting and the collection of official documents from legitimated groups. It is in large part an event-centered approach to documenting reality. More recently, "advocacy journalism" has stressed not just an event in the here and now as observed by a detached audience, but the background of an event as experienced and interpreted by the people involved. Though each type has previously been viewed as the antithesis of the other, the FBC has managed to unify the two in its attempt to construct the meaning of the story of Burma. That is, while plainly an advocate for the exiled NLD party, the FBC has managed to present the story of Burma from such varied and legitimated sources using such a variety of grammars that the story clearly carries an air of objectivity. FBC is adept at what Keck and Sikkink (1998, 2–3, 17, 27) note is the most salient point of a frame—location of a specific, deliberate and intentional cause of the problem (someone to blame). The availability of a specific causal factor renders the problem so defined easier to solve than one which rests on complex, structural problems.

Add to the legitimacy of the story as told through such a journalism perspective the ideal-norms perspective for solving the problem (ending the story), and there is little wonder that FBC has met with some measure of success. Just as the FBC transplanted the journalism perspective from the newspaper to the Internet for purposes of telling the story, it transferred the ideal-norms perspective from television for purposes of solving the problem. Put simply, the ideal-norms perspective refers to the strategy of "sticking with tradition." The argument is that by adhering to traditional norms, ideals and values, any problem with which we are confronted may be effectively solved. In the world of transnational NGOs this means adhering to the principles of democratically elected governments, protecting universal human rights and following the rules of the "global community."

The ideal norms perspective is suitable to the purposes of many NGOs because it enables them to achieve what Keck and Sikkink (1998) call "frame resonance." It is not enough for an NGO to create an internally consistent frame of a situation. Its frame must resonate with broader public understandings of social life and with the broader political culture. In a sense, NGOs are the "moral entrepreneurs" of the international political order (Pfuhl and Henry 1993). They work within the dominant order to define deviant categories, populate those categories with deviant individuals (states), and ban them from the global community until they choose to conform. Nowhere is FBC's adherence to the ideal norms perspective more evident than in its mission statement:

> The Free Burma Coalition [FBC] is an umbrella group of organizations around the world working for freedom and democracy in Burma. Our mission is to build a grassroots movement inspired by and modeled after the anti-apartheid movement in South Africa. Our movement stands 100% behind the leadership of Daw Aung San Suu Kyi and the National League for Democracy [NLD], whom the people have recognized as the sole legitimate leaders of Burma [*www.freeburmacoalition.org*].

The achievement of conformity to these ideal norms (progress), no matter how slow, is, as noted above, an overarching theme in FBC's framing of the Burma problem. While individual stories may detail horrific circumstances or events at moments in time, the network of websites, taken together, defines the problem as one with a clear, reasonable and obtainable solution. This definition is not unwarranted. Without going into extensive detail, it is important to note that FBC offers several examples of instances in which it has been able to alter the behavior or policies of other international actors. These success stories have been attributed by the U.S. Institute of Peace to the ability of FBC to orchestrate "a global grass roots campaign run to a considerable degree on the Internet despite the presence of only a negligible Burmese constituency in the United States" (Danitz and Strobel 1999).

These examples include U.S. cities (15) and states (one) with Free Burma ordinances, laws and resolutions; multinational corporations withdrawn from Burma (25); and U.S. and Canadian universities with Free Burma resolutions and divestiture (19). Corporate divestiture began as early as 1992, but steadily increased, along with city selective purchasing ordinances, beginning in 1995 when FBC went online. In 1996 the U.S. Senate passed the Foreign Aid Bill containing Amendment 5019, which stipulated that bilateral assistance would be limited to "humanitarian aid," that visas would not be issued for Burmese government officials, and that the U.S. would vote against loans and other forms of multilateral aid. In 1997, in accordance with provisions of this amendment, President Clinton signed federal legislation that prohibited any new investment in Burma by U.S. companies. Then in 1998 the International Labor Organization suspended Burma's membership privileges due to "rampant human rights abuses, particularly forced labor, arbitrary imprisonment, torture, extrajudicial killing, and other human rights abuses" (*www.freeburmacoalition.org*). During this period the United Nations also passed a number of "Resolutions on Burma" that stressed the need for all members to uphold the principle of universal human rights. These accomplishments are even more striking when one considers that, for the most part, the activists of FBC are college students and that these campaigns are primarily orchestrated and waged in cyberspace. As the largest grass roots human rights campaign on the Internet, and as nominee for the Robert F. Kennedy Human Rights Award, the FBC has proved its ability to utilize Net logic to accomplish at least some of its goals in spite of its lack of any "traditional" power base.

Another network that has met with some success in using Net logic is the International Federation for East Timor (IFET). Because it adopts the same grammars and perspectives as FBC in framing its problem, the overview of its syntax, vocabulary and use of various inflection devices will be more brief than that provided for the FBC. It serves largely as an illustration, as another example of one blueprint of effective use of Net logic by NGOs. This blueprint is then contrasted with that of the somewhat less effective Zapatista network and with various approaches taken by nation-states.

The IFET web page (*http://etan.org/ifet/*) performs the same key function as FBC's; it serves as the clearinghouse for the most complete and up to date information about East Timor. From this location one can access information on the East Timor Observer Project (including testimonies to various UN bodies, special reports on conditions in East Timor, press releases and statements, weekly project bulletins and letters to the U.N. Security Council, the UN Secretary-General and Indonesian President Habibie), the UN home page for East Timor transitional administration and the websites or email addresses of many of the 129 other organizations billed as East Timor support and solidarity groups.

The extent to which IFET member organizations' syntax follows the "current but ambiguous" format varies. For our purposes here, we will focus on the two organizations with the most prominent Internet presence—

U.S.-based East Timor Action Network (ETAN) and Australian-based East Timor International Support Center (ETISC). The ETAN web page is similar to that of the Free Burma Coalition in that it organizes its information with the goal of calling the individual to action. The initially visible portion of the screen is dominated by an eye-catching photo of a current victim and an adjacent boxed insert that explains "what you can do to help." Scrolling further down the page, one finds information about the background and purpose of ETAN, links to the UN and other support groups, and sporadic news postings. Like the FBC news postings, those of ETAN are ambiguous in scheduling. The activist is required to check in to see if new "action alerts" or news stories have been posted. Finally, at the bottom of the page, one can find links to additional background on East Timor, resources, contacts and legislation.

In contrast, the organization and scheduling of information on the ETISC home page follow the format of the newspaper or magazine, but are adapted to the use of hypertext links. The page consists of a series of news articles down a center column, each of which features one paragraph of information and a hypertext headline that can be clicked to read the full story. Like a standard newspaper, these stories are updated every day, and the user may subscribe to receive the headlines via email. To the right are boxed inserts with links to news items or lengthy reports that warrant special attention. To the left of the news column are links that allow access to background information, including biographies of Timorese leaders, recent Timorese history, ETISC documents on East Timor independence, travel and human rights conditions, documents of the National council of Timorese Resistance (East Timor's resistance leadership organization), lists of activism tools, summaries of the Reg.easttimor asynchronous discussion conference, and the ETISC photo gallery. The ETISC home page is not so much a call to action as it is a format for telling the story of East Timor.

While their syntax varies, digging deeper into these two sites reveals that they are similar to one another and to the Free Burma sites in their use of inflection devices. Both make good use of font sizes; shapes and colors; strategically placed, fast links to current information; and visually arresting video and still photography. In each case, newspaper, magazine, radio and television formats are combined with access to the real time East Timor Chat Room and myriad asynchronous groups (e.g. reg.easttimor, soc.culture.indonesia, bit.listserv.seasia-1, indonesia-1 and so forth) to create a unified frame of the "East Timor problem."

For example, through ETAN, one may access Pacifica Radio's programming on a variety of political issues, including East Timor. Unlike the radio broadcasts for Burma, this broadcast occurs in English and, as such, serves as a companion to and an identity enhancement of the East

Timor activist rather than the East Timor native. The program style is not unlike that of National Public Radio, with an articulate narrator giving the listener background on the situation, interviewing relevant people, and then summarizing and interpreting the information. Similarly, one may access Fastv.com's video coverage of East Timor. This consists of an archive of CNN reports and video clips on various events over a period of time. One can literally view the classic CNN style of news reporting via the computer. Interestingly, even this format, which follows the perspective of "objective journalism," presents content that is entirely within the parameters of the IFET's frame of the Timorese problem. As noted above, this unity, or internal consistency, of content via a number of media formats and inflection devices is the ultimate source of power that NGOs are able to muster via the Internet.

As noted above, ETISC is primarily a forum for telling the story of East Timor. Its effectiveness is due to three specific inflection devices. First, the fact that it is structured like a traditional newspaper legitimates its front page content as "real news." This point is not necessarily as obvious as it first appears. Many a personal home page might carry the same sort of information, but because the story is not contained within the same "official" visual format, it suffers from the possibility that it can *feel* less legitimate. For example, the ETISC site contains links to additional sites on East Timor, some of which are the personal home pages of individuals. While they may be deeply concerned about the problems of the region, their home pages are relatively ineffective. They resemble the "home movie," the low budget television commercial and the amateurish programming one comes across on public access television channels. They are "loud," meaning that they typically have some sort of "wallpaper" as a visual background, on top of which are superimposed a multitude of graphics, photos, icons and text in colors other than black. They are written in first person narrative. Taken together, the grammar of such sites does not lend an air of respectability. While this format (as we shall see in later chapters) may be entirely acceptable for the individual whose home page is designed purely as a "bio" of himself, his activities and interests, it is not conducive to the legitimation of a frame of an international political issue.

Second, ETISC devotes a section of its online space to "bios." Here one can access pictures of the key resistance leaders and read page-long biographical summaries of their activities on behalf of East Timor. These bios typically detail the humble and non-political beginnings of the leaders, the various indignities they suffered that lead them to a life in politics, and the successes and hardships they have met with at the hands of an illegitimate military regime. Though not as effective as FBC's use of video of Aung San Suu Kyi, these bios serve the same purpose. They give the individual viewer a sense that real people are involved in this issue and that the transnational NGOs operating outside of East Timor are working on behalf of the legitimate leaders of the region. Add to that the fact that two of the leaders highlighted have won the Nobel Peace Prize (as did Aung San Suu Kyi), and the message is a powerful one indeed.

Finally, like FBC and ETAN, ETISC makes excellent use of photography as a visual inflection device. Its photo galleries are accessed through a link titled "images joyful and tragic," and the images contained therein juxtapose everyday life activities and scenic landscapes with scenes of torture and massacre. Upon entering the more graphic galleries, the viewer is informed that "the scenes in these photos are being repeated right now." Within each gallery there are series of scenes grouped around specific themes or events and titled "murdered by daylight," "hiding their deeds at night," and so forth. As if the titling and brief interpretation of the galleries was not sufficient to define the situation, one may click on individual photos that then "blow up" in a separate window for close up viewing. Again, the combination of this sort of photography with other media formats serves to create a unified frame of the problem which the individual can scarcely disbelieve.

As one would expect, the vocabulary of these sites is very similar to that found on Free Burma sites. It is a language of sophistication, of struggle, of hope. It is a vocabulary of action and engagement, the goal of which is to draw increasing numbers of individuals into the fold. And, like the vocabulary of Free Burma sites, it serves to uphold the "ideal norms" perspective for solving problems. IFET, as an NGO affiliated with the UN (ETAN is the IFET representative at the UN), adopts the specific vocabulary of the UN in an effort to achieve frame resonance. Nowhere is this more clear than in the IFET Statutes, which state:

> Affirming the critical role of the United Nations in the decolonization process in East Timor, the IFET dedicates itself to effectively work as an international Non-Governmental Organization to mobilize support for the realization of the principles enshrined in the United Nations Charter...
> The IFET upholds the principles recognized by the United Nations Charter ... and asserts that the decolonization of East Timor must be fully in line with those internationally recognized principles [IFET 1999].

Likewise, ETISC defines as its mandate the "support of the people of East Timor in their struggle for self-determination, within the principles of international law in accordance with the resolutions and policies of the United Nations." As with the Burma issue, the perspective of East Timor NGOs is that the "international community" consists of a set of traditional values, beliefs and norms of behavior as enshrined in the declarations of transnational governmental organizations, the adherence to and practice of which serves to legitimate individual nation-states. Sticking with these traditions affords the best solution to the problem. Again, without delving into great detail, NGOs that subscribe to the ideal-norms perspective have achieved a measure of success in the international arena. Where the FBC sees as its primary task the elimination of foreign direct investment in Burma, IFET sees as its main goal the changing of U.S. foreign policy toward Indonesia.

As ETISC noted, "The most significant achievement of the NGO-led campaign has been to keep the East Timor question alive from 1975 (when it was annexed by Indonesia) up until the present" (*www.etan.org*). Doing so has meant engaging in both leverage politics (pressing the UN to intervene on behalf of East Timor) and accountability politics (pressing the U.S. to uphold the democratic process and universal human rights). To date, successes on these fronts have advanced through three of the four stages of network influence—from issue creation and agenda setting, to influence on the discursive positions of states, to influence on policy changes (Keck and Sikkink 1998). Beginning in 1991, when the grass roots East Timor movement began and the Santa Cruz massacre occurred, U.S. policy began to shift against Indonesia. House and Senate members began to issue bipartisan letters affirming support for East Timor's self-determination.

In 1992 Congress voted to cut off Indonesia's military training aid. In 1993 Congress pressured the State Department to reverse its "pro–Jakarta" stance, cosponsor a UN resolution criticizing human rights abuses by Indonesia, and block a transfer of fighter planes from Jordan to Indonesia. That same year, the Senate Foreign Relations Committee adopted an amendment to condition major arms sales to Indonesia on human rights improvements in East Timor, and in 1994 a ban on small arms and riot control equipment was implemented. The prohibition was later lifted, but reimposed in 1996. Though at times violated, the partial ban continued as various Senators continued to press President Clinton to support various UN human rights resolutions. Then, in late 1999, the Senate passed an appropriations bill that restricted U.S. military assistance to Indonesia, linking its restoration to "substantial progress in prosecuting members of the Indonesian armed forces and militia members responsible for the extensive destruction in East Timor following the overwhelming pro-independence vote" (ETAN 1999).

Though these measures of success are not as clear cut as those of the Free Burma movement, they still represent a significant alteration of a U.S. foreign policy that, since 1975, not only ignored human rights issues in East Timor but actively supported Indonesia through the sale of weaponry and by blocking the UN from taking more effective action. Like the FBC, IFET has managed to use the logic of the Internet, a logic that centers on inter-action and engagement across an interconnected web of individuals and organizations, to create a frame of a political situation that is not only pow-erful and internally consistent, but that resonates with broader under-standings of political ideals, values and norms. As we shall see below in an overview of the Zapatista network, it is not entirely the inherent struc-ture of the network as a social form that accords these NGOs power, but their ability to utilize Net logic to achieve their goals. In other words, sim-ply structuring one's organization as a network, while it may be a neces-sary condition for success, is not sufficient in and of itself. At least as important is the ability to understand the logic of interaction via the Inter-net and to use the formats it makes available to create a frame that res-onates with broader political culture.

"Zapatistas in Cyberspace: A Guide to Analysis and Resources," a web page organized and maintained by a University of Texas faculty mem-ber, is the central online location of news about, analysis of and additional links to the Zapatista movement in Chiapas, Mexico.[3] Like the free-burma.org web page, it is a link to links. That is, its content consists of a brief summary of the Zapatista movement as it relates to global neoliber-alism, followed by hypertext links to five pieces of analysis, nine asyn-chronous lists, conferences and newsgroups, and 58 websites. Each link is accompanied by a colorful icon and a short paragraph summary of what one should expect to find at the linked site. However, this is where the sim-ilarity ends. Scheduling of information (the second element of syntax) is unlike that of the other two networks discussed, as is the use of inflection devices and, perhaps most importantly, the type of vocabulary.

In terms of scheduling, two aspects are important—the currency of links and the freshness of the content within those links. Exploration of the links reveals that about 10 of them appear to be "dead" (unavailable at the designated URL). Another 12 contain information that appears not to have been updated since 1998. As noted above, these conditions are detri-mental to the experience of "flow" and, consequently, to the individual's ability to become immersed in the identity of "Zapatista activist." It damp-ens the sense of action obtained in the Burma and East Timor cases; one is easily left with the feeling that "nothing is happening." A final point regarding links is worth mentioning. Whereas the other NGO examples pro-vided links that one could navigate in a serpentine fashion, with most pages having similar lists of links, the Zapatista link system is more similar to the "spokes in a wheel" pattern. Few of the sites listed at the central loca-tion afford access to one another. Thus, one is required to continuously return to the starting point to find a new link.

Regarding inflection, the Zapatista network uses a number of devices not employed by the Burma or East Timor networks. For example, many of the web pages are extremely colorful, using combinations of "wallpaper," large icons, colored fonts and cartoons/caricatures. While much of this references Mexican ethnicity and identity, the end result on some pages (particularly those that have not been updated) is the amateurish or "unofficial" feel described above. Put simply, the validity of the message suffers due to the format in which it is contained. Further, these pages do not generally employ most of the legitimated media formats discussed above. For example, none offer information within the official-looking newspaper or magazine format. While some pages make use of an occasional photo, the existing photo galleries are on individualized pages with little supporting interpretation and few, if any, links to text that could serve to explain them.[4] Finally, they do not make use of audio or video clips. In fact, one has to go through a series of links to arrive at a basic Yahoo.com page that contains news briefs and audio/video clips related to Chiapas. This fact is particularly interesting because both the Burma and East Timor networks made use of audio and video to propagate the messages of prominent resistance leaders. While the Zapatista movement has, in Subcommandante Marcos, an apparently charismatic leader, his communiques are in text form only and usually follow the format of a fable or short story. While these formats may make for interesting reading, they are not as compelling as audio and visual information.

Of all the web links listed at the central location, that of the Mexico Solidarity Network is a possible exception to these generalizations. Its form is very similar to many found in the Burma and East Timor networks in that it is concise, easy to navigate and more official-looking in its use of fonts, colors, icons and links. Interestingly, this network was only started in 1998, four years after the uprising in Chiapas began. Perhaps this reflects a growing recognition on the part of those concerned with the indigenous peoples movement there of the possibility that some forms of Internet presence are more effective than others. Regardless, this network (whose membership now includes about 75 organizations) follows the formula of other successful NGOs. Its page centers on "urgent action alerts," and provides information on simple steps the individual can take to become part of the solution. It also provides information on upcoming events, recent legislative information, links to other resources and the latest news on Chiapas. Incidentally, these news reports are reprints of articles generated by Reuters, rather than individual stories reported by activists that constitute the news of many other Zapatista sites.

Vocabulary, the final segment of Zapatista network grammar, also differs sharply from that of the Burma and East Timor networks. First, of the 58 websites available at the central location, 23 are non–English. This includes two sites, the EZLN and FZLN pages, that represent the dominant forces for change within Mexico. This is in stark contrast to the NGOs affiliated with the other two causes discussed, whose web pages were nearly uniform in their use of English. Many of the non–English pages, not unexpectedly, are Spanish, but there are also several Italian pages, and some German, French, Dutch and Japanese. A possible consequence for individuals not fluent in at least two of these languages is a diminished sense of flow, interaction and understanding of/identification with the goals of the network. Perhaps more problematic is that, unlike the other networks, which employ the vocabulary of "unity," of wanting to belong to the global community, the Zapatista network employs the vocabulary of "revolution." Though it claims to be neither, the movement utilizes a sophisticated Marxist, or socialist, vocabulary of motives. It does not seek to obtain its rightful position in the global order as currently constituted; it seeks to overthrow that order.

As such, the Zapatista network does not conform to the ideal norms perspective for solving problems. Instead, its vocabulary is supportive of a conflict perspective of problem solving, in which activists use a strategy of "debunking" to uncover hidden or underlying realities (Snow 1983). Rather than articulating a specific problem with a direct and deliberate cause (someone to blame), the movement argues for change at the structural level. It attempts to unearth hidden realities of the structural economic system of "global neoliberalism." As Keck and Sikkink (1998) noted, NGOs that attempt such a strategy are less likely to be successful than those that concentrate on a specific, "fixable" problem. This may be particularly true for Internet related attempts at social change. After all, "clicking the mouse" is far more conducive to "shopping for change" (read integration) than it is to revolutionary change of the structural properties of a global economic system. In summary, for better or worse, the use of the conflict perspective for problem solving is less amenable to the creation of frame resonance for a significant portion of the NGO audience than is the use of the ideal-norms perspective. This is evidenced by the fact that, compared to the Burma and East Timor causes, little concrete action (beyond the occasional deployment of human rights observers) has been taken by either individual governments or world bodies like the UN. Perhaps both individuals and states are unclear as to exactly what they are supposed to "do about it."

It appears then that simply adopting the network form, in general terms, is not sufficient for obtaining or exercising political power via the Internet. As the examples above illustrate, reality is far more messy. Not only does it seem possible that some networks are too loosely constituted to be effective, it also appears that despite their newfound power, the most successful networks are those that operate within the parameters of the ideal norms perspective *generated by the democratic nation-state form,* using—online—the grammars of other dominant and legitimated media. Further, the examples above hint at the fact that many uses of the Net within the political order serve to enhance national identity—an identity which the state has historically been able to "harness for its own purposes." That is, successful NGOs do not seek to overthrow the democratic state form, but to marry it to new nations. With regard to the nation-state, a legitimate question then becomes, "is it necessary *at all* to adopt the network form, or is facility with Net grammars and operation within the ideal norms perspective adequate?" In other words, can a hierarchical form such as the state simultaneously remain a hierarchy and effectively utilize Net logic? Or does Net logic necessarily require a shift to the network form? While it is likely too soon to tell, it is instructive to examine and assess some of the Internet strategies nation-states have employed. In so doing we can begin to answer the questions above, to evaluate the state's ability to remain a viable and even dominant international actor.

According to what, at the time of this writing, appeared to be the most comprehensive listing of government sites on the Web, 223 countries and territories maintain some sort of online presence (Anzinger 1999). Their sites range along a continuum of sophistication from "billboard only" to "fully interactive." Billboard sites, of which there are very few, are just what they sound like—single page listings for countries that depict that country's flag, coat of arms, official buildings, and the shape and location of the country. These pages sometimes contain an official photo of the leader as well. However, they have few, if any, links to information or other sources, and no interactive capabilities, such as email. The vast majority of official government sites have progressed beyond this stage and currently fall somewhere in the middle of the continuum. To varying degrees, they offer background information on the social, economic and political structure of the country, press releases and speeches by leaders, and a select assortment of policy-related documents. Still further along the continuum are those countries whose sites allow access not only to select pieces of information but to the full range of government-produced documents via customized search engines. These sites typically also offer the user the opportunity to contact most, if not all, government leaders via email. Finally, at the "fully interactive" end of the continuum are those very few countries that allow not only information searches and email contacts but fully interactive, real time and/or asynchronous group discussions with government leaders, as well as online government services such as tax payment, birth and death registration, and so forth. What follows is an examination of the grammars and perspectives of sites along this continuum, with a special emphasis on those countries at the "fully inter-active" end.

Recall that Net logic consists of multiple media formats, the key com-ponents of which are grammar (syntax, inflection and vocabulary) and per-spective. Beginning with syntax (the organization and scheduling of content), it seems that the state-related web pages, particularly the more sophisticated ones, have some points in common with the more success-ful NGOs outlined above. That is, they organize content around central-ized starting points and operate according to the "current but ambiguous" scheduling model. Consider the organization of content first. Generally speaking, government websites may be divided into a few basic categories: executive branch pages (centering on the president/prime minister and his or her cabinet members); legislative branch pages (each arm having its own page and usually supplying links to the sites of individual members of the legislature); judicial branch pages; individual department/ministry pages (detailing the structure, mission and personnel of a specific govern-ment department); embassy pages; and general, or gateway, pages that serve as central access points to all of the above.

This centralization of information serves some of the same purposes for the state as it does for the successful NGO. Central locations serve as the locus of all "official" information about a given topic. They allow indi-viduals to easily locate and understand information pertaining to their rights and responsibilities vis-à-vis the state (and to compare those rights and responsibilities across the state system). Interestingly, very few gov-ernment sites are "issue oriented" in the same way that NGO sites are. They do not dedicate any significant space to the examination of particu-lar issues, nor do they provide many links to other sources of information (non-official information) on topics. For example, while press releases or reports may be available that deal with the topic of "Free Burma," they do not link the reader to the FBC site for additional detail. This is in sharp contrast to the strategy of NGOs, which always provide links to sources of official, state information on the issues they cover. The upshot is that the frame contained within the official documents is less inclusive and thus less believable. The reader cannot escape the feeling that relevant facts, non-official but real facts, may be missing from these sorts of sources.

Regarding the scheduling of content, states typically follow the "cur-rent but ambiguous" model employed by the successful NGOs mentioned above. While one can never be certain when new press releases, speeches and reports will be issued, one can expect to find the most current "official" information on any topic with which government may be involved. It is important to note, however, that the most current "official" information may lag behind information available from other sources, particularly NGO sources that are single-issue organizations devoted to full-time coverage of a particular topic. Also, while one is continuously able to find new information on most government pages, it is not the sort of information that creates the sense of urgency commonly associated with updates on NGO pages. Logging in and finding a new press release on budget negotiations in the legislature is less compelling than logging in to find an "urgent action" notice about a massacre of protestors in a faraway land. Updates on government pages do not usually afford the possibility for action on the part of the individual. Consequently, identification with the group (state) and its goals are not heightened.

While the differences in syntax between NGOs and states are important in explaining the relative success of some NGOs in using the Internet to alter the behavior of states (and MNCs), even more critical are the differences found in the use of inflection devices. As noted above, new possibilities for inflection (the rhythm and tempo of content presentation), particularly combinations of inflection devices, is what really separates Net logic from other media formats. On the Internet, organizations can combine newspaper, magazine, photography, radio and television formats with asynchronous and real time interactions in a way that enables a highly orchestrated frame. In general, state sites do not take advantage of this opportunity.

Generally speaking, states avail themselves of far fewer inflection devices (media formats) than do the successful NGOs. On all (even the most basic billboard) sites, states use seven devices: a picture of the flag, a graphic of the coat of arms, the national anthem (sometimes in text and sometimes in audio form), a "welcome" message from the head of state (extolling its virtues and inviting the individual to learn about its history, culture and government), short biographies of leaders (with their "official" portraits), scenic pictures of the country (often used as wallpaper and most often found on the pages of smaller, more tropical countries), and the shape of the country, often superimposed with pictures of the flag, official government buildings and so forth.

These items are usually found on the "opening page" of state sites. Beyond that, the vast majority of content on other pages consists of text. Even this does not take advantage of the newspaper or magazine format, as do the successful NGO pages. As Snow (1983) noted, one of the defining attributes of the newspaper form is that its content is tailored to perceived reader interests. The newspaper does not attempt to dictate what sorts of information people want. This is not true of the content on state-run sites. There, content is still selected for the individual based upon what the state feels its citizenry should know (or want to know). Similarly, the core attribute of the magazine form is to provide a framework for and validation of a given identity for the individual reader. States fail to take advantage of this format as well, instead resorting to the inflection devices noted above. Rather than adopting a format that enables the reader (citizen) to feel that he is "part of the game," state pages attempt to instill a national identity by displaying flags, coats of arms and official welcomes from leaders.

Successful NGOs are so because they provide links to additional information and additional organizations. These links are current, fast, and lead to striking, meaningful and highly engaging content. States almost universally lag in this area as well. I have already noted that states, as a rule, do not link their pages to outside organizations where the reader may find additional information. Equally important is the fact that the content internal to these sites, though current, is generally not striking or particularly engaging. Little, if any, use is made of radio and television formats, and photography, which many NGOs use with great effect, is here limited to the official portraits of leaders and to galleries of official portraits of past leaders. Crucially, the "interactive" aspects of these sites are almost universally limited to information searches and email. This is in stark contrast to NGO pages, which either host or provide links to myriad real time chats and asynchronous news and discussion groups through which activists may solidify their identification with the group and its goals. NGO sites begin with action and interaction. They supply highly engaging content, and only as side notes do they provide some background about themselves—their origins, missions and stated goals. The "about us" sections on these pages are relatively minor. In contrast, most government sites are essentially enormous "about us" sections. As a rule, they are neither issue oriented nor interactive in any engaging sense.

At this point, one might be willing to concede that the "strong globalization" theorists are correct, that the state form is withering and that new "actors" will come to dominate the international scene. Two facts lead me to argue otherwise. First, as noted above, democratic states within the state system remain the source of vocabulary (the final element of grammar) and perspective through which the ideas of "global community" and "universal human rights" are constructed. NGOs use (and in the process strengthen) this prefabricated set of rules and resources to achieve social change. NGOs, states and MNCs operating outside of the vocabulary of democracy and human rights, and the perspective of ideal norms, are to some degree at risk for failure (relative loss of power in the political order), regardless of whether they adopt a network form and utilize the various inflection devices that make up Net logic.

Second, there appear to be a handful of nation-states that are beginning, with apparent success, to use Net logic to their advantage. Though this "success" cannot be measured in the same ways one might measure NGO success (in terms of changes in behavior of other international actors), it can be evaluated in terms of the response of citizens. That is, these states appear to be adopting both Net logic and a network form that alters their internal workings in such a way that they become more relevant to the order of everyday lives of citizens and more meaningful as a source of identity. In so doing, nation-states may be capable of securing their external validity.

For example, the official sites for Australia, Israel, Italy and Japan make some use of live video and/or audio feed of legislative procedures. The pages of Canada, Egypt, Hong Kong, New Zealand and the United States offer citizens the ability to download some government forms, comment on select government documents, and conduct some types of business with the government online and via email. Still others, such as Bangladesh, Peru and Sierra Leone, offer some form of real time or asynchronous discussion forums for citizens, with occasional contributions by government officials. And it should be noted that in Peru, the Congressional site on which this interaction takes place was voted among the top 10 "best websites for 1999" by *Expreso* newspaper's magazine, *El Navegante*.[5]

But there are two nation-states whose efforts are so far beyond those noted above that they warrant special attention—Singapore and Great Britain.[6] Because these state sites have more commonalities than differences, their grammars will be discussed simultaneously and in contrast to the generalizations above about other state sites. Though their sophisticated use of myriad inflection devices is what truly separates these from other government sites, a few notes about syntax are also in order. First, both states use a truly centralized site through which the individual may access any government information. This is in contrast to the notion of centralization described above, in which *each branch* or *department* of a government has a central site but is often not tied directly to the others. The Singapore site, *www.gov.sg,* provides a one-stop directory for all ministries, branches of government, statutory boards, overseas missions and special committees. The Great Britain site, *www.open.gov.uk,* goes even further. It offers one-stop access from the European Union level all the way down to local government organizations within the country. Further, many of the ministry-specific sites offer links to outside (non-official) sources. For example, through the Foreign and Commonwealth Office, one can link to various NGOs involved in human rights.

Regarding scheduling, Singapore's main page adopts a regularized pattern of information updates in the same way that a magazine or newspaper would. Front page sections, including "announcements," "news," and "press releases and speeches" are updated each day. Within the site, scheduling is more ambiguous — ministries and branches update their individual pages whenever necessary. Great Britain's strategy is the opposite. The main gateway is updated sporadically, whenever warranted by new information. But some of the pages within follow the format of the newspaper, updating information at regularly scheduled intervals, usually once daily. This is particularly true of the Prime Minister's home page, which will be analyzed in greater detail below. In summary, both sites provide the feel of extremely comprehensive and current information.

Inflection is the strong suit of these sites. With continuous updates and a variety of interactive devices, these sites provide, for the individual, a sense of meaning, purpose and belonging. Like the successful NGO sites, these lead with engaging content and possibilities for interacting, accomplishing goals and effecting change. The "about us" sections are relatively less obvious. Consider first the Singapore site. Its front page mimics that of a newspaper or magazine. The central column of information consists of announcements, news, and press releases and speeches, all of which are updated daily. Further down the page one can gain access to: the "eCitizen Centre," which is Singapore's one-stop government Web information center; the "Government Shopfront," in which citizens may use a Cash-Card to transact business with the government; and other government networks, including LawNet and TradeNet.

Launched in mid–1999 with the goal of delivering all key public services electronically by 2001, the eCitizen Centre and the Government Shopfront provide enormous possibilities for interacting with the state online. At the eCitizen Centre the citizen can find information on business (how to apply for patents, trademarks and technology support, set up and develop a business, rent property and so forth); defense (how to apply for scholarships and job openings, do business with the military, register for military service, etc.); education (how to register for schools, become a teacher, upgrade skills); employment (how to rejoin the workforce, retire, hire new employees, search for a job); family (how to care for elderly family members, register births and deaths, get married); health (how to seek care and hospital services); housing (how to rent, lease or buy a home, how to move); law and order (how to file police reports, pay tickets, obtain legal advice); and transportation (how to use public transit, learn to drive and travel overseas).

At the electronic Government Shopfront, just to name a few options, the citizen can access the Community Chest to make charitable donations for public works and services; the Ministry of Health and the Ministry of Community Development to purchase related books, videos and audio cassettes; the Land Transport Authority to apply for road interpretation plans;

the Ministry of Manpower; the Singapore Tourism Board, the Trade Development Board and the Singapore Department of Statistics to purchase related informational and statistical databases; the Singapore Sports Council to reserve sporting facilities; and the Ministry of Environment to apply for numerous applications and pay fees.

But beyond providing opportunities for interaction with the state as such, the site also appeals to national identity. The right-hand column on the main page consists of a series of colorful icons, most of which direct the individual toward sites where he or she can learn more about the heritage and identity of Singapore. For example, one can visit the Heritage Hub, which is designed to get the user to interactively explore the history and culture of Singapore. Or one can purchase the National Symbols Kit, which is designed to educate citizens about the history of the flag, the coat of arms, the pledge, the national symbol and flower, and even "Singapore shared values." One may also visit the Singapore Song Book and download national songs and accompanying music videos.

Alone, these attempts at promoting national identity might seem superficial. But the Singapore site takes it a step further. Down the left-hand column of its main page it offers links to a number of other sites, two of which are important to the successful promotion of national identity — the People's Association and the Feedback Unit. The People's Association is a national grass roots organization consisting of myriad committees, councils, programs and services. Its mission is to "promote racial harmony and social cohesion through mass participation in educational, social, cultural, sports and recreational and other community activities." While its activities obviously do not take place online, the Association's online presence serves as a central source of information for citizens who wish to become involved in committees, councils and other activities through which they can interact with the government.[7]

The Feedback Unit, on the other hand, operates extensively (though not exclusively) online. Established in 1985 as a means of improving communications between citizens and their government, the Unit provides a number of ways for Singaporeans to contribute their views and suggestions on national issues and policies. Among them are online feedback chat rooms and a website containing interactive content. Citizens can join feedback groups, which are organized by topic and held at regularly scheduled intervals (as opposed to being continuous interactions), and can contribute their views, ideas and concerns. Taken together, the highly engaging content and myriad opportunities for interaction on the Singapore site indicate that states are capable of both adopting the network form and using Net logic to their advantage. In the case of Singapore, it appears that such changes are increasing the relevance of the state apparatus in the everyday lives of citizens and enhancing/legitimating the identity of "Singaporean."

The same appears to be true in the case of Great Britain. The Open Government site for the UK has a considerably longer history. Begun in 1994 by the Central Computer and Telecommunications Agency (CCTA) to support the objectives of the Citizen's Charter on Open Government, this site was designed to provide a low cost, simple to use single point of entry for people to access government information. The service was launched in August 1994, and by the end of that year was being accessed 35,000 times a week. Five years later the service was being accessed 14,000,000 times a week. Now, like the Singapore site, the UK site offers engaging content and interactive possibilities far beyond searching for government documents. From this centralized site one can access public sector organizations from the local to the national level, email government officials, download forms, conduct business and respond to/comment on any number of public documents (in draft form) regarding the improvement of government services.

Far and away the most compelling site within the Open Government system is that of the Prime Minister. This site, titled "10 Downing Street," makes use of an array of inflection devices in much the same manner as the NGOs described above. Like a newspaper, the front page of this site is updated regularly with news. Each week it is also updated with a new audio broadcast about a select social issue from the Prime Minister and with a live feed of Prime Minister Questions in Parliament. In addition to news and broadcasts, the site also features categories labeled "magazine" and "your say."

The magazine is a compelling document. It consists of a series of engaging feature articles, each of which highlights civil servants in some manner. Some give accounts of special assignments (such as the article in the February 2000 issue which discussed the unusual role played by a managerial accountant for a front-line Army unit in Kosovo). Others provide insight into the identities of civil servants (such as the article in that same edition about a civil servant who is also an archbishop). The articles are relatively short, but they are illustrated with color photos of these people "in action" and provide an assortment of quotes, as well as interpretation by the author. The end result is that the reader feels a sense of "being on the inside," of learning some "behind the scenes" information, and ultimately begins to develop a certain affinity for civil servants–he or she begins to recognize that they are "real people."

But the ultimate sense of belonging and purpose derived through this site stems from participation in myriad asynchronous discussion groups. These groups, found in the "your say" area, are of two types: the Policy

Forum and the Speaker's Corner. In the Policy Forum the Prime Minister's Office presents a summary of a specific social issue, related public policy options and a series of opening questions to get the dialogue started. Citizens log in, read this document and then present their views on the issue. The forum is allowed to run for a period of time, and the resulting commentary is presented to the Prime Minister for evaluation and response. This response includes a summary of how the results of the forum will be used to shape policy.

The Speaker's Corner is a more free-form environment. It consists of a number of asynchronous chat forums on over 25 topics, including crime, culture, defense, drugs, the economy, education, employment, the environment, health, parenting and taxation. Rather than responding directly to government questions, citizens interact with one another, and the Prime Minister's Office regularly monitors the groups.

These interactive possibilities, combined with the engaging format of the magazine and live broadcasts, serve the same purpose on this site as they do on NGO sites. They allow the individual to become immersed in the identity and goals of the group, in this case the nation-state. In a sense, this immersion is more valid than that obtained through participation in NGO causes because, generally speaking, at least some of the policies and issues discussed on the government site will be in the immediate experience of and have direct bearing on the people participating. The "cause" is very close to home, in a literal sense.

CONCLUDING COMMENTS:
THE NATION-STATE AND VIRTUALITY

In their 1995 study of local civic networks (public networks designed to serve public interests and to increase public access to information), Law and Keltner found that the most successful networks are those that are easy to use, afford immediate social benefits, and enable users to find things of direct relevance for their lives. When they accomplished these tasks, these networks supported interpersonal relations, community-building and social integration, and raised awareness of and participation in the public process. The authors argued that the success of these networks was due to their inherent ability to streamline communications and decision making through collaborative idea generation and problem solving. In short, these networks were deemed successful because they offered more information to the public with increased speed and efficiency. Recently, this line of reasoning has been applied in comparisons of NGOs and states in a globalized environment, and has led many to conclude that states are in relative decline.

Analysis of the same circumstances through the perspective of media logic indicates otherwise for two reasons. First, merely providing *more* information at an increased speed is not, alone, the reason for the success of those civic networks or of previously "powerless" entities like NGOs. After all, for sheer volume of information, no one can beat the typical government website. Equally important is the fact that the information provided is *more engaging and interactive*. To an extent, successful NGOs adhere to an "entertainment" framework (Altheide and Snow 1979, 19–22). Entertainment refers to experiences that are non-routine (outside the limits of daily, routine behavior). They are "larger than life" experiences that provide opportunities for the legitimated expression of emotion and validation of identity. Entertainment provides, for the individual, a sense of drama: "Traditionally, media have been a source of enjoyment, as is the case with dance, theater and music. Audiences have come to expect that media technology will produce entertainment, and every type of medium has done exactly that" (15).

The Internet proves to be no exception to this rule. As evidenced above, and as we shall continue to see in the chapters that follow, those organizations most successful in adapting their form and content to Net logic are those that provide possibilities for engagement and interaction. They provide entertainment. Further, if one conducts an historical examination of "that which constitutes improvement" of networks and networking capabilities, one finds that "improvement" is synonymous with technical changes that enhance the entertainment aspects of computers and computer networks. Color screens, pull down menus, clickable hypertext links and an assortment of features resulting from improvements in bandwidth compression (faster downloads of files, live audio and streaming video feed), combined with improved interactive mechanisms and customizable screens, make the Internet a user-unique, on-demand and highly entertaining medium. The most successful NGOs—those that achieve at least some of their goals and alter the behavior of other actors—are those that take full advantage of the interactive, entertainment-oriented aspects of Net logic.

The second and related aspect of my argument is that NGO success in the international political arena is thus not the direct result of some inherent power derived from the network form. Rather, it is the result of successful application of Net logic to the framing of a situation. In the end, only two of the six core characteristics of NGO networks appear to simultaneously separate them from the nation-state as a form and be instrumental in their successful use of Net logic. To review, NGOs are generally characterized as 1) voluntary, reciprocal and horizontal patterns of communication that 2) obtain power through the production, exchange and strategic use of "information." They 3) revolve around shared beliefs and values, 4) specialize in a single issue area, 5) seek to frame issues in an attention-grabbing, comprehensible and actionable manner, and, as a result, 6) serve as a source of identity, norms and values for the individual. Of these, only the reciprocal pattern of communication and the attention-grabbing, actionable framing of a situation appear to differentiate the NGO from the nation-state and be instrumental to the successful use of Net logic. Together they allow the participant to develop a strong sense of belonging, meaning and involvement in and commitment to stated goals.

Concerning the first characteristic, it is not at all clear whether voluntary membership in an NGO is in any way relevant to the success of these organizations. In any event, though one is born into citizenship in a given nation, one can always renounce this status. Voluntary membership does not distinguish the NGO from the nation-state. Further, as evidenced above, NGOs have varying levels of hierarchy. The International Federation for East Timor network has the most hierarchical form of those discussed above (with a president, a secretariat who coordinates the independent initiatives of member NGOs, and a consultative assembly that functions as a forum for discussion and analysis of issues) but is also the most successful (East Timor has successfully voted for independence from Indonesia, and the resulting problems are thus legitimated as those that need to be addressed by the UN). The Free Burma Coalition is a less structured network, but one that consists of a few key loci of planning, activity and information. The Zapatista network is the least hierarchical of all and, perhaps not coincidentally, the least successful in obtaining its objectives. NGOs as a group do not fit a single mold. They are usually not completely devoid of some sort of hierarchical decision making process, and though little if any research has been done on this point, it appears that the more successful ones strike a balance between the pure "network" and "hierarchy" forms.

Further, characteristics two (obtaining power through the production, exchange and strategic use of "information"), three (revolving around shared beliefs and values) and six (serving as a source of identity, norms and values for the individual) are not traits that distinguish the NGO from the nation-state. To the extent that all reality is socially constructed, all organizations seek to produce, exchange and use information in a manner amenable to their objectives. Likewise, all organizations and institutions, the nation in particular, revolve around shared beliefs and values and serve as legitimated sources of identity. None of these characteristics distinguish the NGO from the nation-state, and therefore none can account for the newfound success of NGOs in the political order.

Finally, the relevance of the fourth characteristic, specialization in a single issue area, to the successful use of Net logic is questionable. Though specialization may enable a small NGO with few members to affect change on a single issue in a single location, the interconnected and global nature of many social issues may, in fact, give an edge to the state. As it already consists of myriad organizations working on a vast array of issues, perhaps the state need only "network" these organizations together to provide an effective source of cross-issue problem solving. Additionally, it should be noted that the most substantial and most highly regarded (legitimated) NGOs are those that take as their mandate the solution of a broad problem on a global scale. For example, Human Rights Watch is a large, highly regarded organization because it is capable of reporting on a broad array of rights violations around the globe and drawing connections between those violations and the social, economic and political circumstances in which they typically occur.

What is vital to the online success of NGOs and governments alike, and what does currently favor NGOs over governments in a networked environment, is reciprocal communication (interaction) around issues that are framed in an engaging and actionable manner. All social institutions display a level of vitality directly related to their relevance in the everyday lives of the individuals they purport to serve. In this regard, many NGOs have demonstrated a remarkable ability to use the complex grammar of the Internet to achieve their ends. They have managed to make themselves relevant to an increasing number of individuals, a goal that many say the state cannot achieve. Poggi (1990), for example, has argued that the state, in a "globalized" environment, suffers from three key problems: an increasing difficulty in expressing its institutional mission, threats to unity and rationality (where unity refers to the connection of all units within a state, and rationality refers to the state's mode of operation and decision-making), and a "crisis of territoriality" (174–189).

Regardless of the true extent of these problems now, it is not as clear as many have suggested that the Internet will make matters worse for the state. Based on currently available evidence, it seems that states need not (and by definition cannot) do away with all practices associated with the hierarchical form in order to achieve results similar to those of successful NGOs. What is required, and what states are increasingly "catching on to," is reciprocal interaction around issues couched in an engaging, actionable "ideal-norms" framework. Consider first the dual problems of defining a coherent mission and establishing a unified, rational means for operating and achieving that mission. Two points should be made.

First, states are like any other institution in that they are in a constant state of flux. Since World War II, when the development and deployment of nuclear weapons rendered force a less viable alternative, states have sought to reorient their mission from military to "something else." Initially, this "something else" was economic development. Increasingly, it is socio-legal and technological development. The fact of reorientation does not by itself indicate that the state is somehow less viable. Like any other institution, the state is a strategy designed to solve a certain problem—in this case, the problem is how to govern, how to regulate the rights and responsibilities of the individual vis-à-vis the group. As the nature of the problem and the environment in which it occurs vary, we should reasonably expect the strategy for solving the problem to change accordingly. The changing orientation of the state and its mission is indicative not of its weakness but of its resilience.

Second, states are increasingly finding and giving voice to their mission through the logic of the Internet. More often than not, this mission is couched in terms of "customer service," and its implementation is described in terms of the network as a social form. States are increasingly taking it upon themselves to alter their internal workings in a manner that is consistent with the reciprocal, engaging and interactive logic of the Net. In the study of civic networks mentioned above, Law and Keltner (1995, 148) noted that the provision of email is the catalyst for initial and continued use of those networks. Simply put, networks and the information they contain become more relevant to the user as opportunities for interaction increase. Based upon this point alone, I would suggest that states are slowly beginning to adopt their operations to the logic of the Internet. All but the most basic official government web pages provide at least one contact point via email. More often than not, they afford the opportunity to contact not just a department but a specific person responsible for specific issues, policies and procedures. Email represents the beginnings of alterations to the *internal workings* of the state that may serve to enhance its relevance in the everyday lives of citizens and, ultimately, secure its *external significance* within the political order.

But examples of more extensive efforts abound. For example, the government of the Philippines launched the ANGEL (Advisory Network for the Government Executive and Legislature) Project in 1996, the objectives of which are to "set up a network system that will provide comprehensive information and online databases for government planning, legislation and congressional budgeting ... to support the flow and exchange of information among its member agencies."[8] In late 1998 Malaysia launched its vision for "electronic government," the mission of which is to:

> ...lead the country into the digital era. The implementation of EG will dynamically improve how the government operates internally as well as enhance the efficiency and effectiveness of service delivery to the public

at large. The benefits to be derived from the implementation of EG will be enormous. It will improve the convenience, accessibility and quality of interaction with the public and businesses; improve and facilitate information flows, re-engineer processes within the public sector and enhance the quality and productivity of its outputs and services.... The vision of EG is a vision for people in government, business and citizenry working together for the benefit of Malaysia and all its citizens. The vision calls for both reinventing the government by using multimedia/information technology to dramatically improve productivity and creating a collaborative environment that fosters an ongoing development of Malaysia's multimedia industry.[9]

And in 1999 Greece began to develop its Information Society Policy, the goals of which are to offer better services to citizens and firms, achieve a better quality of life for citizens, create a state of the art educational system, realize faster economic growth, promote Greek heritage and culture, achieve equal participation for all citizens, and protect the rights of citizens and consumers. As states use the Internet to streamline decision making and procedures, and to make interaction across the "state-society" divide more reciprocal, engaging and meaningful, they may enhance their external significance and thereby ensure their status in the political order.

Changes to the internal workings of the state with regard to its citizens are only part of the story. Equally relevant are changes to interactions or workings across the state system—diplomacy. Rothkopf (1998) argued that the information revolution creates a new type of political game, one in which:

> ...the actors are no longer just states, and raw power [read military power] can be countered or fortified by information power. The mighty will continue to prevail, but the sources, instruments and measures of that might are dramatically changed.... There was a time when diplomats were the sole interlocutors between countries. Now, unmediated dialogue and information exchange between citizens from around the world occurs 24 hours a day.... The goals, capabilities, and actions of individuals, legitimate NGOs, international organizations, terrorist groups, et cetera will become central to U.S. policy and intelligence. Benign, non-state actors provide policymakers with alternative foreign policy tools. Their influence and ubiquity are dissolving the narrow focus of government-to-government diplomacy and creating a worldwide network that will be a key feature of the environment in which diplomats and generals operate [326].

It is not as if states are unaware of these changes and/or incapable of altering their diplomatic strategies in order to adapt to this new reality. As early as 1995 an official in the U.S. Department of Defense prepared a paper analyzing the potential impact of the Internet on foreign policy and international conflict in which he predicted that the Internet would increasingly be used as a "tool of statecraft" by national governments and that it would play a significant role in international conflicts:

> As more governments recognize the strategic value of this new medium for conveying their message, they will use it as an additional tool in the political process. That is, the current type of information placed on the Internet by official government organizations will be supplemented with politically-oriented material conveying argumentation favorable to their respective positions on issues important to them. When one country involved in a dispute with others begins to use the Internet in this way, and the other countries become aware of this, a catalytic effect will occur, whereby all involved countries enter into the electronic debate in an official way [Swett 1995].

The paper went on to note that the governments of Peru and Ecuador were already beginning to use the Web to bring international diplomacy online. In April 1997 the U.S. Institute of Peace held a conference on "Virtual Diplomacy." The gathering included around 50 experts in international relations, and was designed to assess the challenges to and opportunities for the conduct of international relations resulting from the "information revolution." Participants readily acknowledged that "we in the United States face the need to transform our institutions, which grew up in another time." The conference was part of an ongoing project in which the government works with NGOs, academic institutions, and the business community to find ways to meet the challenges of new media.[10] Given these sorts of developments, it is difficult and perhaps unwise to assert that the state system is in crisis. Though change is slow and cumbersome, states do appear to recognize the importance of realigning their missions and internal workings in ways that coincide with Internet logic, and are taking the first steps toward that goal.

That leaves us with the "crisis of territoriality," one which is supposedly exacerbated by the rise of the Internet. There appear to be three possible outcomes of networked computing in terms of community and, ultimately, territorial sovereignty. First, one can create an entirely new community without regard to physical boundaries. Second, one can replicate a physical (or already imagined) community in an attempt to strengthen it. Third, one can dissolve a physical (or imagined) community through the creation of a virtual one that supercedes it. This third outcome, it should be noted, is never the stated or intended goal of online communities, nor does it appear to be a regular result. That is important to remember, because a key argument of "strong globalization" theorists is that the "spaces of places"—territory, geography, national borders, and the nationally organized identities to which they correspond—are increasingly irrelevant.

As noted in Chapter One, this sort of result has long been presumed regarding new communications technologies. Much has been made about every new invention's status as a "revolutionary technology" with the capacity to dissolve time and space. The important thing to keep in mind about communications media is that, while they can be used to overcome such physical barriers, they do not force the transcendence of "mental" or ideological boundaries on the part of their users. People have historically related to each other through shared space, shared interests or shared goals. For those with shared interests and goals, the Net (like other media) allows the problem of shared space to be overcome. It does not *lead to* uniformly shared interests and goals. Therefore, while we can expect to witness the development of a "global community" in some form, we should not anticipate that this new identity will result in the erosion of other memberships and identities.

Examination of online interaction bears this out. Rather than exchanging one membership for another, people continuously add community memberships to their identities. Consider first the notion of building new communities without any physical (space-time) boundaries. This sort of community building is a commonplace occurrence in individual real time chat rooms and various sorts of asynchronous discussion groups. It is also occurring on a Net-wide basis. The identity of "Netizen" indicates that people increasingly conceptualize the entire Internet as a nation of some sort. When one stops to consider that the nation is largely an imagined community, it makes sense that the logic of the Internet affords increased possibilities for imagining community at the global level in the form of "global civil society." Clearly, networked computing can be used to create an entirely new community without physical (space-time) barriers. It should also be noted that these new identities, in contrast to what proponents of "Internet addiction" claim, do not serve as replacements for face-to-face memberships. As most people report that the time they spend online was previously used to watch television, it seems that the only relationships that may be replaced are the vicarious ones experienced through regular viewing.

This point is particularly relevant in the case of national identity. Just as "the neighborhood" and "the city" as imagined communities are not eliminated when their members simultaneously imagine themselves as part of "the nation," the national community is not supplanted by the imagined "global community." Quite the contrary. While affording new modes of interaction through which global community may be imagined, the Net is simultaneously replete with examples of replicated national communities. Countless websites seek to reconnect individuals that, though they share a national identity, are scattered across the globe. Most seek to provide a space where people can share ideas, discuss (national) concerns, meet old friends, make new ones or simply "hang out." To that end, these sorts of sites provide news centers, photo galleries, real time and asynchronous discussion groups, locator services (such as "white pages"), and links to information on face-to-face social clubs around the world.

This sharing of national identity online centers on culture, social issues and problems as they relate to and are bounded by a specific, legitimated state structure within specific territorial boundaries. Citizens imagine the nation online just as they do in face-to-face contact—in a manner that legitimates and reinforces the idea of state sovereignty: "All over the world people leave behind their homelands to explore opportunities in other countries.... Through the World Wide Web, [they find] a way to be a part of the world they left.... Expatriates can read newspapers from their homelands published daily on the Web.... There is an active community of expatriates and a new sense of belonging for those that left home.... For those connected via the Web, the term expatriate no longer applies in the traditional sense as it is now possible to stay connected to one's culture while becoming an active part of a new country.... Breaking the one way communication model of the past [has] fostered a sense of participation in a way that previously was impossible" (Church 1996).

In at least one instance it has been argued that the national community created online is more real, more complete, than that created through face-to-face interaction. Ian Buruma (1999) noted that "China" has alternately been understood as a state, a nation, a geographical area, a culture, an ethnic idea, a sentimental notion and a myth:

> The "Chinese problem" is not new. During the long history of the Chinese people, China has often been divided into separate states. And the Chinese people, even those commonly defined as Han Chinese, were made up of various ethnic groups. Even the Chinese spoken language, the one thing all Chinese might be thought to have in common, consists of many dialects which are distinct enough to be classified as separate languages. And yet the myth of One China has been tenacious. It is an idealized China, a cosmological idea rather than a nation-state, in which all Chinese live in harmony.... China also exists as a sentimental notion, celebrated in kung fu movies and pop songs, mostly made in Hong Kong. But sentiment alone does not make for a political community. A nation, in the modern political sense, not only needs common institutions of government but common mass media, where issues of shared interest are reported and discussed, freely in a democracy, or as a form of indoctrination in a dictatorship.
>
> So if we define China as a political community, there are two Chinas, and perhaps, if we include Hong Kong, even three. But the Internet may have changed all this. One might argue that China, as an imagined political

community in which all Chinese can take part, albeit without common institutions, only exists in cyberspace. There, for the first time, Taiwanese, mainland Chinese, Hong Kong Chinese, and overseas Chinese read the same papers, follow the same debates, and talk about politics on a daily basis [9–10].

While there can be little doubt that individual nation-states (some more than others) and the state system as a whole face new challenges brought on by advances in networked communications technologies, it is unclear at this point that the institution is in danger of imminent demise. Preliminary investigation reveals that, though their responses may be slow relative to NGOs, states are well aware of the challenges they face and are attempting to adapt and survive. Perhaps what is most clear about the overview of findings and conclusions in this chapter is that little with regard to the Internet and the status of the nation-state in the political order is obvious or self-evident. A great deal more research is needed. The nation-state is one of the broadest forms within the political order and comes in many types, each of which encompasses numerous institutions and groups that require in-depth analysis. Further, this chapter excluded from analysis entirely the transnational governmental and multinational corporate forms, which clearly add complexity to the mix. This chapter has served merely as a starting point, as an argument about how to best organize and coordinate future research on the role of the Internet in the political order. Using media logic as an organizing principle, any number of additional questions might be answered, including:

1. What are the implications of Internet use in everyday life for the political order? Can we make connections between how people use the Internet to construct and interpret political reality every day and the future significance or role of the state? If we understand these uses and their consequences, can we arrive at a better definition of "globalization" or "global community"?

2. Regardless of the advantages that may accrue to the network as a social form, does the state continue to serve certain purposes or to possess certain strengths that only the state can? If so, what are those purposes and strengths?

3. To what extent can online activity aimed at fostering national identity accomplish that goal? Is such national identity in conflict with the idea of global civil society? Is it the sort of identity that the state can still "harness to its purposes"?

4. Can we, instead of lumping NGOs together under the broad rubric of "network form," classify NGOs as "types" along a continuum, relative

to an ideal type, in order to better understand what characteristics are amenable to Net logic? Can we create a similar classification scheme for nation-states, as they, too, come in a variety of types?

5. What are the implications of Net Logic for various political processes, such as campaigning and policy formulation? That is, what can studies of the logics of web pages, real time chat rooms and asynchronous discussion groups tell us about the likely outcomes of conducting the political business of polling, campaigning, debating, voting and interpreting public policy online? Will certain sorts of candidates (or policies) have an advantage over others in online campaigning? Will the interactive nature of the Internet induce more or less critical examination of policy and campaign issues?

6. What are the dominant Internet patterns of interaction and information distribution regarding the political order?[11] Are these likely to change as new "push" technology enables a greater degree of selectivity of information on the part of the individual? That is, will individuals actively seek out information on issues previously of little interest and opinions different from their own, or will they customize their online interactions to include only those issues and opinions with which they are in agreement? What are the implications of such choices for the political process?

NOTES

1. These figures were obtained from NUA Internet Surveys Ltd. and were current as of early 2000. See *www.nua.ie* for details and for updated statistics.

2. These figures were obtained from Matrix Information and Directory Services, Inc. and were current as of early 2000. See *www.mids.org* for details and updated statistics.

3. This Web page is available at: http://www.eco.utexas.edu:80/Homepages/*Faculty/Cleaver/zapsincyber.html.*

4. An exception to this is the gallery posted by Scott Sady, which contains both interpretation of the photos and links to other sources, and is electronically available at *http://burn.ucsd.edu/~ssady/.*

5. At the time of this writing, this comment was electronically available at *http://www.congreso.gob.pe/eng/inicio.htm.* 2/17/00.

6. Interestingly, many of the new functions and goals that governments have taken on in Great Britain and Singapore are being tackled by private enterprise in the United States. GovWorks.com, GovNetworks.com and e-thepeople.com are three private companies whose websites offer "civic chats" on public policy issues, directories of government agencies, information on campaigns and the future of online voting, information databases on a variety of policy issues, polling data, and signatures for petition. The interested reader is referred to *http://www.govworks.*

com, http://www.govnetworks.com and *http://www.e-thepeople.com* for additional details.

7. Additional information may be found at *http://www.pa.gov.sg/*.

8. The interested reader is referred to *http://www.opnet.ops.gov.ph/angel.htm* for additional details.

9. At the time of this writing, Malaysia was in the process of implementing its "first wave" of pilot projects, including: driver and vehicle registration, licensing and summons services, utility bill payments, Ministry of Health online information, electronic procurement, online Prime Minister's Office, Human Resources management Information System and a Project Monitoring System. Upon completion, Electronic Government would encompass intra-government (interconnected IT infrastructure, electronic registration and archiving, paperless workflows, re-engineered work process, IT literate officials), business to government (24 hour one-stop shopping for government information and services, IT based processing of business to government transactions, accelerated and transparent decision making, customer-oriented services) and citizen to government (24 hour one-stop shopping for government services, invisible boundaries among departments and online participation in the political process) relations. This information and further details are electronically available at *http://www.mampu.gov.my/EG/MainPage.htm*.

10. The interested reader is referred to the details of the conference, electronically available at *http://www.usip.org/virtual_dipl.html*.

11. Naewon Kang and Junho Choi, "Structural Implications of the Cross-posting Network of International News in Cyberspace," *Communication Research*, 26 (August 1999): 454–481. In this article the authors published the results of research conducted to ascertain the patterns of international news distribution in cyberspace via the Clarinet news system. They argue that patterns of news distribution and consumption change along with technology, and that currently they display a "world systems" distribution. That is, certain countries are recognizable as "core" countries, while others are semi-peripheral or peripheral in status. They also note, however, that these online rankings according to news distribution do not necessarily correspond to those countries' statuses in "real life." What remains unclear is what the implications of "online status" are for the state system.

CHAPTER FOUR

The Corporation
in the Virtual World

There is a revolution under way, and mastering the Net has moved front and center on Corporate America's agenda. The Internet model, with fewer harder assets, a direct pipeline to customers, and freedom from the hierarchical management structure of most of corporate America, offers a new level of speed and operational efficiency for those who master it— and huge dislocations for those who do not. Throughout corporate America, executives are suddenly waking to the realization that those who do not move fast to get in on the game risk having their lunch eaten by tiny rivals who may have barely existed just a few years ago [Byrnes and Judge 1999, 78].

By the early 1900s, Max Weber, perhaps the preeminent theorist of the economic order, had outlined the evolution and key attributes of the capitalist system of production and its defining organizational form, the corporation. He argued that the economic order, previously arranged according to various types of "political capitalism," had, beginning in 17th century Europe, transformed itself into a second type–"modern industrial" or "rational bourgeois" capitalism. In contrast to political capitalism,[1] in which the opportunity for profit depends upon preparation for and exploitation of warfare, conquest, and the political administration of foreign geographic regions, modern industrial capitalism is characterized by a specific type of production establishment, the corporation:

> Essential to modern capitalistic enterprise, according to Weber, is the possibility of rational calculation of profits and losses in terms of money. Modern capitalism is inconceivable without the development of capital accounting ... rational bookkeeping constitutes the most integral expression of what makes the modern type of capitalist production dissimilar to prior sorts of capitalistic activity such as usury or adventurers' capitalism...

> Necessary to the existence of capital accounting in stable productive enterprises [are] the basic prerequisites of modern capitalism: 1. The existence of a large mass of wage-labourers, who are not only legally "free" to dispose of their labour power on the open market, but who are actually forced to do so to earn their livelihood. 2. An absence of restrictions upon economic exchange on the market: in particular, the removal of status monopolies on production and consumption [such as existed, in extreme form, in the Indian caste system]. 3. The use of a technology, which is constructed and organized on the basis of rational principles—mechanization is the clearest manifestation of this. 4. The detachment of the productive enterprise from the household [Giddens 1971, 179].

Whereas many observers argue that multinational corporations and/or transnational non-governmental organizations are likely to wrest political power from the clutches of the nation-state, thereby undermining the entire sovereign state-oriented political order, observers of the economic order propose no such takeover. When it comes to the economic order, it seems that the Internet Revolution is not quite so revolutionary in its purported consequences. That is, no one argues (or even suggests) that these defining aspects of Weber's "modern rational capitalism" are called into question because of networked computing and "globalization." In fact, most suggest, implicitly or explicitly, that the Internet serves to enhance these features of modern capitalism. The corporation, that social form which epitomizes Weber's idea of rationalization and which has long been assumed to be the dominant actor in the economic order, is expected to prevail.

This is a curious expectation, because, as Weber went on to note, the rational organization of free labor within the economic order and the corporation is merely a single example of a more general, more fundamentally important type of social organization—bureaucracy:

> Bureaucracy involves an organization devoted to what is from the point of view of the participants an impersonal end. It is based on a type of division of labor which involves specialization in terms of clearly differentiated functions, divided according to technical criteria, with a corresponding division of authority hierarchically organized, heading up to a central organ. Bureaucracy is a mechanism founded on discipline. It is the fitting of individual actions into a complicated pattern in such a way that the character of each and its relations to the rest can be accurately controlled in the interest of the end to which the whole is devoted. It is by far the most efficient method or organizing large numbers of persons for the purpose of performing complicated administrative tasks [Parsons 1968, 506–507].

It is precisely this characteristic of the bureaucratic, hierarchical nation-state which is deemed untenable by proponents of "strong globalization" theory. However, when the same properties are accorded to the structure of the economic order, observers anticipate that the bureaucratic corporation, unlike the bureaucratic state, will somehow overcome these problems through adaptation.

Regardless of the validity of this disparity in expectations, the debate about the economic order is not about whether modern rational capitalism will survive the Internet Revolution, but about what specific form the corporation will take in its inevitable victory. A few observers have attempted to point out that changes to the economic order are neither as speedy nor as wide-ranging as those purported in the quote that opened this chapter. For example, in her review of what would appear to be the most innocuous border in terms of globalization, Ceglowski (1998) points out that even the U.S.–Canadian border presents substantial problems for companies operating or trading in both countries. Taking the argument of "strong globalization" (in which goods, services, capital and information flow across seamless national borders, and in which choices over where to produce, shop, invest and save are no longer confined within national borders) as a starting point, Ceglowski analyzed cross-border trade and investment between two countries (the U.S. and Canada) with few, if any, barriers to trade, close geographic proximity, and common social, political and cultural traditions. Yet even under these conditions she found that the border "matters a lot" in terms of quantity of trade (within compared to across the border) and persistent consumer price differences.

> Globalization often conjures up an image of a worldwide society—no boundaries, no borders, no barriers. Economically speaking, in a truly borderless world, financial capital, production activities and labor would flow as easily between countries as they do within a country. However, this picture of an economic global village is not quite accurate. Despite expansion of international economic activity in recent years ... a barrier-free world has not been achieved.... Evidence of greater economic integration is not the same as evidence that national borders no longer matter for the worldwide distribution of goods and services. Although this distinction may appear to be simply a matter of degree, it is important. In a truly borderless world, the strength of the economic ties between markets would not depend on whether they are located in the same country. In particular, consumers and producers within a given country would not trade more among themselves simply because of shared nationality [17].

Similarly, Walter (1998) questions claims that multinational corporations dominate both the economic and political orders. He argues that globalization theory—specifically, the assertions that the state has lost the power to tax and regulate capital movements, and that immobile workers and citizens are powerless against mobile firms—is questionable:

...such broad claims are exaggerated. The anomaly is that global firms
often fail in their demands that important host states adopt inward investment rules or regimes allowing their full operational flexibility... The core
of the globalization argument is that increasing capital mobility raises the
bargaining power of firms vis-à-vis immobile states, citizens and factors
(primarily labor). In this "structural" version, by a process of regulatory
arbitrage states are pushed into spontaneous or unilateral liberalization,
which coincides with the interest of capital agents... [But] in the face of
their structural weakness, transnational corporations have resorted to old-
fashioned political lobbying, particularly of their parent [home] governments. In a brave new world in which mobile capital could simply
compete away restrictive state policies it did not like, there would be no
need for such corporate lobbying and diplomacy [288].

Nevertheless, we once again find a great deal of certainty among proponents of "strong globalization" that the corporation can and will change
forms in order to survive drastic and fast-paced changes in the economic
order. In general terms, and this should come as no surprise, the network
form is perceived as offering the greatest possibilities for survival in the
new economic arena. Arguing that the Internet has altered the nature and
structure of competition, observers claim that organizations that can
become networks are much more likely to find new "niches" in which they
might survive. What characteristics of the network form are likely to make
survival possible?

A new form of organization—delayered, downsized, and operating
through a network of market-sensitive business units—is changing the
global business environment.... In industry after industry, multilevel hierarchies have given way to clusters of business units coordinated by market
mechanisms rather than by layers of middle-management planners and
schedulers.... These market-guided entities are now commonly called
"network organizations" ... [Snow, Miles and Coleman 1992, 5].

Implicit in this description of the network is a basic assumption about
what the corporation (or any other organization) actually is. It is the same
assumption made about the defining attribute of the nation-state, though
it is less obvious. The corporation, regardless of the form it adopts, is seen
first and foremost as a rationally orchestrated, *bounded* unit. In the same
way states are said to exist within defined geographic boundaries for the
purpose of governance, corporations are said to exist within membership
boundaries organized for the rational pursuit of profit. As a consequence,
theorizing about the changing corporate form focuses on alternative strategies (and the expected gains in efficiencies thereof) of structuring membership.

In economic terms, the corporation is seen as a mechanism for coordinating production and transactions. In its pure hierarchical form, the corporation is characterized by consolidated ownership, supervision and command within formally mandated frameworks for interaction, with authority being an important basis for action/interaction. Membership within this form is static; people are hired into specific units, or divisions, within the corporation, and there they are expected to remain. In contrast, the pure network is ruled by "shared values." Coordination of exchange results from a sense of mutual obligation, shared values and beliefs, and long-term, reciprocal interaction. Membership within this form is very fluid. People come and go as they please, regrouping in different configurations as warranted by the objective at hand. In its purest form, there is no central unit or division or headquarters around which activity revolves.

Any number of observers have proposed variations on these pure forms, and in every instance the variations revolve around who is to be considered a "member" of the "organization." For example, Tapscott (1998) suggests that corporations (hierarchies) are being replaced by e-business communities (EBCs). These EBCs, networks of suppliers, distributors and customers that conduct communications and transactions via the Internet, are differentiated according to control (self-organizing v. hierarchical) and value integration (high v. low). Accordingly, they adopt one of four possible forms: open market (self organizing with low integration), aggregator (hierarchical with low integration), value network (hierarchical with high integration) or alliance (self organizing with high integration).

An even more membership-oriented theory of new organizational forms is that of C. Snow, Miles and Coleman (1992). They propose that organizations are re-forming in three variations of the pure network: the internal network, the stable network and the dynamic network. In the "internal network" form, units or divisions already present within a hierarchical corporation cross those institutional boundaries to work together on a project by project basis. Because the corporation does not "outsource" work, it does not outsource membership. In the "stable network" form, there is still a "core" corporation, but a portion of the work (and therefore the membership) is outsourced to a set of outside vendors. Finally, the dynamic network represents the closest approximation to the pure network. While there is still a "lead" organization, that company outsources the majority of its work/membership; it "identifies and assembles assets owned largely or entirely by other companies."

What these propositions about new corporate forms fail to take into account is the fact that organizations, corporations included, are not "rational," stand-alone structures that can be defined in terms of "who is a member" and "who is not." Organizations are organized sets of inter-human behaviors (Martindale 1966). They are systems or patterns of behavior which arise when pluralities pursue their individual and collective aims in common. Accordingly, the appropriate unit of analysis is not the individual, not "possible configurations of membership," but behavior, "how the objective of the interaction is defined and how it is achieved." The corporation, like the nation-state, is first and foremost a psychic phenomenon. It is capable of being imagined in any configuration suitable for obtaining the desired objective. Again, given the media culture within which all organizations operate, the most salient question is not "who will win the competition among the powers?" but "who is most capable of taking advantage of the Internet as the 'interaction medium'?"

The generally accepted response to this question is that the corporation is somehow inherently more capable, at least compared to the state. This is despite the fact that both share a history of being hierarchical, bureaucratized forms. It is also despite the fact that every theory of the new "network" form actually yields examples of multiple sub-forms and myriad cases in which some hierarchical corporations have successfully converted to a more networked form while others have not. In short, the pat answer denies the complexity of the situation. It treats the corporation, like the state, as a single, pure form about which blanket statements of viability can be made. Where the state is seen as having an inherently unchanging nature, the corporation is seen as inherently malleable. Arguing that the Internet forces a conversion to networks from hierarchy is overly simplistic. There are myriad forms of hierarchy, just as there are multiple forms of networks. Some hierarchies display network qualities, and many networks contain elements of hierarchy. Thus, it is not enough to say that corporations must convert to network form or perish. Rather, we need to continue our examination from the previous chapter. Is it the network form alone (in whatever specific format it exists) that affords economic power? Is the network form more conducive to utilizing new media logic through which economic power is obtainable? Only by examining enough instances in which the network form has come into conflict with the hierarchical corporation, been adopted by the corporation, or successfully rejected by the corporation will we be able to shed additional light on the future configuration of the economic order.

NET(WORK) LOGIC AND THE ECONOMIC ORDER

In order to better understand the position of the corporation relative to the NGO and the state in the process of "globalization," it is instructive to begin by comparing and contrasting a handful of these organizations with one another. Doing so illuminates the strengths and weaknesses of corporations in terms of Net logic, and lessens the likelihood of making blanket statements about the "competition among the powers" that are untenable in light of detailed analysis. Of course, any attempt to assess the overall status of the corporation relative to the NGO and the state is fraught with methodological difficulties. When examining the state and Net logic, one is working with a finite and known set of data. It is possible (and I did) examine each and every state's Web presence. Similarly, transnational NGO websites represent a stable and relatively small portion of total sites on the Web from which a meaningful sample may be selected.

The corporation, however, is another matter. There are no centralized locations for information about corporate Web presence, and the population fluctuates every day. For practical purposes, the data set for this type of research is infinite. Further, corporate Web presences may be designed to focus on business-to-consumer interaction or business-to-business interaction. This was not the case for states or NGOs, whose websites were directed specifically to the individual (citizen or activist, respectively).

Given this dilemma, I have elected to limit the analysis in this chapter in two ways. First, I will focus strictly on business-to-consumer relationships. A 1999 survey of 300 information technology executives conducted by *Information Week* Research found that the most common "transformational initiative" underway at companies regarding the Internet was interaction with customers: "Above all, transformation is about customers — changing the means by which companies find, sell to, service, and communicate with them" (Wilder 1999, 44). Second, when choosing the handful of companies to be analyzed in this chapter, I have elected to rely on rankings and ratings supplied by outside sources. In selecting the group of companies astute in the uses of Net logic, I have relied on rankings provided by Forrester Research and Gomez Advisors, two companies that specialize in analysis of the Internet consumer marketplace. I then compare and contrast this group of companies with a handful of those expected to dominate both the political and economic orders in the age of globalization — the Fortune 500 and the *Wall Street Journal*'s "World's Largest 100." If assertions about globalization are correct, we should expect to see the companies currently dominating the world economy readily adapting to the network form and to the use of Net logic in furthering their stated objectives.

Both Forrester Research and Gomez Advisors rate sites across a number of categories. While the exact order of rankings can vary, it is most often the case that the "top five" companies in any given category are similar.[2] Amazon.com, not surprisingly, was consistently rated highest in the areas of books, music, videos, toys, games and "general merchandise."

Drugstore.com, LandsEnd.com, eBay.com and CharlesSchwab.com were consistently at the top of the rankings in the categories of health, apparel, auctions and investing, respectively. Though they are rated according to such parameters as "ease of use," "customer confidence" and "relationship services," the most important attributes of these companies, which I argue are more directly responsible for their online success, are less utilitarian in nature. These are the corporations that, regardless of their relatively small size and lack of importance in the "global economic order," have something that the Fortune 500 generally lack to date. They have an ability to conform to the logic of the Internet. Accordingly, it is this grouping of companies that will be examined collectively and then compared to those companies argued to "rule the world."

To reiterate, Net logic, like any other media logic, consists of both grammar (syntax, inflection and vocabulary) and perspective. While other media combine grammars and perspectives to create unique formats, the Net is capable of meshing these individual formats together in a variety of ways to create a unique framework for ordering social reality. Where radio is the companion medium and film the emotion medium, the Internet is the interaction medium. The five companies listed above—Amazon.com, eBay.com, drugstore.com, LandsEnd.com and CharlesSchwab.com—are similar enough in their successful uses of the grammars and perspective of the Net that they may be analyzed as a group.

Regarding both grammar and perspective, these corporate sites are every bit as complex as the successful NGO and state-related sites discussed in the previous chapter. However, complexity should not be confused with mimicry. Comparing the perspective of these corporate sites to that of NGO and state-related sites, one is immediately aware of a different "feel." Where NGO and state sites are serious in nature, operating first and foremost through the "ideal norms" perspective and utilizing "entertainment" only as a means to further those objectives, the ".com" sites listed above are purely fun—they epitomize the presentation of social order through the entertainment perspective. This should come as no surprise. Over time, the activity of shopping has increasingly been used and defined as a source of socializing, quality time and escape. Shopping is, first and foremost, a form of play. It is a means of relaxing, of escaping the serious side of daily life, and, when in the company of others, a means of creating quality time with friends and family. In fact, it was this very understanding of the nature of shopping that led many to believe, in the early days of the Internet, that people would *never* shop online. What was overlooked by the skeptical was the highly interactive and engaging nature of the Internet as a medium of communication. The Web as a shopping environment has enormous potential to combine for the consumer the entertainment he or she has come to expect from both the shopping experience and the mass media experience.

The companies which most successfully exploit that potential are those that have figured out that the two most important attributes of the entertainment perspective present in Net logic are customization and community. Each of the companies listed above uses a common grammar to afford the individual a highly customized shopping experience, an experience of socializing and community, and sometimes both. What follows is an analysis of the common attributes of these companies' grammars and how they are used to achieve these experiences.

Recall that grammar consists of syntax (the organization and scheduling of content), inflection (the rhythm and tempo of content presentation) and vocabulary. With regard to syntax, the organization and scheduling of content on these successful corporate sites can be described as centralized and current/regularized, respectively. Remember that the centralized nature of NGO sites meant that one site served as the central location for access to complete information about a particular issue. The centralized nature of the state site, on the other hand, implied self-containment—individuals need not look elsewhere for "official" information. The centralized organization in the present context more closely resembles that of the typical nation-state site than it does the typical NGO site. Here, centralized organization refers to the fact that the "home page" is a "headlines only" page—like most nation-state sites, it offers nothing of substance. Instead, this page consists of a series of links to other within-site pages, on which one may browse product categories, search for specific items or engage in the social activities offered by the site. These sites do not conform to the network form in that they do not serve as central locations for information about and purchases of the many products they offer. Rather, like the typical state site, they attempt to offer the customer a "total experience," thereby implying that there is no need to look elsewhere for the products and services they offer.

In terms of scheduling, these sites are current and regularized. The main pages are typically updated each day with new releases, sale items, features and shopping ideas in each of the main product categories. These regular and frequent updates to the main page ensure that the consumer experience of the site will be fresh, thereby encouraging frequent returns and purchases. The exception to this is the Charles Schwab site. Here, as with the online sites of other established investment houses, we have a curious blend of "serious" and "play" activity. Investment sites online are clearly consumer-oriented. They are shopping sites. But, due to the subject matter, they must give off the impression of being serious in nature. This is particularly true of sites that represent long-established, traditional brokerage firms. Those that are most successful find a way to apply the entertainment frame to the serious business of investing. One of the ways Schwab accomplishes this is by updating its page less frequently than do other shopping sites; only the market charts (DJIA, S&P500 and NASDAQ) are updated constantly. This less frequent changing of the look of the main page lends an air of permanence to the Schwab site that is not required in the fields of apparel, books, online auctions and so forth.[3]

While organization and scheduling of content are important, once again it is through the use of inflection devices that companies have the opportunity for economic success. Inflection refers to the rhythm and tempo of content presentation. As I have stated before, the Internet as a medium of communication is in a class by itself because it affords users the possibility of combining myriad inflection devices in a manner previously unavailable. Where the successful NGO uses these devices to orchestrate an experience of a particular social problem and an identity of activist, and the successful state uses them to orchestrate an experience of nationhood and an identity of citizen, the successful corporation uses inflection devices to create the experiences of play and community and the identity of "unique, ideal self."

Inflection devices on these corporate websites range from font type, size and color to the stable, ever-present menu bar, to color graphics and photos of products, to innumerable hypertext links. Each of these devices serves to guide the customer through the site, presenting him or her with an easily managed, enjoyable and engaging/interactive shopping experience. Sale and feature items are often highlighted with colored text and accompanied by small photos or color graphics depicting the products. In a sense, these sale and feature items are the equivalent of "action alerts" on the NGO pages. They are presented using similar inflection devices, with the expectation that emphasizing those points will not only call the individual to action but will cause him or her to further investigate the site.

Overall, what is most striking about these pages is their uniformity of appearance. On each, the corporate name and logo may be found at the top of the page, almost always in the left-hand corner. Next to the company name, and stretching the full width of the main page, one may find the site menu bar. These menus consist of a series of tabs, each of which will take the customer to a specific product or service category. In terms of rhythm, the most significant aspect of this menu is its constant presence. No matter where one is within the site, one has instant access to all other primary within-site pages simply by clicking on the appropriate menu tab. This feature enhances the experience of "flow" within a site by eliminating the need for the customer to backtrack in order to search for a new item. The direction is always forward.

Below the site menu, the remainder of the main page is organized into three columns of information, all of which are brightly (but not loudly) colored. The center column is that which is typically updated daily. It contains information on featured and sale products. The left-hand column typically consists of a series of hypertext links offering the customer direct access to product categories by browsing, to special features and services of the site that are typically less often utilized than those found in the main menu, to company information, and to "help" and customer service information. Finally, the right-hand column serves as a place holder for information that is not readily categorized in the other areas of the page. On the Amazon.com site this is the area reserved for customization of the page, an important inflection device to which we will return momentarily.

In terms of inflection and the overall appearance of these pages, one should not overlook what is *not* present on any of these sites—the extensive use of text. Compared to the NGO and state-related sites, these corporate sites offer almost nothing to read. There is little, if any, "official" background information about the product, no news, no press releases, nothing that would slow the tempo of the visitor's movement through the site from product to product. This point about inflection is directly related to vocabulary, the final element of Net grammar. Because the objective of these sites is to move the user from purchase to purchase, not only is there very little text, but what text there is makes use of elementary vocabulary. This is in contrast to the successful NGO and state sites discussed in the previous chapter, which are issue-oriented and use a sophisticated vocabulary to match. The vocabulary of the sites discussed here is everyday life in nature, precisely because its locus is within the chat rooms and discussion forums populated by community members.

Again, the exception to some of these rules is the Charles Schwab site. It, too, has the corporate name and logo in the top, left-hand corner of the site, a full-screen tab menu that remains present on within-site pages and an organization scheme of three columns of information. However, it quite obviously lacks the ability to promote sale and feature products. So, rather than organizing its columns of information around products, it organizes them around services and information. Naturally, as a result, this site relies on text as a source of information for the customer more than the other sites do. This, however, does not mean that the site is "dry." It still uses a number of inflection devices, most of which are designed to customize the investment experience of the individual, to which we will return momentarily.

At this stage of website development, most any corporate site centered on consumer goods will naturally attempt to attract and keep customers by advertising featured items and sale prices, and by offering a general ability to search and browse the sites in order to find the desired goods. Where our selected sites excel is in the use of inflection devices that customize and/or make social that experience. Because these inflection devices are so vital to the success of these sites, a separate overview of each is instructive.

Consider first the drugstore.com site. This site contains three customization features and two interactive/community features that enhance its success. Regarding customization, the site enables the individual user to 1) set up an account by providing minimal personal information; 2) maintain a personal shopping bag; and 3) manage pharmaceutical, health and insurance information online. Account setups are remarkably easy on this site, requiring minimal information input and time to complete. Once this is accomplished, the site greets the individual by name upon each return. Through this account the user may maintain the other two customized features—the shopping bag and the pharmacy. The personal shopping bag remains with the user regardless of what within-site page he or she is on. As the user moves through the site, each purchased item is placed into this ever present shopping bag, making it easy to view the items selected and their corresponding prices. Once an order is placed, the customized account system can be used to review past purchases, cancel the order or check the delivery status. Similarly, the customized account allows access to a personal pharmacy area in which the user may maintain health profiles (drug allergies, medical conditions, current medications), review prescription histories and maintain insurance plan information for all account members.

In addition, the site contains two highly engaging inflection devices that give the individual shopper a sense of interaction with others: monthly newsletters and 24-hour customer care. Newsletters covering issues such as store updates, new products, special offers, tips on wellness and nutrition, and beauty tips are available via email. Upon receiving these email newsletters, the user may "click" on the hypertext links contained within and be transported directly back to drugstore.com to take advantage of the new information. Finally, the 24-hour customer care system allows the user to access product information and to interact directly with a pharmacist regarding health and medication issues.

Turning to the LandsEnd.com site, we find still other devices that effectively foster a customized and interactive shopping experience. Like the drugstore.com site, the LandsEnd.com site offers a personal account option. While this does not afford a personalized greeting each time the user enters the site, it does allow the individual to maintain a personalized address book and reminder service, both of which enhance the sense of "flow" one obtains from the shopping experience. In the personal address book one can maintain the names and addresses of individuals frequently shopped for. The reminder service allows one to choose dates and occasions one wishes to be reminded of via email. The reminder service then forwards the email at an interval predetermined by the user so that purchases may be shipped at the proper time. The second, and more engaging, customization device is the Personal Model. This feature allows female shoppers to construct a model that accurately reflects their physical characteristics (hair color, height, measurements, face shape). This Personal Model may then be stored in the personal account and "brought back to life" each time the shopper returns to the site to try on articles of clothing.

The LandsEnd.com site also contains unique inflection devices in terms of interactivity. Like the drugstore.com site, it allows users to sign up for newsletters that contain product news. More interestingly, this site contains the Lands' End Live and Shop with a Friend features, both of which allow individuals to interact in real time while shopping. Enabling the Lands' End Live feature allows the shopper to interact with a customer service representative, either by telephone or by live text chat. The customer service representative may then aid in the selection of various products. Alternatively, the Shop with a Friend feature allows two shoppers to explore the site together. Again, each may communicate with the other via telephone or via live text chat, and can simultaneously move through the site, selecting products for purchase together.

The defining customization device on the CharlesSchwab.com site is the ability to create a completely customized page, the MySchwab page, that one can then use as the default starting point each time the web browser is enabled. Like the drugstore.com page, a registered MySchwab page greets the individual by name each time the site is entered. It also presents, in a concise format, a page of customized hypertext links and information snippets, as selected by the individual. This customized starting point can include categories such as "my watch list" (symbols, current price and price change of selected stocks), "my news" (headlines), "my weather" (for the user's local area), "my reminders" (a personal planner), "my cartoons" and "my local events finder," among many other categories.

In terms of interactivity, the CharlesSchwab.com site effectively utilizes three inflection devices not reviewed in the sites discussed above: investment videos, the Learning Center and the live investment forum. These are some of the basic media formats (video, Q & A, and real time chat) used by successful NGO sites and discussed in the previous chapter. Here, though they are put to different uses on the surface, they ultimately serve the same purpose—to stimulate commitment to a particular social reality presented in a highly orchestrated frame.

Consider first the investment video. The site uses a series of five videos in which Charles Schwab speaks to the individual investor "one to one" about the process and benefits of investing wisely for retirement. Each video corresponds to a specific stage in the life cycle/investment process, from "starting to plan" through "in retirement." The format is very similar to that used in videos by the Free Burma Coalition of Aung San Suu Kyi. They depict Charles Schwab, up close and personal, addressing a specific issue to an unseen interviewer and dispensing information about the importance of investing, the problems that result later in life from a lack of financial planning, and various ways to begin and sustain an investment regimen. The tempo of these videos is slow, and the presentation is designed to convince even the most ill-at-ease that he or she, too, is capable of successfully planning for the retirement years. Overall, they give one the feeling that a caring, fatherly figure will be there at all stages to assist in the investment process.

To that end, the Schwab site has orchestrated the Learning Center, an online, self-paced tutorial program designed to help individuals of all experience levels enhance their investment skills. These courses follow a basic question and answer format. They introduce the topic, lay out the learning goals, and then move through series of hypothetical case studies in which various investment questions are asked and answered. Each course concludes with a review "quiz" to make sure that the student has achieved the desired learning goals. Interestingly, these courses bear some resemblance to the question and answer format of the NGO pages, in which the individual moved through a series of questions (and corresponding explanations) about the issue at hand.

Finally, the Schwab site makes regular use of the live chat format in its regularly scheduled "investor forums." Each forum highlights a specific investment topic, and members of the Schwab community may log in and ask specific questions of the featured speaker. These forums are held at regularized times. Specific days of the week are always dedicated to specific topics (e.g. Wednesday forums are dedicated to retirement), and the site maintains a list of upcoming events for up to two months in advance. This stable, unambiguous format fits with the logic of the investment site quite well; it emphasizes structure and planning, two qualities that investors value when making important financial decisions.

Though the eBay.com site, through its "my eBay" feature, offers customization features similar to that of drugstore.com and LandsEnd.com, this site truly excels in its use of inflection devices that enhance a sense of community. Specifically, the site employs real time and asynchronous discussion forums, "About Me" pages, and the "Safe Harbor" and "Feedback Forum" features to orchestrate a sense of community identity among members. The real time chat rooms are both general and topic-specific. In either case, they function as communities in much the same way as real time chat rooms found elsewhere, especially those in the Internet Relay Chat system. Here individuals can join together in a setting that functions as the "third place" [Oldenburg 1991]. They can talk about everything and nothing in particular, banter, and generally enjoy the company of others without the prospect of "serious" discussion. In contrast, the asynchronous discussion forums are more serious in nature. Here community members can discuss issues of relevance to the management of the eBay community. They can discuss "pet peeves," suggest means of improving the community and get advice on how to be a better community member.

The "About Me" pages serve a dual function. Every registered member of the eBay community is afforded the opportunity to set up an "About Me" page within the site. On a practical level, these pages serve as virtual storefronts through which community members can peddle their wares. But they also serve a second, more community-oriented purpose. They are the means by which each individual can design and promote his or her individual identity within the community. These sites typically center on the kinds of items the individual likes to trade and collect. In so doing, they promote that individual's status (level of expertise) within the community and thereby contribute to community stability. They lend the impression that the person represented is trusted, knowledgeable, respected.

If that were not enough to promote a sense of safety in this online auction world, eBay also makes use of "Safe Harbor" and the "Feedback Forum" to ensure a level of trust that might otherwise be unobtainable. Safe Harbor is the site's "comprehensive safety resource and protective arm." It covers the various policies individuals must abide by if they wish to retain community membership, and explains the means of social control available when those policies are violated (e.g. fraud prevention, insurance, I.D. verification, authentication services, dispute resolution and so forth). It even provides a short list of "community values" to which all members are expected to adhere. The "Feedback Forum" is perhaps the most prominent and immediate means of effective social control within the community. It consists of a searchable database of community members. Each member who has traded online receives feedback from the other party involved. This feedback becomes part of the individual's "permanent record" and can be accessed by others who are considering trading with him or her. In short, this feedback ultimately represents the individual's track record of trustworthiness.

Finally, we turn to the Amazon.com site, perhaps the quintessential example of a site that effectively combines customization with community in its adoption of Net logic. Again, this site offers a customization feature like those above in the form of a "my account" section. Here one may manage personal information, cancel and track orders, and review a comprehensive purchase history. But the Amazon.com site uses a more important customization device. It reserves the entire right-hand column of the three column home page layout for a "New for You" section that is unique to each and every user. Not only is the user greeted by name upon entering the site, he or she is presented with an array of recommendations, new releases and "quick picks" based upon past purchases. Like other areas of the site, this customized portion is updated often enough that the user may anticipate fresh recommendations on a very regular basis.

When it comes to community, Amazon.com shares a number of features with eBay.com. Key community features of this site include "Member Pages," "Only for Friends," and asynchronous discussion forums. Member Pages, like the eBay.com "About Me" pages, serve as personal storefronts. Here, however, the wares being peddled are not collectibles but thoughts and opinions. These pages typically include the individual's name, a brief bio, a photo and an email address, but the vast majority of space on these pages is dedicated to book (and other product) reviews: "Pack it full of your ideas, opinions and recommendations... It's a great way to hear other viewpoints and open up your mind to things you may never have considered before." Embedded within these Member Pages are special areas called "Only for Friends." This area can only be accessed by friends and family members who are invited by the individual. Here one can provide more intimate details regarding purchases, opinions of the product and any regrets about the purchase, all with the intended effect of helping others within the "friends circle" make better choices in the future.

Finally, Amazon.com makes available a series of asynchronous discussion forums. These forums are topic-specific and typically revolve around specific products and categories of products. They are designed as education areas in which an individual may seek guidance from others about the benefits and drawbacks of products before purchasing them. Beyond that, however, they serve as places in which people who are interested in product categories or related hobbies can share their experiences.

All of these sites, regardless of the specific combination of inflection devices they employ, have managed to combine the personalization of the shopping experience with a sense of interaction and belonging. This is an impressive feat, and one that even the most successful NGO and nation-state websites have failed to accomplish. Though some of those sites represent mastery of the community aspect of Net logic, none are characterized by the personalized experience one achieves when visiting the sites discussed above. The end result of this combination of customization and community is the feeling that one is doing something more than "just shopping." These sites accomplish, in a self-contained framework, what NGOs must use the network form to attain—fast links to meaningful, engaging, interactive content.

In terms of the grammar of media logic, inflection devices are those strategies that emphasize a particular aspect of social reality as ordered and presented through a specific medium. The corporations discussed above have successfully combined a number of these devices to simultaneously emphasize the personal and membership attributes of what would otherwise be a mass, but solitary, experience. They do so by regulating the rhythm and tempo of the site. Customization and community devices alternately speed and slow the rate at which one moves through the site. Personalized greetings and customized main pages (like those of Charles Schwab.com and Amazon.com) immediately grab the attention of the user. They make for a speedy and compelling entrance to the site. Customized account setups, shopping bags and information management capabilities likewise speed the exit of the shopper once he or she has finished shopping. But in between, personalized experiences like the LandsEnd.com "Personal Model" and interactive/community experiences obtained through chat rooms, discussion forums and the like serve to slow movement through the site. The shopper is afforded the ultimate play/entertainment experience—the ability to enter and leave quickly, with the option of lingering over an array of meaningful, engaging content in between.

As Seybold (1998, 46) noted, most companies follow five general stages of e-business. These stages are in parallel with those I described for nation-state sites in the previous chapter, and include: 1) Supplying company and product information (the billboard site); 2) Providing customer support and enabling interactions (typically billboard plus email and search engines); 3) Supporting electronic transactions; 4) Personalizing interactions with customers; and 5) Fostering community (through real time chats or asynchronous discussion forums). The final two stages, making the online experience both personal and social, separate the successful corporations discussed above from those that are less successful in the use of Net logic. It is to the analysis of a handful of such companies, highly successful by more traditional measures, that we now turn.

The "top ten" companies from Fortune 500 rankings combine with the "top ten" from the *Wall Street Journal* "World's 100 Largest" to form a list of 15 unique corporations.[4] Of these 15 corporations, three are automobile manufacturers, two are oil and gas companies, one is a retail store, one is a holding company for consumer packaged goods, one is a manufacturer of durable consumer goods, and the remaining seven are technology companies. A survey of the websites of these corporations reveals several commonalities regarding their respective abilities to utilize Net logic. Accordingly, the discussion that follows consists of key generalizations about these sites for purposes of comparing them with the successful sites discussed above, as well as to NGO and state sites. When warranted, exceptions to these generalizations are discussed in greater detail.

In terms of both grammar and perspective, these large corporate sites have more in common with state sites than they do with the ".com" sites discussed above. Like the state sites discussed in the previous chapter, their organization (the first component of syntax) is centralized and "official"; main pages are structured to contain all official information regarding products, organizational structure, financial/investment information, corporate history and public policy statements. This is in stark contrast to the sites discussed above, which gave scant attention to these types of informational categories (a point to which we will return in the discussion of inflection devices).

The scheduling of information on these sites (the second component of syntax), however, is unlike that of any other site types discussed elsewhere. All of these sites contain a "news" section. Sometimes the news is placed directly on the front page, other times it is in a link on the menu bar. In any event, these news sections are very current and are updated regularly (usually daily). The scheduling of information across the rest of these sites, though, is not current. Many of the sites may be appropriately categorized as "stage two" or "stage three" in Seybold's classification of e-business stages. They supply company and product information, and typically provide extensive search capabilities, some customer support and support for some electronic transactions. However, these stages of engagement/interaction do not require that the site be updated regularly. That is, once the product information has been uploaded, and search engines enabled, sites at these stages are low maintenance. The effect is a website that is stale, or "boring." Sites that are infrequently updated do not engage the individual and consequently do not provide any incentives for frequent return visits.

Use of inflection devices across these sites is indicative of these fundamental syntax frameworks. There is no uniform "look" across these sites. While all have a menu bar across the top or down the left-hand side of the main page, these menu bars are generally not continuously present as one moves through the site as they were in the ".com" sites analyzed above. Without this inflection device, movement through the site is less rhythmic, and the tempo is generally slow. The user, lacking the ability to leapfrog through the site and maintain a forward direction is instead forced into an "up and down" experience of the site. Information is layered, or nested, within these sites and thus exhibits the "Zapatistas in Cyberspace" spokes-on-a-wheel format discussed in the previous chapter. This problem is exacerbated by the fact that many of these sites combine business-to-consumer with business-to-business information. Though the technology sites prove more adept at separating these categories, many of the others lump these information categories together. As a result, the consumer is forced to weed through product and service information of little or no relevance. Again, this serves to detract from rhythmic, upbeat movement through the site.

Overall, however, the most problematic aspect of these sites is that they do not customize and/or make social the experience of them. Unlike other successful sites, these generally do not use personalized greetings, ever-present shopping bags, customizable pages, photography, video, audio, fast links to engaging content, real time chats or asynchronous discussion forums. There are some exceptions to this rule, both successful and unsuccessful, that are worth noting, primarily because they point to what is, across the board, a basic inability (to date) on the part of otherwise highly successful MNCs to effectively utilize Net logic.

Consider first the use of video, a device astutely employed by successful NGOs and a few state sites. Of the 15 Fortune 500 and Largest 100 surveyed, only General Motors uses video on its website by offering webcasts from an auto show. While such an idea is intriguing in the abstract, as it provides a way for concept car enthusiasts to participate in the auto show without having to travel to do so, there are two problems with the way the video is used on the website. First, it is billed on the main page as a "news flash." This is despite the fact that, at the time of this writing, these videos were already four months old. The user is promised "news," only to be disappointed. Second, and more importantly, the videos are "press release" in nature. That is, they depict a corporate official on stage in front of a large audience, announcing plans for the future and then guiding the audience through a slide show. It is not particularly engaging to view a slide show second hand through a webcast, particularly when it is "old news."

A second problem in the use of inflection devices that these sites suffer is in their use of hypertext links. Some sites, including General Motors and General Electric, have links that are either "dead" or that point the user to capabilities that have not yet been enabled. The second of these two problems is more annoying, as the user is lead through several layers of information only to find that, ultimately, the service he or she was attempting to employ is "coming soon." Further, some of the sites offer links to internal pages from which the user cannot easily return. For example, on the Chrysler site, it is not possible to view a "demo" of a car model and then return to the previous page by hitting the "back" button on the browser. Hitting the "back" button serves only to reload the same "demo" page. This is particularly problematic on sites that do not offer the continuous menu bar. Without either of these options, the user is forced to "right click" the "back" button and select a previous page from the list that appears.

Needless to say, such link problems frustrate the experience of flow and cause the user to wonder whether a return visit to the site is worth it.

Regarding chat rooms and discussion forums, some of the technology sites (e.g. Intel and Microsoft) provide asynchronous forums for IT professionals. As a rule, however, these large corporate sites do not provide community areas for the general public. The exception to this rule is the Royal Dutch/Shell website. Here one may participate in a series of uncensored public forums on a variety of topics, including sustainable development, human rights, diversity and equal opportunity, and climate change. Specific topics across broad issue areas are kicked off by corporate employees and, in terms of sentiments conveyed, are essentially unfettered expressions of opinion by anyone who wishes to participate. Under their policy of "open communication," the employees responsible for maintaining the discussion forums engage in regular dialogue with the corporate critics that frequent the forums and attempt to present an acceptable image of the company. Even more remarkable is the fact that Royal Dutch/Shell, in addition to deliberately providing an open forum for public hostility toward oil and gas companies in general, also provides a series of links to outside sources on its forum issues. This is in stark contrast to other large corporate sites that, when they provide links to outside sources at all, provide them to sources of information that are consistent with that corporation's frame of a particular situation.

In general, then, these corporations make few attempts to employ the many inflection devices made possible through the logic of the Internet. Though home pages are colorful enough, few attempts are made to combine customization and community features in ways that support either the entertainment perspective utilized by the ".com" sites or the ideal norms perspective utilized by NGOs. Instead, like many of the less-than-successful nation-state sites, these large corporate sites make extensive use of text in order to provide "official information." As noted above, this text-based information revolves around five general areas—products, organizational structure, financial/investment information, corporate history and public policy statements. Interestingly, with the exception of the finance/investment category, these are the same categories of information to which nation-states devote the majority of their site space. And the end result is generally the same; one can acquire a good deal of "official" background information, but the sites are not particularly compelling.

This extensive use of text is closely related to the vocabulary (the final element of grammar) and perspective employed by these sites. Without exception, the vocabulary is sophisticated in nature (as is that of NGO and state sites) and at least attempts to revolve around the "ideal norms" perspective for problem-solving (as do NGO and state sites). Unlike the ".com" sites discussed above, these Fortune and World's Largest sites use media (the Internet included) to engage in a conversation with NGOs and nation-states. They attempt to promote a specific corporate image that is simultaneously in keeping with the capitalist values of free enterprise and the democratic nation-state values of universal human rights in a "global community." Here, as with no other organizational type yet discussed, we have a curious blend of objectives. Clearly, within the capitalist framework the defining organizational principle is the pursuit of profit. However, when capitalist organizations find themselves operating within the political and normative orders, orders operating according to other principles, it seems they must at least make an attempt at an image that conforms to those principles. The corporations under discussion here do so by presenting "about us" sections that speak the language of the NGO and the state—the language of community involvement, common values and corporate responsibility.

In principle, the objective of presenting such an image is sound. But again, poor understanding of the logic of the Internet dooms many of these efforts from the start. Rather than incorporating an array of available inflection devices into the presentation, these sites rely on text, the presentation of which can only be described as "canned." They contain brief "bios" of the companies, which invariably describe them in abstract, visionary terms; histories of the companies, which outline their remarkable achievements; and an assortment of "public policy" segments, which are typically divided into "community giving" and "living our values." The overall tone of these areas is that of the "official" press release, making it difficult to believe any attempts at personalization or genuine concern. In the end, though the perspective supposedly adhered to is ideal-norms, the visitor to the site is left wondering how the corporation can successfully adhere to both global community values and the pursuit of profit. This dilemma, combined with the fact that these sites are also ineffectual in their use of inflection devices to promote customization and community, calls into question the assumption that the corporate form is somehow more inherently capable of adapting to globalization than is the state.

CONCLUDING COMMENTS:
THE CORPORATION AND VIRTUALITY

Recall from the previous chapter that Law and Keltner (1995), in their study of civic networks, found that the most successful networks were those that are easy to use, afford immediate social benefits, and enable users to find things of direct relevance for their lives. They went on to suggest that these features were a direct result of an ability inherent in the network form to streamline communications, decision making, idea generation and problem solving. In short, successful civic networks are so because they are speedy and efficient. This argument is, in essence, precisely that used in the quote that opened this chapter. When theorizing about the "new corporate form," observers generally claim that corporate success via the Internet is derived from increased speed and operational efficiency, a "direct pipeline" to customers, and freedom from hierarchical management structures typically associated with traditional corporations.

Preliminary evidence documented in this chapter reveals that this argument is only partially true. The attributes of the successful online corporation mimic those of the successful online civic network. The most successful corporations are those that enable customers to find relevant products (customization) and afford social benefits (interaction within an online community). However, the two points I argued in the last chapter apply here as well. First, corporate success in the online world, like NGO or nation-state success, is derived not from pure efficiency gains brought about through increases in transaction speed and decreases in transaction costs, but from the ability to adopt Net logic in the framing of activities and goals. For corporations, the activity is consumption and the frame is entertainment. Successful online corporations are so because, through inflection devices designed to simultaneously personalize and make social the experience of shopping, they provide a non-routine experience of what is, in fact, a very commonplace activity. They create social spaces online that serve as "third places"—places that offer meaningful, relaxing, interactive and entertaining experiences apart from those afforded by home (the "first place") and work (the "second place") (Oldenburg 1991).

Second, and relatedly, success in this new economic order is not the direct result of some inherent power derived from the network form. Three circumstances point to the truth of this statement. First, examination of the corporate structure of the most successful ".coms" discussed earlier reveals that they are rather hierarchical in structure. While they may not be as bureaucratic as nation-states or many of the "traditional" corporations, they are by no means networks in the sense that successful NGOs are. Second, there is evidence that some traditional corporations (two of those found in the top ten slots of the Fortune 500), while they remain hierarchical in structure, are beginning to effectively utilize Net logic to create websites that are customized and interaction/community oriented. Third, the brief history of the World Wide Web is replete with examples of network-like ".coms" that have failed. Whether such failure is a result of an inability to use Net logic remains unclear. But it certainly cannot be attributed to their inability to convert from an hierarchical to a network form of organization.

Let us begin by examining the first point—the degree of hierarchy in the structure of successful ".coms"—in greater detail. Seybold (1998) has argued that success in the realm of e-business depends upon a core set of objectives, all of which revolve around the end customer. She argues that corporations must target the right customers, make it easy for customers to do business with them (by redesigning and streamlining "customer facing" processes from the end customer's point of view), provide a "360 degree view" of the customer relationship internal to the company, deliver personalized service and foster community. Interestingly (and, according to this preliminary investigation, correctly), she does not claim that a corporation must adopt a certain form—the network form—to accomplish these goals. And, by all accounts, the successful ".coms" analyzed here do not appear to be particularly "networked" in structure.

CharlesSchwab.com and LandsEnd.com are the online arms of two relatively old (over 25 years) corporations, and they both have the hierarchical structure of traditional firms. CharlesSchwab.com has a board of directors (12 members), an executive management committee of 17 members (two co-chief executive officers, seven enterprise presidents, a chief financial officer, general counsel, a chief strategy officer, a chief information officer, a chief marketing officer, a chief administrative officer and two executive vice presidents) and 124 senior vice presidents. LandsEnd.com also has a board of directors (seven members), a president/chief executive officer, two executive vice presidents, a chief financial officer, general counsel, treasurer, two senior vice presidents and 12 vice presidents. Clearly, both of these corporations operate effectively with a rather hierarchical system of administrative departments and divisions. Yet they are also successful at adopting the logic of the Internet to suit their business objectives.

The pure ".coms" analyzed above, drugstore.com, Amazon.com and eBay.com, do not differ significantly in their structures. Even though they are considerably younger, they still display all of the major hierarchical components of organization noted above. Drugstore.com, for example, was incorporated in early 1999. It has a board of directors (eight members), a president/chief executive officer, a chief operations officer and four vice presidents. In operation for only one year at the time of this writing, drugstore.com had over 400 employees, had acquired competitor Beauty.com, and had entered into strategic alliances with Rite Aid Corporation (for the online prescription service) and General Nutrition Centers, Inc. (for exclusive online product distribution). Amazon.com, begun in mid–1995, has an even more hierarchical structure. It, too, has a board of directors and the standard "chief" and "vice president" positions. But it is also organizationally differentiated into three business segments—U.S. Books, Music and DVD/Video; Early Stage Businesses; and International. Further, the company employs over 7600 people and has entered into strategic alliances with Gear.com, Pets.com, HomeGrocer.com, Greenlight.com, Living.com, Audible, Ashford.com, Della.com, Kozmo.com, NextCard and Sothebys for the purposes of advertising and supply chain management. Like the others, eBay.com has the traditional officers—chief executive, chief operations, chief information and numerous vice president positions. What is most interesting about eBay is that it was begun in 1995 as a sole proprietorship. It became so popular, however, that its founder elected to incorporate so as to bring more structure and more administrative control to the process. By late 1998 eBay held its initial public offering and has been growing ever since.

Moore (1998, 78) has claimed that the new economic order is defined by "business ecosystems." These ecosystems consist of "networks of complimentary functions" made up of customers, suppliers, producers and even competitors. He argues that businesses successfully operating within these ecosystems focus on market development and are replacing the traditional business form, the multi-divisional ("M-form") firm that operates with administrative control in mind. From the perspective of this research, such a description of the "new economic order" is questionable for two reasons. First, it is unclear how "new" this new economic order actually is. Corporations have long sought to secure optimal shareholder value through both vertical and horizontal business integration. As evidenced above, the most successful pure ".coms" are, to a large extent, "M-form" in nature as well. As they age, they continue to expand. Expansion leads to further bureaucratization in the form of additional business units and additional layers of management within those units. And while some may argue that the strategic alliances entered into by drugstore.com and Amazon.com are primary examples of "business ecosystems," in the end they are first and foremost an attempt to acquire, through the bureaucratic legal process, administrative control.

Second, there are a few traditional corporations that are not only highly successful by conventional standards but also make effective use of Net logic without abandoning the hierarchical form. Ford Motors and Walmart hold two of the top ten positions in the Fortune 500 (Walmart also holds a top ten position in the "World's Largest 100" list, which is based not on revenue but on market capitalization). Successful by any traditional standards, examination of their web pages reveals that they are also effective in using the Net as the interaction medium.

Consider first the Walmart web page. The main page boasts the standardized appearance of the successful retail ".coms" discussed above. The Walmart name and logo may be found at the top left-hand corner. Below that, stretching the width of the page, is the menu bar, which consists of a series of tabs, each of which takes the user to a specific service or department. The remainder of the main page is organized into three vertical columns. The center column, updated regularly, contains seasonal and/or event-related feature and sale items. The left-hand column provides a stable listing of departments for browsing. The right-hand column affords access to the features that customize the shopping experience. Though the site does not currently host the community features that Amazon.com and eBay.com do, it does a nice job of customizing the shopping experience through its "My Walmart," "Shop My Way" and "Photo Center" features. These engaging, entertaining aspects of the site contribute significantly to its high rankings by both Forrester Research and Gomez Associates; Walmart.com is a close second to Amazon.com in the category of general merchandise.

Lest one begin to suspect that only retail corporations are capable of effectively utilizing Net logic, we now turn to a brief examination of the Ford Motors website. Organization of information within this site is divided into four key categories (products, news, people and "for owners"), each of which is easily navigated and contains the kinds of information one would expect it to contain. This seemingly obvious point should not be overlooked, as many of the Fortune 500 websites analyzed above are problematic in terms of rhythm and tempo precisely because they do not effectively categorize the information and services they provide. But beyond effective organization of content (syntax), the Ford site makes effective use of inflection devices to foster a sense of personalization and community.

In terms of customization, the "Buyer Connection" and "Owner Connection" features are effective. Using Buyer Connection, one may browse through different automobiles by category, make/model or geography. Or one may use the "build" device to create a customized "dream vehicle," feature by feature. Once the virtual vehicle is completed, Buyer Connection allows the user to apply for financing, request price quotations from selected dealers and store the virtual vehicle in the "Buyer Garage" until purchase time. Entertaining as this feature is, the Owner Connection is even more so. Billed as a "personal reserved parking space on the Web," the Owner Connection affords registrants access to a host of customized information packages and services, as well as to an online community of other Ford owners. Customized features include maintenance records and service reminders, online owners' manuals, warranty guides, customized screen savers, discounts and special offers, local traffic updates, and online shopping.

Registration with Owner Connection also allows users to participate in interactive/community portions of the site, including online surveys about Ford automobiles, email with Ford employees and the Interactive Info Center (a help feature of the site). Finally, the Owner Connection portion of the Ford site includes a feature called "Owner Stories." Though not as developed as a discussion forum in terms of fostering community, the Owner Stories feature allows registrants to swap personal stories about their experiences with their cars. These stories are typically "testimonials" (along the lines of those used on NGO sites) and consist of instances in which the car got the owner "out of a jam" or in which, when something went wrong, Ford service personnel "made it all better."

One final point should be made about both the Walmart and Ford websites. Like the other large, "traditional" corporations analyzed above, each uses a portion of its site to deal with serious public policy issues. However, the manner in which they do so is quite different from the "canned" press release format described above. Rather than filling these portions of their sites with official policy statements about issues such as diversity, health and safety, and the environment, both Walmart and Ford present specific examples of programs and events in which they participate in order to solve these problems. Most often, descriptions of this involvement are "community oriented," meaning that the corporations define themselves as members of the communities in which they operate, and depict their employees in situations of community involvement. Overall, this framing of the issues is more engaging and more believable than the policy statement approach taken by most other large corporations. The approach makes it easier to see the corporation as a collection of involved individuals rather than as a behemoth with questionable intentions. In short, these sites more effectively conform to the "ideal norms" perspective for solving social problems.

Given the conflicting evidence about the importance of adopting the network form for the effective utilization of Net logic, what might we conclude about the future impact of the Internet on the corporation and the economic order? In order to answer this question, one must keep in mind that the corporation, like any other institution, is first and foremost a strategy designed to solve a certain problem. In a capitalist economic order the problem is how to organize the flow of work, materials, ideas and money in an effort to optimize profit (or shareholder value) in the face of competition. Like the state, the corporation is a bureaucratic form precisely because, as Weber noted, bureaucracy is actually the most efficient organizational form for the coordination of large functions over large areas.

As I noted at the outset, most of the debate regarding the economic order revolves around how the corporation of the future will structure membership in response to "globalization." Yet surprisingly, though globalization seems to imply the necessity of coordinating more and more functions across larger and larger geographic areas, observers seem to be in agreement that the economic order will come to be dominated by "network" (non-bureaucratic) organizations. It is this contradiction, I suspect, which has resulted in a great deal of confusion about the future of the corporation. Ultimately, the exact meaning of the term "network" remains unclear.

What exactly are the core properties of this new network form? This question remains largely unanswered for one key reason—the sociological and economic conceptions of "the network" do not coincide. The sociological notion of the network is closely allied with the definition used in the last chapter in the discussion of the transnational NGO. The NGO is viewed by many as the quintessential sociological example of the network form, as it is based on shared beliefs and values, characterized by voluntary, reciprocal and horizontal patterns of communication, populated by actors committed to a specific cause or goal, and capable of generating information quickly and accurately and deploying it effectively. One need only recall this definition of the network form from the previous chapter to be convinced that the successful ".coms" are really nothing of the sort.

In contrast, the economically based concept of the network describes a form guided by laissez-faire market principles and efficiency. In this version of the network form, "...individuals or small groups use networks of personal contacts and contractual relationships to bring together the resources needed for each venture. It is, indeed, the classic form of market organization, allowing resources to be put together quickly when an opportunity for profit presents itself and dispersed when a venture is completed" (Hendry 1999, 569). Malone and Laubacher (1998) have offered, as an example of this form, the Linux community, "a temporary, self-managed gathering of diverse individuals engaged in a common task.... Tasks are not assigned and controlled through a stable chain of management but rather are carried out autonomously by independent contractors. These electronically connected freelancers, or e-lancers, join together into fluid and temporary networks to produce and sell goods and services" (144).

Based upon preliminary evidence offered throughout this chapter, it seems clear that the successful ".coms" do not conform to this economic definition of the network either. These highly successful entities are not free-form linkages among independent contractors. They are legal entities with unique identities. They are corporations. The only thing that distinguishes them from the more traditional form is that they have figured out how to successfully utilize the logic of the Internet. They are entertaining. Further, continuing for a moment with the Linux community as an example, two points should be made. First, it should be noted that the product of this community is not sold for a profit. It is one thing to produce computer programs as a network of hobbyists, and quite another to design a system to be marketed and sold for profit. Second, it should be noted that a cursory glance at the many information technology publications now available reveals that many technology professionals have doubts as to the quality of the product(s) created by the Linux "network." Relative to UNIX, the Linux operating system is considered to be less reliable, less stable and less robust. In short, it may well be that the Linux community, like the Zapatista network discussed in the previous chapter, is simply too loosely connected to prove successful.

While there can be little doubt that traditional corporations face a host of new challenges and opportunities due to the advent of networked computing, it is unclear at this point that this institution will have a significantly different role in either the economic or the political order in the future. Preliminary investigation reveals conflicting assumptions about and evidence of adoption of the "network form" as a prerequisite for the survival of and success in a globalized economic order. Globalization theorists have generally argued that hierarchical structures are uniquely ill-adapted to change. If this is, in fact, the case, then how can globalization theorists argue that corporations (hierarchical by definition) can adapt to changing environmental circumstances and thereby come to dominate not only the economic order but the political order as well? Proponents of strong globalization also argue that when these hierarchical structures do adapt, they will take on the form of networks. The question then becomes: How can a temporary collection of individuals, coming together strictly for the purpose of profiting from a single venture, ever muster enough economic and/or political clout to challenge the authority of the state (or even the NGO)? Finally, if the transformation underway is about becoming a network, about breaking down barriers between what is inside and what is outside the company, how can such a transformation be seen as a harbinger of efficiency and success for the corporation, but a harbinger of loss of sovereignty and political demise for the state? These are but a few of the conflicts found within the assumptions about globalization and the economic order.

If we expect to straighten out this confusion and to better understand the roles of the network form and Net logic in the economic order, a great deal more empirical research is needed. Many of the research questions proposed in the last chapter with regard to the state and the NGO would also prove helpful to explore with regard to the corporation, including:

    1. What, exactly, constitutes the network form? From an examination of different hypotheses about the nature of the corporate form, it appears

that what gets theorized about as *the* network form is actually a cluster of forms, some of which conform more closely to the ideal type than others, and all of which display the properties of the *hierarchical* and *market* forms to varying degrees. Is it possible to reconcile the sociological and economic conceptions of the network?

2. What would a series of case studies on the structures of and success ratios of specific corporations tell us about the relationship between degree of network structure and success in the economic order?

3. How different are the current attempts at vertical and horizontal integration from those at the turn of the last century? Are the "networks" that result today qualitatively different from those formed decades ago by corporations seeking to capture and expand market share? If so, in what ways?

4. Regardless of the advantages that may accrue to the network form, does the corporation continue to serve certain purposes or possess certain strengths not attainable through conversion to the network? If so, what are those purposes and strengths?

5. Can we document specific instances in which "communities," such as the Linux developers, have successfully competed with established corporations or altered the behavior of other actors in the economic or political orders? If so, to what can we attribute the success?

6. What are the implications of Internet use in everyday life for the economic order? That is, how do the network form and Net logic re-present the ideas of work and organizational membership? Are "virtual teams" within organizations effective? Can networks foster a sense of personal identity in the same way that corporations can? Can corporations "harness" those identities to "suit their purposes" in the same way that states harness national identity?

7. Given their relative shortcomings in the use of inflection devices, what are the implications of Net logic for corporations attempting to exert power in the political order? Can they compete effectively in the framing of issues with the state and the NGO?

NOTES

1. Weber identified four types of political capitalism—imperialist, colonial, adventure and fiscal—each of which afforded the opportunity for profit through political expansion, exertion of prerogatives over conquered territories (trade monopolies, compulsory labor, etc.), exploitation of political prerogatives (leasing rights to coin money) or simply through raids for treasure in foreign lands. See H. H. Gerth and C. Wright Mills, *From Max Weber: Essays in Sociology.* New York: Oxford University Press, 1946, for additional details.

2. Weber identified four types of political capitalism—imperialist, colonial, adventure and fiscal—each of which afforded the opportunity for profit through political expansion, exertion of prerogatives over conquered territories (trade monopolies, compulsory labor, etc.), exploitation of political prerogatives (leasing rights to coin money) or simply through raids for treasure in foreign lands. See H. H. Gerth and C. Wright Mills, *From Max Weber: Essays in Sociology*. New York: Oxford University Press, 1946, for additional details.

3. Ratings from these companies were, as of the end of 1999, electronically available at *www.forrester.com* and *www.gomezadvisors.com*.

4. Not surprisingly, the E-trade site more closely parallels the grammar of other shopping sites. E-trade syntax, inflection and vocabulary operate exclusively through the entertainment perspective. While many investors find this framework acceptable for investing "play" money (that which they can afford to experiment with and lose), many others apparently find this framework unacceptable. As a result, many polls related to "best websites" for online investing reveal a preference for traditional, "stodgy" houses such as Merrill Lynch, Fidelity and T.D. Waterhouse.

5. Since the last ranking of Fortune 500 companies was published, two of the companies (Exxon and Mobile) merged, reducing the total number by one. In addition, four of the companies ranked in the top ten of Fortune 500 are also ranked in the top ten of the "World's 100 Largest," reducing the total number of companies from 20 to 15. Note: Fortune 500 rankings are based on revenue, while World's 100 Largest rankings are based on market capitalization. Companies in the top ten slots on these lists were as of the close of 1999.

CHAPTER FIVE

Church, University and Family in the Virtual World

Interestingly, observers of institutions within the normative order do not place the same emphasis on the Internet Revolution that observers of the political and economic orders do. Though many have argued that changes in production technologies embodied by the Industrial Revolution brought about changes in the structure and function of institutions within the normative order, a similar connection has not been argued between changes in communications technologies and the normative order. To the extent that communications technologies are typically examined within this realm, it is in order to assess the detrimental effects of so-called mass media on the individual.

Throughout history, as the reader will recall from Chapter One, critics of mass media have argued that media usurp the legitimate authority to engage in the socialization of the individual from the church, the school and the family. Emphasized are the detrimental effects of mass media upon the *individual*. With the exception of religion, examination of how such media are used to transform the very structure and functioning of *institutions* is practically nonexistent. Such examination is precisely the goal of this chapter. Accordingly, it begins with an outline of the basic functions of the three core institutions of the normative order—the church, the university and the family. Then, from the perspective of media logic, it examines the ways in which the Internet is used to transform the manner in which these institutions accomplish their respective social functions.

Consider first the arena of religion. A system of beliefs, practices (rituals) and shared symbols directed toward the "sacred" or "supernatural," religion has long been understood by sociologists to be the universal institution through which people address the ultimate meaning of human existence. Religion provides emotional comfort in times of confusion or distress. It stabilizes social life by providing ultimate guidelines, values and norms applicable to the conduct of everyday life, and thereby ensures social cohesion, solidarity and control. Ultimately, religion provides, for the individual, a sense of identity and purpose, and answers questions about ultimate meaning.

While the ultimate function of religion is always the same, the social form it takes is not. Once again, it was Max Weber (1964) who pointed out that religious social forms are of four types (ecclesia, church, sect and cult) and may be classified along a continuum according to organizational features, the degree of similarity between group norms and values and those of larger society, and whether the group claims to be uniquely legitimate. For purposes of this chapter, we are concerned with the "church" and "sect" as social forms. The church (or denomination) is an established and formally organized form characterized by large membership, relative wealth, extensive bureaucratic regulations, formal training programs and career plans for its employees, and abstract, intellectualized moral standards and conceptions of God. The church readily seeks accommodation with larger society, and is thus a socially accepted organization within the context of religious pluralism.

The sect, in contrast, is a smaller, less formally organized group that has separated from a denomination (church) and has negative tension with larger society. The leaders of sects acquire their position through charisma rather than through formalized training. Where members of the church may try to make abstract moral standards "fit in" with everyday life, members of the sect place religious convictions ahead of what others around them may believe via a literal interpretation of Scripture. Typically, sect members seek to escape the formality of the church form in order to have a more personal "experience" of God. They reject the intellectualized approach of churches, stressing instead personal salvation, direct experience of divine power and the emotional expression of religious beliefs. Sect leaders and members actively recruit new members through the promise of salvation and personal fulfillment. In the upcoming sections we will explore these two social forms from the perspective of media logic, examining the extent to which each appears to be capable of successfully utilizing Net logic, and theorizing their respective likelihoods of success in the normative order in the future.

Since the Industrial Revolution, education has been another core institution of the normative order. It is a modern society's formal system of instruction and serves to transmit cognitive skills, knowledge and values from one generation to the next. In a sense, the educational system is an extension of the family—as society became more technologically and socially complex, families could no longer be expected to pass along all of the knowledge and skills the individual would need throughout his or her lifetime. Formal schooling under the direction of specially trained teachers is a strategy for solving that problem. Further, formal education has served the purposes of social integration (forging a unified whole with a common language, national identity, cultural experience, belief system and value set from a collection of culturally diverse individuals), conformity to conventional social norms, the establishment of social relationships (peer group networks and potential marriage partners), social control, and reproduction of a status hierarchy (education as gatekeeper). For all of these reasons, education has been and continues to be central to the normative order.

In this chapter, analysis is confined to that particular social form characteristic of higher education, the university. While primary and secondary education organizations clearly attempt to incorporate the Internet into the classroom, it is at the university level, where "virtual" institutions are popping up in record numbers, where we are currently most able to observe any fundamental changes in social form. In Weberian terms, the university can be understood in much the same way as the corporation and the church. As a form, it is characterized by bureaucracy, the "rational" pursuit of goals, abstract thought and formalized training of its leaders. Successful movement through this form prepares the individual for, and in fact perpetuates, bureaucracy in other areas of life. As Weber (1946) notes,

> Educational institutions ... are dominated and influenced by the need for the kind of "education" that produces a system of special examinations and the trained expertness that is increasingly indispensable for modern bureaucracy.... Today, the certificate of education becomes what the test for ancestors has been in the past ... a prerequisite for equality of birth, a qualification for canonship, and for state office.... The development of the diploma from universities ... and the universal clamor for the creation of educational certificates in all fields make for the formation of a privileged stratum in bureaus and offices.... When we hear from all sides the demand for an introduction of regular curricula and special examinations, the reason behind it is, of course, not a suddenly awakened "thirst for education" but the desire for restricting the supply for these positions and their monopolization by the owners of educational certificates [240–241].

In the upcoming sections we will analyze two successful virtual universities, assessing their abilities to use Net logic, examining the extent to which they are similar to or break away from the traditional university form, and theorizing their likelihood of success relative to "brick and mortar" universities in the future.

Finally, we will examine the family as a core institution of the normative order. Interestingly, the family is the most difficult institution within the normative order to define in specific terms. This is largely because the form it takes changes rapidly over time as individuals use it to solve different problems in an ever-changing social environment. Traditionally, "family" has been understood as people who are related by blood, marriage or adoption. Consisting of at least two people, the family is argued to be "any sexually expressive or parent-child relationship, in which people have a sense of mutual commitment, provide mutual aid and support, and identify with other members of the group" (Thompson and Hickey 1994, 319). While such definitions do not truly illuminate the nature of family or its changing form, examination of the functions that the family has performed over time does.

The family is argued to be the foundation of social order because it performs several basic tasks, the most important of which is the socialization of children. The family is considered the "first" agent of socialization, meaning it typically has more influence over the behavior, attitudes and beliefs of the child than does the church, the school, the child's peer group or mass media. As the primary agent of socialization, the family is responsible for creating new members for society and for integrating them into the norms and values of larger society. But the family solves other social problems as well. It is used to regulate sexual activity (by limiting partners to a monogamous relationship and prohibiting incest); to transmit ascribed social status and standing within the community; to care for the young, the old and the ill; and, most recently, to provide members with material and emotional support, fulfillment and a sense of belonging.

Over time, the dominant family form in Western industrial societies has evolved from "extended" to "nuclear" (two heterosexual parents and at least one child). However, other family forms are increasingly considered legitimate strategies for solving the problems outlined above as well. Such forms include the single parent family, "blended" families (in which at least one of the adults is a stepparent), cohabitation and gay/lesbian couples. These modifications in family form have generally been attributed to changes in the economic order and in reproductive technologies, and typically ignore the role played by media. As Thompson and Hickey (1994) note, those who analyze the relationship between family and media (particularly television) focus not on changes in social form but changes in quality of functional performance. "Television has been accused of wrecking the family, causing divorces, destroying children's minds..." (336). Unanalyzed are the ways in which the logic of television is used by the individual to understand and legitimate both family form and function. With regard to the Internet and family form, that type of analysis is precisely the goal of the upcoming sections. Three ".com" websites and many personal home pages concerning the family are analyzed to ascertain the extent to which they conform to Net logic, and the possible implications for the future of the family as a social form.

In conclusion, while there has been a great deal of theorizing as to the effects of the Internet Revolution on institutions of the political and economic orders, little has been done with regard to institutions of the normative order. This is somewhat surprising, as these institutions—religion, education and family—are perhaps most directly relevant to people's everyday lives. In the remainder of this chapter I seek to partially fill this void. Through the lens of media logic I examine the extent to which the church, the university and the family are adopting the logic of the Internet in order to fulfill their social functions, and whether such adoption demands (or is at least enhanced by) a fundamental change in social form. In short, the questions addressed here are the same as those addressed in chapters three and four: Does the network form accord those who adopt it any advantages (power) in the normative order? Is the network form more conducive to the adoption of the logic of the Internet? Are the church, the university and the family required to adopt the network form and/or the logic of the Net as the interaction medium to secure their external significance in the normative order? It is to these questions that we now turn.

NET(WORK) LOGIC AND THE NORMATIVE ORDER

Religion

> Overall, religiosity in the United States has been stable in recent decades. But a great deal of change is going on inside the world of organized religion. Membership in established churches ... has plummeted by almost 50 percent in the last three decades. During this same period, membership in other religious organizations ... has increased just as dramatically or even more so... As the most church-like organizations become more worldly in their orientations, people abandon them in favor of other, more sect-like religious communities... [Macionis 1993, 491].

Because religion, in whatever form it takes, is so fundamental to the establishment of social order and meaning, sociologists have spent a great deal of time attempting to explain this transformation and to predict what it may mean for the future of the institution. In general, they agree that the key contributor to this change in religious affiliation and expression is the marriage of religion and mass media. No sooner had electronic broadcasting via radio "officially" begun in 1912 than fledgling stations started experimenting with the transmission of religion-oriented programming. In

January 1921, Pittsburgh station KDKA transmitted the first live radio broadcast of a church service. It was a success. By 1925, 63 religious organizations held radio licenses (Erickson 1992, 2), and in 1990 there were more than 1370 religious radio stations in operation (Schultze 1990, 73).

But the "mediazation" of religion goes back further than the advent of radio. As Schultze notes:

> The rapid popularization of a media gospel began in the early nineteenth century. Numerous preachers and Bible teachers challenged the existing social and religious authority of college-trained clergy by creating emotionally stirring messages for popular audiences. These new evangelists changed the standard conventions for proclaiming the gospel. First, they deintellectualized the message, simplifying it for mass audiences of common folk. Second, they replaced the genteel language of the educated clergy with vernacular speech delivered in easily understood oral styles, including storytelling and anecdote. Third, they dramatized the delivery of sermons with voice and body, transforming the pulpit (if there even was one) into a stage for popular religious drama in which the preacher was the main character. The effect of these changes was to create engaging messages and styles of delivery that both attracted large audiences and moved them emotionally [35].

In short, by the time radio was invented, certain forms of religious organization were fully prepared to adopt its logic. The most prominent of these were Fundamentalist and Evangelical organizations, which, in time, overcame broadcast restrictions imposed by the Federal Council of Churches (which represented Protestantism, Catholicism and Judaism) in what Erickson (1992) has explained as the battle between the "liberals" and the "conservatives":

> The mainstream-vs.-outsiders struggle in religious broadcasting came to be defined as a battle between the "liberals," those religious orders that had been assimilated into current U.S. society and had been known to interpret the Scriptures in a manner that gave breathing space to social changes and shifts of attitude, and the "conservatives," those worship groups that adhered to a more traditional, frequently fundamental interpretation of the Scriptures, that were generally opposed to sudden changes in society and social mores… [8].

In Weber's terms, it was a battle between the church as a social form and the sect. In the late 1940s the battleground shifted to television. Success in this visual medium meant abandoning, for the most part, sermon-like presentations adopted for radio logic. Christian Broadcasting Network (CBN) and Trinity Broadcasting Network (TBN) began using many visual formats easily recognizable today, including news and interview programs, variety shows and magazine-style shows. In 1977 the Angel Award was established by the Religion in Media Association as the equivalent of the "Emmy" for religious broadcasting. Presented locally and nationally on an annual basis for the "best" religious radio and television programs, films, recordings and other media, the Angel Award was a clear indicator of what Altheide and Snow (1979) have termed the "entertainmentization" of religion. The "best" programming is that which operates according to the entertainment perspective, providing the individual with a vicarious, larger than life experience outside the parameters of everyday life.

Sociological research is replete with examples of the ways in which religious orders, particularly fundamentalists and evangelists, successfully adopted the logic of television to secure their external significance. A lengthy review of such examples is unwarranted here. What is of concern is the general fact that "conservative" religious orders have proven more capable than the more "liberal" orders of adapting to the logics of new media as they are created. The sect as a form has been more successful than the church. The key question at this point is whether this trend will continue regarding the Internet. Will the sect, as a social form, prove more astute at adopting the interaction framework (logic) of the Internet than the church? It is to a review of select websites that we now turn in an attempt to answer this question.

Because Christian Broadcast Network (CBN), Trinity Broadcast Network (TBN), Falwell Ministries and the Billy Graham Evangelistic Association (BGEA) have been generally recognized as the most successful adopters of media logic in the past, our examination begins with a review of the websites of these organizations. These sites are then compared to those of churches not generally known for their successful use of media logic, the Catholic Church and the Church of Jesus Christ of Latter-Day Saints. Finally, all of these sites are compared to that of an individual church with a local congregation that also broadcasts its activities live online.

Of the four organizations traditionally adept at adopting media logic, only CBN currently exhibits real facility in the use of Net logic. In both grammar (syntax, inflection and vocabulary) and perspective, the CBN site (*www.cbn.org*) best utilizes the Internet as an *interaction* medium. Consider first the syntax of the site. In terms of the organization and scheduling of content, CBN is a centralized, self-contained unit. That is, like the state and business sites discussed in previous chapters, it is not network in form, as it has no links to pages outside the CBN organization. In terms of overall appearance, CBN is organized in much the same manner as the successful ".com" sites discussed in Chapter Four. The organization logo is found in the top, left-hand corner of the main page, below which is content organized into three vertical columns and updated daily. The center column consists of hypertext headline links to feature articles, columns and other news pieces. The left-hand column contains the ever-present site menu bar (one which follows the individual from page to page and allows him or her to instantly jump from page to page within the site without having to "go home"). This menu bar allows one to instantly link to all of the major content pages and services within the site. The right-hand column contains graphics-enhanced links to special features, services and alerts. In short, the page is structured like a high quality online magazine.

In contrast, the syntax of the TBN (*www.tbn.org*), Falwell Ministries (*www.falwell.com*) and BGEA (*www.billygraham.org*) sites does not take full advantage of Internet capabilities. Like the CBN site, these are also self-contained (without links to outside sources of information or interaction). In and of itself, this is not necessarily a problem. However, the internal organization of content is poor. Rather than providing fast, descriptive and compelling links to internal content on the main page, these sites tend to bury access to internal information in a non-descriptive pull-down menu on the home page. As these links are initially invisible to the user and offer no graphics or text to describe the content, the new visitor to these sites would have little reason to investigate further. Additionally, with the exception of the Falwell site, these sites lack the ever-present menu bar. One cannot hop from one internal page to another without first hitting the "back" button on the browser. Some of the links in these three sites are "dead," and others lead to information that has not been updated for some time. All of these elements of syntax contribute to poor flow within these sites and, in general, do not offer the user a compelling reason for repeat (let alone frequent) visits to the site.

Regarding inflection, the rhythm and tempo of content presentation, CBN is again ahead of TBN, Falwell Ministries and BGEA. All of these sites offer several ways for the individual to become more involved with the "work of the Lord." These opportunities include online prayer requests (in which the individual submits a brief synopsis of a personal problem via email and asks for those within the organization to pray for him or her), charitable donations, in-home Bible training and study, email access to a regular newsletter, and online searching for Scripture relevant to a wide array of personal problems. The Falwell site is perhaps most astute at offering opportunities for involvement. Much like the successful NGO page, the Falwell page is dominated by a series of "action alerts" that briefly lay out an issue or problem in dynamic terms and then offer a letter to write or a petition to sign—the solution to the problem is just a click away.

But beyond these opportunities for involvement, these pages are surprisingly lacking in their use of the wide array of inflection devices that the Internet makes available. The TBN home page consists of a series of 12 icons arranged by topic in a four-by-three grid pattern. Clicking on each icon takes the user to a page that is essentially a billboard. That is, the internal pages are heavily laden with text and offer the user almost no opportunity to explore the topic further or to interact in any way. Each icon leads to a dead-end path. The Falwell and BGEA pages suffer from the same problem. Desired content is not easily located from the main page, and when one does arrive at the desired page, the presentation of the content can only be described as stale. Surprisingly, for organizations well known for facility with the grammars of television and radio, their web pages are almost devoid of stimulating audio-visual information. For example, Falwell Ministries is well known for its television production of the Old Time Gospel Hour. Not only is the link to Old Time Gospel Hour not prominent on the main Falwell page, when one does arrive at it, one finds that only archived shows at least six months old are available for viewing. There are no recent shows and no ability to broadcast the show live via the Net. The Billy Graham site offers information about television specials but no archived shows or live events. And its famed Hour of Decision radio program, though ostensibly accessible online, is marred by network congestion or failed connections and is often simply inaccessible. For its part, the TBN site offers no audio-visual information at all.

The CBN organization proves more astute in its use of inflection devices. In addition to the slick, magazine-like format of its main page filled with colorful graphics, photos, fonts and hypertext links, this site's internal pages make extensive use of photography, audio and video. For example, upon entering the "news stand" portion of this site, the user has the option of clicking on individual news stories. Several of these are accompanied by gripping photos, and the occasional story is even presented in video format for the user with the appropriate software. Alternatively, the user may simply click on the video of CBN news and be instantly transported to a news show formatted in precisely the same manner as those found on television.

Similarly, entry into the "outreach" and "worldreach" sections of the site reveals compelling stories of need from around the world and explanations of how CBN is working to solve an array of problems, all in a slick, magazine-style format. Stories are accompanied by professional photography designed in much the same way as the photography used on the NGO pages—alternately showing "before and after" scenarios in order to point out that solutions to the problems portrayed are obtainable. Further, one may view a series of video clips that mimic traditional television "infomercial" portrayals of people, usually children, around the world having their problems solved through the work of CBN.

Finally, the CBN site includes an online shopping experience called Family Central. Designed in the same way as the successful ".com" sites discussed in the previous chapter, Family Central is a customizable shopping source for family oriented books, music, videos and even many technology products. The site uses photos and color graphics to enhance its product displays and is generally easy to shop. This is in stark contrast to the other sites under discussion, which, when they do offer a shopping feature, tend to simply list items for sale category by category, without pictures or links for enhancement.

On all four of these sites, vocabulary (the final element of grammar) is closely tied to perspective. Altheide and Snow (1979, 199–216) noted that the ideal-norms format of television, combined with the entertainment perspective, is the very foundation of media religion. The same holds true for online religion. As one might easily guess, these sites conform strictly to the "ideal norms" perspective for problem solving. They serve notice to the individual that, in order to solve both personal and social problems, we must all stick with tradition. We must stand by traditional norms, values and beliefs. In order to accomplish this, these sites approach problems with a rather simplistic vocabulary. They argue that problems are readily solvable if people will "give themselves over to God" and "do what they know is right." However, the vocabulary of the CBN site differs from the other three in one important respect. It is less religious in nature. Where TBN, Falwell Ministries and BGEA constantly invoke specific passages of Scripture, the CBN site tends to use vocabulary that one would simply classify as humanitarian in nature. CBN site vocabulary is also less political in nature, particularly when compared to the Falwell Ministries site. The Falwell site, with its action alerts, petitions and political analysis, is centered on tying religious belief to policy outcomes. CBN site vocabulary is nonpolitical in nature. In fact, the site is not even linked to the website of Pat Robertson's other venture, the Christian Coalition, the vocabulary of which is decidedly political in nature. The presentation of content described above, when combined with a relatively non-religious and apolitical vocabulary, could easily lead the uninitiated visitor to believe that the CBN site is not "that religious." It might even allow the initiated but cynical web surfer to remain at the site and peruse its contents in greater detail than would probably be the case at any of the other sites. While no information is available as to whether this approach has made CBN more successful in its online venture than other religious sites, the idea is certainly worth exploring in greater detail.

Before moving to an analysis of other online religious organizations, it is vital to note what is absent from these Evangelical sites. None of these four sites have even attempted to either customize (personalize) the online religious experience for the individual or to foster any sense of online community. As noted in the previous chapter, customization of the online experience is one of the keys to success for businesses operating online. Customization affords the individual an experience of a unique self and a sense that someone "out there" is interested in his or her needs and concerns. Considering the fact that the defining objective of these Evangelical associations in the past has been to deliver a more "personal experience of God," it is surprising that they make no attempts on their websites to continue that tradition.

Even more surprising is the lack of online community at these sites. The defining logic of the Internet is interaction, particularly interaction in a many-to-many framework. Yet CBN, TBN, Falwell Ministries and BGEA offer no chat rooms, bulletin boards or discussion forums—frameworks for interaction so vital to the success of NGOs, businesses and even nation-states discussed in previous chapters. As Schultze (1991) noted, Evangelism via the television format has traditionally constituted an "invisible church" in which

> The enjoyment of the show substitutes for the enjoyment of interpersonal relationships that exist in a real congregation. Because the tube cannot provide dialogue and touch, it cannot sustain fellowship and genuine trust among viewers. Its congregants never meet one another, so they share only a viewing experience, not a relational one. Any interaction is mediated through the show. The televangelist decides what viewers will know about each other—who watches, why, how frequently, when, and with what contributions. He controls the flow of messages from one invisible viewer to another... Televangelism's communication is essentially a series of monologues designed to create the impression of membership, relationship and even accountability [208].

While such a framework proved highly successful for televangelism, it flies in the face of the logic of the Internet. Whether these associations, given their social form, can adopt to Net logic remains to be seen. We will return to this point in the concluding section of this chapter.

With this brief analysis of traditionally media-adept religious orders behind us, we now turn our attention to the examination of two orders not commonly known for their astute use of media logic, the Catholic Church and the Church of Jesus Christ of Latter-Day Saints. The official pages of these two sites, *www.vatican.va* and *www.lds.org,* respectively, leave something to be desired. Like the less developed nation-state and business sites, these pages are overtly "official" in their grammar. Each main page is decidedly religious in appearance, depicting historical religious figures and symbols, and each serves as the starting point for what are largely billboard sites. From the main page of the Catholic Church, one may access official information about Vatican museums, the Vatican city-state, the Roman Curia, and the Vatican library and archives. Only the "multimedia" page, on which the individual may access select audio and video archives (with an occasional live presentation), uses any inflection devices other than text. This self-contained (non-network), infrequently updated site is devoid of all other inflection devices—variety in font, color, photography, hypertext links and interactive forums—so successfully used by other organizations.

Similarly, the main page of the Latter-Day Saints organization is essentially a series of billboards. On this page one may access "official" documents and statements of beliefs, such as "articles of faith," the "importance of families," "the family guidebook," and other documents relevant to the establishment of the church and its views on various topics. This site is completely text-based. There are no chat rooms, message boards, magazines, photography or audio-visual resources. There is not even an email contact point. This site, like the official Catholic Church site, is designed not to elicit a response from the user but to disseminate official information.

Though the Evangelical sites reviewed above have their shortcomings, they are generally more in keeping with the logic of the Internet than either the official Catholic Church or LDS sites. If this were where the story ended, we would expect that those sect-like organizations would continue to draw members away from more traditional church-like organizations. However, further online exploration of the Catholic and LDS traditions reveals that this will not necessarily be the case. Each is also represented by myriad "unofficial" sites, many of which have been much quicker to adopt the logic of the Net. For our purposes here, we will confine our examination to a single Catholic site, Eternal World Television Network: A Global Catholic Network, and a single LDS site, LDS World.

The Eternal Word Television Network (EWTN) site is a web-based extension of a global Catholic television network (www.ewtn.com). Like other religious pages examined, this site is non-network in its organization of content. However, unlike some of the others, the site content is also very current. The look of the main page, though overtly religious, is updated regularly, as are the "what's new" and "news" sections within the site. Further, this site is considerably more advanced in its use of inflection devices than is the official Catholic Church page. It contains a photo gallery of several individual exhibits depicting various activities of the Pope, an online magazine entitled *Life on the Rock* that imitates the television news magazine show in format, and an assortment of audio and video presentations.

Unlike the official Catholic site, audio and video resources present programming from an assortment of people and places, not just from the

Vatican. For example, one television show viewable live over the Internet (and in archive form) is Mother Angelica Live: "EWTN's original, live viewer call-in show with Foundress Mother Angelica offering practical and witty solutions to life's challenges. Join Mother Angelica ... for family night and Bible study.... Mother Angelica and her guests teach the Faith, probe current issues, and take your phone calls." In addition, one may log in daily and receive new audio prayers, homilies, reflections and "inspirational messages," and may even use the computer as a radio (the companion medium) by activating the continuous play of religious music available on the site.

While these and other audio-visual devices bring EWTN up to par with CBN, the Evangelical site most astute in the uses of Net logic, this site takes things one step further. In its *Life on the Rock* online magazine, this site offers two means of interaction not available on any of the sites previously discussed. First, the site offers a Bulletin Board on which one may post prayer requests. When posting this request, the individual has an option to post his or her email address as well. Most people take advantage of this option, thereby enabling other users of the bulletin board to contact them directly via email to pray. Second, the site offers a Question & Answer board on which the individual may post questions about the application of Catholic teachings to particular life situations. A board moderator then responds directly online to the question posed. While this arrangement does not yet allow for the many-to-many interaction format, it does at least provide one-on-one interaction in a public setting that all other participants have access to. These sorts of activities, combined with the call-in video and audio shows available online, make this the most interactive site examined thus far.

Turning now to a brief examination of an alternate Latter-Day Saints site, LDSWorld (*www.ldsworld.com*) is a vast improvement over the official LDS site in terms of conforming to the logic of the Internet. Its use of syntax and inflection resemble that of the ".com" sites discussed in the previous chapter. Rather than presenting the user with a home page filled with religious symbolism, this site looks more like a newspaper, with its three-column presentation of information and services. The center column, filled with news articles and "what's new" features, dominates the page. To the left is a menu bar with links to all of the main internal pages, and to the right is a series of hypertext links to special features, including "hot spots," "calendar" and the "daily quote."

Within its site, LDSWorld makes use of many other inflection devices, including photography, audio and video (both live events and archives), an online magazine (which is very professional in format and serves to legitimate the LDS cultural identity), email newsletters, and so forth. The objective of this site is to serve as *the source* for information and guidance regarding the Church's teachings and its role in larger society. In order to accomplish this, the site affords what no other religious site examined so far does—a level of customization and links to the "outside world." Individual users may register with the site. Registration means that the user is greeted by name upon entering the site and that he or she has access to other features within the site, including an email newsletter and a personal email account. In addition, registered members are eligible to contribute content to various areas of the site.

This site, unlike other religious sites, also offers a searchable database of links to other web pages, some of which are religion-oriented and some of which are not. All links residing within the database have been approved by LDS, and the topics range from humor to business to genealogy to news. Because links are screened, the user cannot access sites that do not meet with the approval of LDS officials. Nevertheless, even this level of networking is non-existent on other religious sites and makes it conceivable that a member could set his default browser home page to the LDSWorld site and browse only within the web made available through it. (It should also be noted that this site offers a shopping option different than any other religious site. Rather than building its own store of items, LDSWorld has built a store that consists of a series of links to other, non-religious online stores, including Sharper Image, Dell Computers, Hickory Farms and many others. This feature adds to the site's ability to serve as the default browser home page.)

In summary, EWTN and LDSWorld offer their users something that the official sites of the Catholic Church and Latter-Day Saints do not; they offer entertainment. Through a combination of customization features, audio, video, photo galleries, news articles, and interactive databases and bulletin boards, these non-official sites, while still adhering to the ideal-norms perspective, entertain the user by making the experience of religion more interactive and thus more engaging. These non-official sites bring a measure of balance back to the battle between the "conservatives" and the "liberals," the sect and the church, discussed above.

This ongoing battle between church and sect is further affected by the Internet in that it affords the individual local church the possibility of effectively using media for the first time on a national—and even global—basis. The small church may now move beyond the occasional broadcast on local radio and public television to a world audience. At last count there were over 29,000 web pages on various faiths and practices, over 6500 denominations and sects (within Christianity alone), and over 800 individual churches (within Christianity) with their own home pages capable of disseminating all manner of religious information and beliefs around the world.[1] Let us briefly examine the features of one such church in order to better assess the role of Net logic to the future of religion.

The Salem Baptist Church of Chicago is located on that city's South Side. It is also located at *www.sbcoc.org.* With a congregation of over 10,000 members, some of whom are "virtual" and dial in from around the world, it is successful in both formats (Mowatt 2000). In terms of Net logic, the leaders of Salem Baptist Church have grasped what no other religious leaders discussed so far have—the Internet is a medium of interaction. Not only are the in-person sermons at this church highly interactive (as one can readily see by viewing archived sermons online), but the virtual church reflects this level of interactivity as well. While this site has a few shortcomings (some of the pages are slow to load, some links take the user to pages that are still under construction), it has captured the essence of Net logic with its broadcasts, real time chat rooms and asynchronous discussion forums.

Viewing sermons online, whether archived or real time, gives one the sense of really being in church. These broadcasts are unlike their counterparts on the Evangelical pages because the live audience interacts with the minister, rather than just sitting passively in row after row of chairs. The feel is that one is ensconced in a cozy, "real" church setting, not in an auditorium, which is often the feeling derived from viewing Evangelical broadcasts. A sense of community is evident in these events, and it is a sense that is enhanced through participation in real time chat rooms and asynchronous discussion forums that the site also hosts. In the chat rooms, as in most other real time events, one finds polite, friendly and lively conversation about almost any topic at all or about nothing in particular. The asynchronous discussion forums, as is usual, are more topic-oriented. Here people share their concerns and questions about faith and an assortment of life issues and problems. Though this web page is relatively simple compared to many of those analyzed above and lacks the slick, professional magazine format of the CBN and LDSWorld pages, it makes up for these shortcomings with its ability to instill in the individual a sense of community, belonging and commitment. Sermons and message boards use a relatively simple vocabulary and adhere to the ideal norms framework for problem solving while simultaneously providing entertainment and interaction. This site is fun, pure and simple.

EDUCATION

In contrast to the case of religion, sociological research into the adoption of media logic within the realm of education is practically non-existent.

This is not to say that education and media are not closely allied institutions. They are, particularly in the area of "distance education." Matthews (1999) has noted that, as early as the 1840s, Sir Issac Pitman was using shorthand to deliver correspondence courses by mail. By the early 1900s the University of Chicago had established a department of correspondence teaching, and the University of Queensland had founded a Department of External Studies. Further, the university, like the church, used non-text media as quickly as they were invented to secure its institutional significance in the normative order. The idea of mixed-media "distance education" reaches as far back as the invention of the radio and motion pictures, and the university has been relatively quick to adopt other media since that time, up to and including the Internet:

> The earliest reference I can find to a "university of the air" is in an American radio magazine dated May 1922: "The people's university of the Air will have a greater student body than all our universities put together." Full of enthusiasm for this "new-fangled medium," men were busy prophesying a bright educational future. Here was a miracle machine to carry teaching into every home.... In 1913, Thomas Edison proclaimed the motion picture as the agent of complete school reform. Almost every new product of communications technology has been tried out somewhere, sometime, on education—open-circuit television, long-distance instruction by computer, talking typewriters, stereovision, radiovision, 16 mm film, 8 mm film, Super 8 mm film, single concept loops, filmstrips, floppy discs, talking books, teaching machines. And everywhere a curious confrontation has occurred—old world with new technology [Hooper 1974, 178–180].

Nevertheless, explorations of this relationship between education and media tend to revolve around the "how to" format; the focus of research is on how to better utilize various media within the educational process. Left unexamined is the extent to which the university conforms to and reproduces media culture, and the implications of such conformity for the future of the form.

As noted at the outset of this chapter, exploration of the relationship between education and media here is confined to that social form known as the university. Even this methodological limitation does not afford the possibility of discussing a statistically significant portion of the population, as the majority of higher education institutions in the United States (around 3700) have distance learning programs, and about 25 percent of those offer accredited degrees and certificates that can be obtained exclusively through some form of distance education (Matthews 1999). For this reason, exploration of the relationship between the university and Net logic will be confined to two cases, the Open University of the United Kingdom and Jones International University, headquartered in the United States. The Open University (OU) is significant because it was a pioneer in the use of mixed-media in distance education and because it allowed for distance education on a massive scale. It continues those traditions today, making significant use of the Internet (and other media) to reach over 200,000 students. In short, OU set the standard for distance education for those that followed. Jones International University (JIU) is significant because it is the world's first and only fully accredited, completely virtual institution of higher education. Using only Internet technology (including forums, chat rooms, and streaming audio and video), JIU has been accredited by the North Central Association of Colleges and Schools even though it lacks any "brick and mortar" campus (OU, though primarily a correspondence university, does have over 330 regional study centers available to students).

The Open University was founded in 1969 and began admitting students in 1971. From the beginning, it was a media pioneer. In the early years its core technologies were radio and television, but it also relied heavily on original and creative print media to reach students. In assessing the implications of these print media, MacGibbon (1974) early on anticipated the argument of media logic:

> I am convinced that the OU course books have opened up not merely a new and fruitful approach to student book design; they have defined the place of the printed page as a teaching aid in relation to other media. The impact of the course books is immediate: they contain pictures, colour, and unusual layout, novel features for most undergraduate texts. The generous use of pictures, even to the extent that they are not always essential to the text, is notable if only as an indication that visual media, television and colour magazines are now accepted as fairly respectable purveyors of serious ideas.... More important than the pictures, however, are the layout and typography, the application of magazine design techniques to achieve a highly specific and sophisticated educational objective. These are not textbooks, but teaching aids which serve as a substitute for lectures, seminar, reading guide and notebook, providing a course in themselves, many of them quite independent of the television and radio programme [165].

The ability of the Open University to effectively utilize media logic continues, as evidenced by their online presence (*www.open.ac.uk*). Perhaps the most important point to understand is that the organization of this site's content is truly web-like. The main page offers three basic categories of information—"spotlight" (which includes information on courses, qualifications, residential schools, research projects, business connections, OU television access and student views), "news" and "about us"—all of which are updated frequently, and each of which is linked directly to the other categories in a variety of ways throughout the site. Though this site does not have a standardized, ever-present menu bar, these interconnections of internal pages serve the same purpose; they enable the user to "surf" the site, topic by topic, in the order he or she chooses without having to return to a central location for access. The result is the same sense of flow obtained by surfing the hypertext links on the best NGO, state and business web pages discussed in previous chapters.

Accordingly, the effective use of hypertext links as an inflection device is the greatest success of the OU site. Visible links are available within text documents on the site, but hidden links in icons and pictures that require the user to "mouse over" the area in order to find them are also dispersed frequently throughout the site. These "hidden" links serve largely as a redundant system; clicking on them sends the individual to the same internal pages made available through visible links. But "mousing over" the many blinking icons, photos and other graphics within the website to find possible links makes the site more fun. It is sort of like a game to see if one can find links to new, unexplored places within the site.

Interestingly, the OU site does not yet make use of streaming audio or video feed to convince the casual surfer to investigate the site further. Instead, it relies heavily on text-based documents, particularly the "frequently asked questions" format and the "testimonial." For example, the "student experience" section of the page leads the prospective student through a series of commonly asked questions about life as an OU student by presenting a colorful, checkerboard style page filled with blinking icons. Clicking on these icons allows the user to view the "question and answer" formatted information in a separate pop-up window. In this way the user may research life at the Open University by area of concern, rather than being guided through a prearranged "list" of questions and answers as he or she seeks out the most pertinent information. Other areas of the site (for example, the "courses and qualifications" section) also use a text-based frequently asked questions format to draw the prospective student in. Again, though, these areas of the site are never simply dull lists of official information (like those found on so many nation-state sites), but are tailored to the individual interests of the user via hypertext icons that take the user anywhere within the list he or she wishes to go.

Accompanying these FAQs are the photos and testimonials of OU faculty, staff and students. These testimonials get to the heart of the feel of the OU site through their use of a vocabulary (the final element of site grammar) that is simultaneously sophisticated and inviting. Faculty and staff testimonials discuss the mission of OU—the opening up of a whole new world, via education, to people for whom higher education was previously inaccessible. Student testimonials are akin to brief autobiographies. They succinctly tell the story of a student's life circumstances before enrolling in Open University and contrast those circumstances to where they now find themselves. They present different types of people from all walks of life, all of whom have found studying at the Open University to be challenging and instrumental to their success in life. Life as an OU student is realistically portrayed as demanding, occasionally frustrating and always rewarding in the long run.

This upbeat vocabulary, combined with the personal accounts of real-life OU students, supports the ideal-norms perspective traditionally associated with higher education (educational achievement equals a productive life). This format, though not as technologically sophisticated or as emotionally compelling as extensive use of photo galleries and streaming audio and video, in the long run serves its purpose. It is elegant in its simplicity, reaching a less technologically savvy potential student body through traditional means of persuasion. However, for the enrolled student, the picture is quite different. Actual students are involved in a university setting that makes extensive use of audio-visual strategies, online communications and conferencing, and a virtual desktop.

As the key concern here is utilization of online technologies, we will focus on what could be described as the "backbone" of OU's virtual presence, the FirstClass system. FirstClass is the university's electronic conferencing system. It affords users access to email, private conferences (asynchronous discussion forums), university-wide conferences and personal records (including information on current, future and past courses, progress toward the degree, and access to the email of a personal counselor), all of which may be tailored to the individual's needs and interests. In so doing, FirstClass serves as the virtual equivalent of the classroom and student body community found at the traditional brick and mortar university. Like most other virtual communities, FirstClass is managed through a series of FAQs that instruct the new user on how to navigate the system, how to interact with others and how to seek additional help. Its success, like that of any other community, depends on the individual's willingness to abide by community rules as described in the system's "Code of Conduct" document. For the actual student, it is the FirstClass system that ultimately makes Open University successful in adopting the key aspects of Net logic—interaction and community.

Thirty years after Open University was founded, Jones International University became the first fully accredited, completely virtual institution of higher education. Coming into existence during the Internet Age, JIU relies almost exclusively on computer networking technology for achieving its institutional mission. Where OU began in a text-based environment and worked diligently to develop cutting edge print media, JIU concentrates its efforts on adopting the logic of the Internet. Despite the different times in which these organizations came of age, and despite the different overall appearances of their web pages, they use similar strategies for attracting prospective students—FAQs and testimonial evidence.

The JIU site, in its overall appearance and syntax (organization and scheduling of content), has more in common with the ".com" sites discussed in Chapter Four than it does with the OU home page. The university name and logo are located in the top, left-hand corner of the page, an ever-present menu bar serves as the defining organizational principle for internal content (divided into categories, including academics, student services, corporate education, faculty and administration, and alumni), and additional page content is organized vertically into three columns. In terms of inflection (the rhythm and tempo of content presentation), however, JIU is very similar to OU. The site makes extensive use of the FAQ format and testimonial evidence to attract the prospective student.

For example, upon entering the page, one may take a "virtual tour" of the university via an FAQ document. This document pops up in a separate window and guides the prospective student through commonly asked questions. It does so in a way that emphasizes the legitimacy of the organization (it is an accredited university with faculty and content experts from high quality brick and mortar universities), the personal attention one receives at JIU compared to the large, traditional university, the convenience of studying online and, most importantly, the interaction in the virtual classroom with other smart, successful students from all over the world. These are the elements that make the JIU experience exciting and community-oriented. Other FAQ documents, found in the "academics," "student services" and "faculty and administration" areas of the site, reiterate these claims and are supported by testimonials from students and alumni. Like the OU testimonials, these operate with a vocabulary that appeals to the ideal-norms perspective for solving problems. They are miniature autobiographies that depict individuals leading more productive lives, thanks to their studies at JIU. Because the prospective audience for these testimonials is different (OU has no admissions requirements and is designed to serve the under-served and disadvantaged), JIU students and alumni are depicted as individuals who, already successful, could have pursued higher education "anywhere" but chose JIU because of its convenience.

For the enrolled student, JIU is more advanced than the Open University in its ability to successfully utilize the logic of the Internet. Where OU still relies heavily on print, radio and television media to serve its students, JIU operates completely online. Though students are required to purchase books and the occasional video in order to prepare for class, the classes themselves are taught exclusively online. Each course has its own web page inside the JIU site that hosts online assignments, course related online resources, additional content material (the course syllabus, updates and so forth) and the course forum, which is where "the action" occurs. The forum, like the conference in the OU system, is an asynchronous discussion group where students discuss with the instructor, and with one another, the current course topic. While the instructor is responsible for opening each initial topic, students are also capable of suggesting and opening topics for discussion.

Because of the particular technological framework employed by JIU, the forum resembles the television "talk show" format in many important respects. In the traditional university setting, the instructor typically lectures extensively and occasionally reserves time for questions and answers. In a virtual university, he or she serves more as a "host." Like the host of a talk show, the instructor plans what the general topic for discussion will be and attempts to orchestrate the dialogue so that it adheres to the major issues to be covered. However, as the stated objective of the virtual university is "collaborative learning," and as expert "content providers" are primarily responsible for the design, structure and content of the course, the instructor is essentially prohibited from dominating the forum to the exclusion of the thoughts and opinions of others. Students are expected to interact with one another extensively and are expected to learn from one another in addition to learning from the instructor. The instructor, like the talk show host, is a "facilitator" of that learning process, not the absolute source of knowledge on the topic at hand.

Regardless of how one feels about the legitimacy of this arrangement, the important point to remember is that the online teaching situation, by virtue of the logic of the Internet, demands it. All successful online ventures ultimately rest on their ability to use an assortment of inflection devices to generate interaction and maintain a sense of community. The online university is no different. If it expects to be successful, it must conform to the logic of the Net as a medium of interaction. Simply logging into a course forum to read static "lectures" delivered by the instructor would defeat the entire point of online education. The founders, administrators and faculty members of JIU understand this point, and have created a web presence that embodies online success. Course forums are interactive, engaging social spaces in which students recognize each other as individuals and, in time, develop a strong sense of community.

FAMILY

> The evolution of the family has been a slow but continuing process of selection, test and occasional rejection in the search for a more suitable

structure of unity in a prevailing social culture ... the human regard for family is so fundamental that it has always evolved to meet the needs of its members. The family has never been rejected; it has merely changed in form [Kay 1972, 7–8].

As noted in the introduction to this chapter, the family as an institution has changed form over time as it has been used to solve different social problems. In Western industrial societies the general problem to be solved has changed from economic survival and legitimation of the class structure to satisfaction of the emotional and identity-oriented needs of group members. As the problem changed, so too did the dominant form the family takes. From the "extended" family that embodied hierarchy (particularly in the feudal era), the family has become far more "network" in form. It has become what Cooley described as a true primary group, "...those [groups] characterized by intimate face-to-face association and cooperation. They are primary in several senses but chiefly in that they are fundamental in forming the social nature and ideals of individuals.... Perhaps the simplest way of describing this wholeness is by saying that it is a 'we' ... the bond in a primary group is based upon an intrinsic valuation of the other as a person, not from anticipation of specific benefits" (Coser 1977, 307–308).

Homans (1950) noted additional characteristics of the modern Western family that point to its network-like structure when compared to the pre-industrial family:

> The growth of civilization has meant that activities have been steadily taken away from the family and turned over to other organizations. Or better, other organizations have arisen by a process of differentiation within kinship. Today, about the only activities left to the family are the sexual relations of husband and wife, the care of young children, cooking, and the maintenance of a household. Farming, fishing, clothmaking, education and religious ritual have all gone from it ... the emotional ties between persons do not exist in a vacuum but are a function of the activities they carry on together and of the way these activities are organized.... Today, the jobs that a married couple carry out together are much fewer. The partners choose one another on grounds of romantic love ... but when the dream of romantic love has faded, they have to rely upon sexual relations and mere companionship to form the foundation of their marriage.... In the old-fashioned family, the activities did not have to be contrived; they were given.... Because the activities of the family are no longer complex enough to require centralized control, the father has lost his job as boss.... From being a sort of god, he has become a mere equal and familiar [276–277].

In short, the family has transformed itself from hierarchy (based upon "top-down" mandated frameworks for interaction, command and authority) to network, the foundation of which is shared values and beliefs, and within which interaction is horizontal, reciprocal and coordinated out of a sense of mutual obligation and long-term commitment. As Homans went on to note, however, this change in form resulted in increased ambiguity regarding norms of interaction and behavior between husband and wife, and between parents and children. Armed with a new structure and institutional mission, the family struggled to define the appropriate behavioral norms by which to integrate the two. For this, they turned to mass media, particularly the magazine and the television.

Each of these has a complex logic all its own, the details of which are beyond the scope of this discussion.[2] What is most relevant is that the magazine, as the subculture/identity medium, and the television, as the cultural mainstream, have been and continue to be used for the purposes of defining and constructing "family" and to understand and legitimate *how* the family should function. To those ends, the magazine, especially the "women's magazine," has served as a source of practical "how to" information on family life, while the television has depicted corresponding "ideal types" of family life. Both of these types of information about how the family should function are now readily available on the Internet. Magazine-type information is available on sites such as *www.family.com*, *www.parents.com* and *www.igrandparents.com*, while ideal-type families traditionally found on television are now portrayed "straight from the horse's mouth" on personal family web pages found on sites such as homestead.com. It is to a brief examination of the grammars and perspectives of these two types of sites that we now turn.

Turning first to the "how to" sites, it is important to note than in both grammar and perspective these sites closely resemble the traditional print magazine. In terms of syntax (the organization and scheduling of content), the main pages of family.com, parents.com and igrandparents.com are centralized and current/regularized. With features and tips updated daily, and with advertising and departments that link to other potentially relevant web pages, each of these sites aims to serve as the central location for all relevant information on "how to be a family." The promise inherent in this centralized, regularized presentation of content is that the busy parent is guaranteed a fresh experience each day from a definitive source. There will be no time wasted on stale information or in searching online for the needed resources.

Like the cover of most any print magazine, these sites rely heavily on the use of color, graphics and "teaser" headlines to capture the attention of the potential reader. They are centralized in the same sense that the successful ".com" sites discussed in the previous chapter are; they are "headlines only" main pages that offer no immediate substance but promise a great deal of relevant ideas and information to the user who turns the page. Snow (1983, 83) noted that print magazines are designed to be read front to back, but are, in fact, commonly thumbed through in the opposite direction. Knowledge of this fact helps determine the internal organization of articles and advertising in the traditional magazine. Designers of these online magazine-style sites have no such knowledge, as the whole point of hypertext is that the user may access information on a site in order of relevance and interest. This feature necessitates that, internally, content and advertising on these sites be centralized by the main page (the "cover" page) via a system of redundant hypertext links.

Specifically, feature articles, tips and advice columns are made available on the "cover" page via both direct access (clicking directly on an icon or a feature article headline) and an ever-present menu bar that leads the user to the general department in which the feature may ultimately be found. This system of abundant and redundant hypertext links increases the likelihood that the user will at least "thumb through" a significant portion of site content. In addition, advertising is placed in banner form at the top and bottom of internal pages. Such placement is necessary because, unlike the print magazine, in which a page of advertising is visible next to a page of content (whether the reader wants to see it or not), advertising on the Web is relatively invisible. Placement of banner ads at the top and bottom of internal pages (and these banners are usually blinking or scrolling) ensures that the reader will see the message and that he or she may conveniently "click" on the ad, if he or she chooses, without having to scroll around in the article. Add to these features the fact that most articles are available on a single page (without having to click "next" at the bottom of the screen) and are accompanied by photos and/or graphics, and the syntax of the family.com, parents.com and igrandparents.com pages very closely resembles that of the traditional print magazine.

Turning now to inflection (the rhythm and tempo of content presentation), one finds that these sites again mimic the print magazine in that they rely heavily on boxed inserts, bold font styles and colors, artwork (graphics and icons) and photography. Unlike other successful sites discussed in previous chapters, parents.com, family.com and igrandparents.com make no use of audio or video. Yet, like the print magazine, they emphasize a commitment to a particular subcultural identity, the "good family." To a large extent this is accomplished by combining a particular writing style with photos, graphics and even cartoons that capture the essence of the article. Like the print magazine, these photos, icons and graphics are used on the "cover" page to heighten interest in a particular feature. Within the site they are used at the beginnings of articles and are sprinkled throughout to hold the reader's attention. Often, "mousing over" these photos and graphics will reveal additional hypertext links.

Unlike the print magazine, however, the writing style on these sites is less narrative in structure and pace, and more declarative. While the features "tell a story" in a sense, they do not do so in the traditional manner. They are typically very short, factual and incisive, eschewing background detail, flashback sequences, meandering story lines and authorial ruminations on "the meaning of it all." They are more like short "news" reports based on individual experience and universalized through the vocabulary of identification. In terms of tempo, this written format is extremely fast. Were it not for the liberal use of photos and graphics, the user could easily speed through the content of a site and come away feeling less involved and less committed to the perspective offered. However, the liberal use of visual data slows the tempo considerably in two respects. Initially it causes the reader to pause to consider the information available in the artwork. Then, for those items that are "clickable," it causes the reader to investigate the matter further. Overall, then, the liberal use of photography and graphics serves to capture the attention of the reader, slow the tempo of movement through the site, and regularize the rhythm of the act of "surfing" through, all of which leads to a fuller emersion in the site content.

Additionally, these sites are capable of taking inflection one step further than do print magazines. Like the successful nation-state, NGO and corporate sites discussed in previous chapters, these sites customize and/or make social the user's experience of logging in. In so doing they further enhance the emotional involvement of the user in the content of the site and in the cultural identity ("good parent") derived therefrom. In short, customization and community features on these sites turn the reader into a member. For example, registering with parents.com (a quick process that does not require dissemination of extensive personal information) allows one to tailor some content areas to particular concerns. A section entitled "your view" is then available on the "cover" page that includes features, tips and other resources directly relevant to the content areas selected during registration. Other customization devices on this site include a childbirth planner (an electronic planner/organizer with nursery checklist, budget calculator and birthplan worksheet), a health records section (an electronic recordkeeper for doctors' appointments, illnesses and vaccinations) and a "baby book" (an electronic scrapbook of baby's early years). Similarly, registration with the igrandparents.com site allows one access to an email newsletter, email birthday reminders and a personal, customizable, within-site private area entitled "my grandchild" within which one may store and update all relevant information about grandchildren.

Registration at these sites also affords the user access to a community of users with similar concerns, interests and cultural identities. Real time chat rooms are one forum in which this interaction can occur. Though they can be free-for-all discussions among regular members, these are typically moderated forums that feature special guests who are experts in a particular area of family life (pregnancy, behavioral problems, balancing work and family, and so forth). These chats occur at regularly scheduled intervals, announced well ahead of time, and afford the community member the opportunity to "hear," firsthand, an expert solution to a specific problem. In a sense, these events follow the logic of the television daytime talk show in that they present audience members with a chance to interact firsthand with someone they would otherwise not be able to access, all within the structure of a controlled, moderated forum. Even the chat room "lurker" who chooses not to post questions directly can glean information from the conversation which he or she can then apply to his or her own life circumstances.

The second framework for interaction, one which has been discussed extensively in previous chapters, is the asynchronous discussion forum or bulletin board. Discussions are divided into general topics, within which members may start and maintain an unlimited number of specific topic "threads." For example, topics in the igrandparents.com site include childhood development, health and safety, values and traditions, and things to do, among others. Far and away the most commonly used forum in this site is the "tough subjects" category, within which grandparents seek and offer advice within a community of peers on a wide range of problems relating to their grandchildren (and children as well). Even though this site had only been in operation approximately three months at the time of this writing, this community area of igrandparents.com had already developed a large company of regular users who quite evidently feel free to discuss all manner of extremely personal troubles online.

The family.com site has the most developed range of asynchronous discussion forums. Within broad topics such as "all about you," "family ties," "your kids," health, learning and travel, one can choose from over 70 discussion boards, and more are being added all the time. Like the asynchronous forums on igrandparents.com, those here allow community members to talk to one another in intimate detail about an assortment of problems related to family life. Discussion threads and the messages within them may be short or long, detailed or general, to the point or meandering. Regardless, they serve the same function as topic-specific forums everywhere; they are a place not to chit-chat but to discuss and resolve specific problems.

Turning now to vocabulary (the final element of grammar) and perspective, we again find that these sites have a great deal in common with print magazines designed to reach a general, middle class audience. In examining the perspective(s) employed, one must ask, "what shared values and norms are employed?" What is valued by the readership of a particular magazine (user of a particular website), and what are the norms of behavior that guide the reader (user) in his or her quest to obtain the desired goals? In the sites discussed here, two overlapping strategies are evident — the construction and maintenance of group (cultural) identity and the ideal-norms strategy for solving problems. In terms of identity-building, the defining value, or element, on all three of these sites is "kids." First, it is evident from a study of site content that, in order to constitute "a family," the group must include children. If the group does not currently include children, it must either be trying to (in which event there are abundant resources on how to conceive and what to expect) or it must have moved well beyond that point (as is the case when the children are adults living independently away from home). As long as one subscribes to this defining value, then one can belong to any family form, including dual income, single parent, extended family, blended family and even homosexual family, and be capable of constructing and maintaining a favorable identity via these sites. Though one could argue that such a value is self-evident in sites entitled "parents" and "grandparents," it is important to note that any online search for "family-oriented" informative websites almost universally supplies links to sites that revolve, first and foremost, around children. Though sociologists and the census may count individuals, groups of assorted people living together, and even married couples without children as "families," family-oriented web pages do not.

There is a second interrelated aspect of identity-building via these sites. Whatever family form one belongs to, the ability to claim the identity of "good parent" rests on one's ability to obtain and make use of absolute knowledge. The good parent reasons his or her way through childhood illnesses, behavioral problems at school and home, and multiple childhood developmental stages, and is simultaneously knowledgeable in the arts of sandbox construction, craft making and gardening, and capable of throwing the best birthday party, planning the greatest family vacation and whipping up nutritious meals in 15 minutes. This "good parent" is an ideal type to which participants generally subscribe, and one which they can work toward as active members of these sites. They can log on at their convenience, find out what the next potentially huge problem with their child may be, what the vacation hot spot for families is, or just what they may easily prepare for dinner that night and, in so doing, be one step closer to being the ideal parent.

But the perspective employed is even more complicated than that. In order to be a good parent and belong to a good family, one must adhere to the ideal-norms perspective for solving problems. This is an interesting point because, more than any other institution discussed so far, the family has changed form to meet the new challenges of a changing social environment. Nevertheless, the recipe for being "a good family" is still to stick with middle class tradition. And the vocabulary employed on all of these sites is essential to conveying how this is to be carried out. Instrumental to "good parenting" are "firmness," "specificity," "negotiation," "consistency" and "rationality." Parents who are firm with their children, who are consistent, who are capable of negotiation and who never let their emotions get in the way will produce "good kids." Their goodness will evidence itself in the choices they make regarding lifestyle and in how they eventually raise their own children in conformity with the same strategies.

These magazine-style sites are not the only sites from which parents can learn "how to be a good family." As noted earlier, companies like homestead.com host huge numbers of personal family web pages, many of which are available for viewing by the general public. In many respects, though their logic differs considerably from that of television, they ultimately serve the same function as television shows that revolve around family. They present their audience with a peek into the private moments of an ideal type.[3] How do they accomplish this? It is to a very brief overview of the general nature of the grammar and perspectives of such pages that we now turn.

Though there are vast numbers of personal family sites created by families of varying backgrounds, socioeconomic class and structure, all sites researched for this work (50 sites were randomly selected) adhered to the same basic grammar and perspective. Regarding the organization and scheduling of content (syntax) of these sites, all can be described as organizationally simplistic and randomly (but frequently) updated. By organizational simplicity I mean that these sites, as one would expect, are far less complex in their structure than sites constructed by "formal organizations" of any type. Many consist of a single page that contains all family information. Others are organized as a main page with very limited links to separate pages that contain photo albums or even the identity-related information of individual family members. Regardless, these sites lack many of the organizational properties (menu bars, redundant links and so forth) instrumental to the success of other types of sites. However, many of these sites are interesting nonetheless. The level of interest they are capable of sustaining has a great deal to do with the inflection devices they utilize (a point to which we will return momentarily) but also with the frequency with which they are updated. Surprisingly, many of these sites are very active. Their authors update them frequently (if irregularly), and these frequent updates contribute to their appeal. One can begin to "follow" certain favorite sites, observing how the children grow, what sorts of activities the family becomes involved in, how different areas of their lives are progressing, and the like. The story is ongoing.

Again, however, it is the use of inflection devices that enables these sites to serve as ideal family types, if not in structure (membership) than at least in life *style*. Generally speaking, family sites make heavy use of color, font style and size variety, background wallpaper, music, icons and graphics. In terms of overall appearance, most sites use these devices to the point that they become "busy" or "loud" in much the same way as did the various sites connected by the Zapatistas in Cyberspace site discussed in Chapter Three. Upon entering the typical family site, one is immediately struck by a colorful wallpaper selection, on top of which are fancy and colorful fonts, blinking graphics, scrolling messages and some clickable hypertext links. Often this visual spectacle is accompanied by an automated musical selection that plays continuously until one leaves the page. All of these features are specially selected by family members because they convey the desired impression of the family—its lifestyle, background and values. More often than not, the selected wallpapers, graphics and fonts are oriented around one of two themes—nature or romance. Accordingly, many fonts are in cursive (something unheard of elsewhere on the Web), and there is an abundance of flowers, country scenes, cupids, angels, hearts, puppies, kittens, flying birds and the like. Musical accompaniments generally consists of selections from the "love songs" category.

All of these devices combine to serve as background for what is clearly the dominant inflection strategy on personal family pages—photography. Photographic strategies on these pages are of two types, portraiture and documentary. Family portraits, whether taken by a family member or by a professional, are generally used to open the site and are often accompanied by a short paragraph introducing the family to the visitor and welcoming him or her to the site. As one would expect, these portraits depict family members nestled closely together, everyone happy. More extensive use is made of the documentary strategy, which constitutes the vast majority of photography on all sites. These pictures document either a special event as it happens (family vacations, weddings, birthdays and so forth) or the everyday life activities of individual members. Typically, each of these photos is accompanied by a brief but descriptive narrative statement that explains to the outsider what he or she should see in the photo. In other words, the narrative gives the visitor the appropriate context within which to define individual members and the family as a whole.

In order to do so, the vocabulary that accompanies these pictures is decidedly "we" in nature—in precisely the sense that Cooley (1909, 23) meant when he argued that the family is a primary group. The vocabulary, though depicting each member as a unique individual, makes claims about the family as a unit. The people depicted in photos on these pages are not collections of individuals. They are family. Interestingly, this vocabulary is used to depict problems within the family as well. In arguing that these pages present the "ideal type" family, I am arguing not that they present an idealized, unobtainable family in either structure or function, but that they present a group which conforms to the ideal-norms perspective for solving problems. Narratives hint at problems that arise during the course of daily family life in a way that announces "we are regular folks who have problems, but we always stick together." Sticking together, serving as the source of warmth, comfort and identity in an increasingly uncertain world, has been the defining function of the family since the Industrial Revolution. It is tradition, and these websites portray families that adhere to that tradition come what may.

CONCLUDING COMMENTS: CHURCH, UNIVERSITY, FAMILY AND VIRTUALITY

Considering the significance that religion, education and family hold for the everyday lives of people everywhere, it is remarkable that these institutions, and the forms they take, have received scant attention from theorists of the "new global order." In debates about the nature of the "new corporate form," the powerfully networked NGO and the supposedly impotent bureaucratic nation-state, institutions of the normative order are nowhere to be found. In an attempt to ignite discussion about the future of such institutions, we turn now to a brief synopsis of what the evidence to date of their respective abilities to conform to Net logic tells us about their future form and significance.

Sociological research on media (particularly television) and religion in the past has yielded interesting insights into the relative popularity of the sect in recent decades. Any number of observers have noted that sect-like religious organizations have been adept at popularizing their belief systems by applying the entertainment framework to the practice of worship while maintaining adherence to the ideal-norms perspective for solving problems. This trend is perhaps best summarized in the work of Erickson (1992), when he points out that:

> The 1980s saw an upsurge in electronic religion's audience for a multitude of reasons. One was the ever-growing availability of cable television,

bringing a wider variety of sectarian programming to areas that had previously relied on two or three local stations or the fuzzy signals from faraway channels.... Another reason for the increase was a general disenchantment in mainstream religion, with many parishioners feeling that ideology in the big, established churches was changing too fast to suit them, and that these churches were not addressing such vital concerns as the growing crime rate and decreasing respect for moral values. Syndicated conservative speakers did not solve these crises, but they addressed the issues in a loud, clear, decisive voice, usually proposing a back-to-the-good-old-ways solution.

The electric church will continue to be regarded by many viewers, both the faithful and the cynics, as a source of entertainment. But this last aspect of the industry should not be regarded as wrong or nontraditional. It merely takes things full circle from the days thousands of years ago when music, dance, and drama all began to grow out of religious ceremonies. There always has to be some way to keep the audience coming back [14–17].

In terms of institutional form, it is clear that the sect has been more successful than the church at adopting the logic of television. However, it is less clear whether this will continue to be the case with regard to the Internet for three reasons. First, with the exception of CBN, the successful "electronic churches" of the television age do not conform to the logic of the Internet. They offer no customization features on their websites, no opportunities for reciprocal communication and no chance for community-building. The one-way transmission of information so taken-for-granted in mass media, yet so detrimental to success in the online world, continues. Second, the more church-like forms (Catholic Church and LDS), which have been relatively less successful at adopting the logics of other media, are gaining ground in the online world. Though the official sites of these churches are still sorely lacking, the unofficial pages of these churches are highly engaging and interactive and provide multiple opportunities for meaningful interaction and community-building. EWTN and LDS World are two prime examples of this change. Finally, individual local churches, such as the Salem Baptist Church of Chicago, are increasing in popularity as they adopt to the logic of the Net.

The sects that have been so successful in adopting the logics of other media cannot be defined as networks. But they did not have to be in order to be successful in television or even radio. Yet they also cannot be defined as hierarchy in the sense that we have discussed that form in earlier chapters. In Chapters Three and Four the hierarchical form was, by definition, bureaucratic. As Frankl (1987, xiii) rightly notes, these sects are structured as non-bureaucratic hierarchies; they are oligarchies. As the medium of interaction, the Internet demands that all institutional arrangements, regardless of form, afford quality opportunities for community-building, for active engagement with "the other." In the arena of religion, as in others already analyzed, it remains unclear what role social form will play in the ability to become successful in the online world. CBN conforms to the logic of the Net relatively well, yet it has not changed form at all in order to accomplish this. It is an oligarchy. As such, it would appear that oligarchic and even dictatorial forms of organization may potentially be successful in the online world. Such a conclusion has important implications beyond the arena of religion. It flies in the face of those who predict that nation-states operating within either of these frameworks must necessarily be toppled by the Internet, and, accordingly, warrants serious investigation. The more one examines online successes and failures across a range of activities, the more one is forced to conclude that adopting a specific structure, altering the "internal workings," may be less critical to success in a "globalized" world than conforming to the defining organizational principle of the dominant medium of communication.

The same argument may be made in the arena of higher education. Regarding organizational structure, Open University is the classic model of an hierarchical, bureaucratic structure. In fact, it is hard to imagine an organization less network in form, and yet it is highly successful in its use of media logic. As Ferguson (1976) noted,

> The structure is not essentially different from that of other universities. The governing body is the Council. The Council is charged by the Charter with "advancing the interests of the University, maintaining its efficiency, encouraging teaching, the pursuit of learning and the prosecution of research therein." The Council consists of the University Officers, the Chairman of the Academic Advisory Committee, four members appointed by the Privy Council, three members appointed by the Committee of Vice-Chancellors and Principals, three members representative of local education authorities and one of education authorities in Scotland, one member appointed by the Royal Society, one member appointed by the BBC, the Pro-Vice-Chancellors, six members appointed by the Senate, two representatives of the part-time teaching staff and two of the students, and a few coopted members.... Much depends on the substructure. In early days this was relatively simple. Now it is inordinately complex... [126].

In addition to the Council, there is a Senate of about 400 members, a General Purposes Committee, a Finance Committee, a Staff Board, an Estates and Buildings Committee, a Planning Board, an Academic Board and a Student Affairs Board, not to mention the various boards unique to each academic department. The activities of all personnel must be regularly coordinated through a formalized system of bureaucratic procedures as they work together to develop cross-discipline teaching tools for courses across the curriculum. This organization is a bureaucratic hierarchy.

The same can be said of Jones International University. Though completely virtual and highly adept at the use of Net logic to secure its external significance (official accreditation being the key designator of this), JIU is similar in structure to the Open University. It has a seven-member governing board, two nine-member academic advisory boards, the standard corporate offices, and a host of faculty members, administrative officers and content experts, all of whom must coordinate their work through regularized, bureaucratic procedures. In fact, a cursory glance at the requirements for accreditation reveals that only a bureaucratic hierarchical form is capable of becoming accredited. In short, the virtual university does not present a challenge to the organizational form of the traditional brick and mortar university. Rather, it challenges the traditional university to better conform to the engaging, interactive, collaborative and entertaining framework of the Internet.

As for the family, that institution was already network structured by the time the Internet came along. To whatever extent social form is relevant to success in the online world, the modern family form was ready-made to adopt the logic of the Internet as the interaction medium. Like the NGO and the successful ".com," the family was not required to overcome structural issues of the past in order to conform. This, in part, may help to explain the proliferation of both family-oriented magazine style web pages and personal family home pages. With "work" as the defining organizational principle of the family long gone, and "play" being the primary means by which the modern family is evaluated as properly "functional," it seems only natural that the Web, through the entertainment framework, would both instruct the family on how to be "functional" by playing together and provide case study examples on how this is to be accomplished. Not only is the process of interacting *within* these types of sites fun and engaging, but they provide instruction on how one's actual family may be properly fun and engaging as well.

In terms of social form within the normative order, there exists a striking lack of knowledge about which are the most successful at securing their external significance in an age of globalization. Those who study the institutions of education and family have had little, if anything, to say in the past about the implications of communications technologies for changing institutional forms. Those who study the marriage of religion and media made great strides in explaining the shift in popularity from church to sect due to television, but have largely ignored the ways in which the Internet may affect that particular "balance of power." And it appears that globalization theorists ignore the normative order altogether, focusing their attention on the battle between the state and the corporation. Because these institutions of the normative order are vital not only in the everyday lives of people around the world but as foundations for social order at the macro sociological level, it is important that we begin asking and attempting to answer the many important questions raised by this brief analysis. From the perspective of media logic, such questions are closely related to those outlined in previous chapters and include:

1. What are the implications of Internet use in everyday life for the normative order? Can we make connections between how people use the Internet to construct and interpret social order and meaning and the future significance of organized religion, education and the family?

2. What are the implications of Net logic for various normative processes such as the definition of a society's moral foundation, the practice of worship and the transmission of social norms through the process of socialization?

3. Will institutions of the normative order become even more prominent due to the many-to-many interaction pattern of the Net? If so, what does this mean for actors in the political and economic orders? For example, will the state, the NGO and/or the corporation find itself challenged by a "globalized" system of education or "mass culture," as many structuralists argue?

4. Is it possible for the oligarchic or dictatorial form to prove just as effective in the use of Net logic as the network? Is there something more than "wishful thinking" in the arguments of those who profess that such forms are doomed by the many-to-many interaction pattern of the Net?

5. What could detailed study of family-related websites tell us about the future form and institutional mission of the family? That is, will the intact nuclear family remain the ideal type, or will other structures be equally valid? What are the implications of the Internet for the rebirth of the extended family form? Will the institutional mission be altered? Will the family gain or lose in strength relative to other institutions?

6. Does the completely virtual university have any advantages in its ability to conform to Net logic relative to the traditional brick and mortar institution? Or vice versa? If so, what are those advantages? Is the education received from a virtual university significantly different in quality or type than that received at a physical university? If so, in what way? And what are the implications of the virtual education for the economic and political orders of the future?

7. Will organized religion gain or lose membership due to the Internet? What can an examination of online worship, via virtual or replicated physical churches, tell us about the relative strength of the church and the

sect? What are the implications of these possible changes in the arena of religion for actors in the political and economic orders?

NOTES

1. These figures are current as of mid–2000, and were derived from the section on Society and Culture (subsection Religion) within the *www.yahoo.com* web page.

2. The interested reader is referred to Robert P. Snow, *Creating Media Culture* (Beverly Hills: Sage Publications, 1983).

3. These sites also host password-protected family pages on which family members may post family trees, photo albums, and family news and events, as well as hold real time text (and voice) chats and asynchronous forums. While there are important implications of this practice for the family form of the future, for our purposes here we are concerned with the public family pages that serve as ideal types.

CHAPTER SIX

The Self in
the Virtual World

As we enter the postmodern era, all previous beliefs about the self are placed in jeopardy, and with them the patterns of action they sustain ... the very concept of personal essences is thrown into doubt [Gergen 1991, 7].

Arguments about the future of the self, like those embodied in the quote above, are most commonly made by observers who align themselves with the theoretical orientation commonly called "postmodernism." In order to understand their claims, it is necessary to have a basic understanding of what postmodern theory, and the postmodern society, look like. This is no elementary task, for it is perhaps the defining attribute of "postmodern theory" that its contributors and contributions constitute only the most loosely affiliated modes of thought. In short, it is easier to define what postmodern theory and society are not, rather than what they are.

Postmodernism refers simultaneously to four matters: the historical moment from the conclusion of World War II to the present; the multinational forms of capitalism; a movement in the visual arts which rebels against classic realism; and a form of theory that is post-positivist, interpretive and critical—one that rejects traditional scientific methods and the notion that theories and hypotheses may be tested or disproved according to rational, universal scientific principles. Born out of criticism of Enlightenment reason and scientific objectivity, postmodernism attacks universalism, elitism and formalism, is open to the experience of the "other" (previously oppressed minorities), and posits a postmodern society in which culture is organized around technologies of communication that blur the distinctions between the real world of objects and images of those objects (simulacra). Such a society is argued to be structured by symbolic or linguistic meanings, meanings which may be manipulated to create a reality that is a staged production to be judged against its media counterpart. In this production, the universal, abstract notion of "self" is replaced by a self that is individuated according to all manner of social categories (gender, ethnicity, consumer class and so forth). Objective existence is no longer. The self (and, in fact, all social reality) exists only to the extent that—and in the manner that—we think, write and talk about it. In fact, it is arguable that this purported loss of a "core" or "essential" self is the defining social problem in postmodern society:

> All postmodern theories emphasize the fragmenting character of culture and the blurring of differences marked by symbols. Individuals are seen as caught in these transformations, participating in, and defining self from, an increasing array of social categories, such as race, class, gender, ethnicity, or status, while being exposed to ever increasing varieties of cultural images as potential markers of self. At the same time, individuals lose their sense of being located in stable places and time frames [Turner 1998, 608].

Postmodern theorists have as their primary concern the sociology of culture; and because technology is a central "agent of change" in human culture, many focus their efforts on understanding the role that technologies play in this shift from modern to postmodern society. With regard to communications technology and the self, the postmodern statement is perhaps best embodied in the work of Gergen (1991). In *The Saturated Self*, Gergen argues that media, particularly radio, film and television (his book is pre–Internet) lead to a state of "social saturation," in which the individual is exposed to an ever-expanding range of relationships with other people. "Through the technologies of this century, the number and variety of relationships in which we are engaged, potential frequency of contact, expressed intensity of relationship, and endurance through time all are steadily increasing. As this increase becomes extreme, we reach a state of social saturation" (61).

Social institutions, beliefs and practices reflect the postmodern condition of social saturation. Small, face-to-face communities, in which one's ability to affect change was constrained in space and time, give way to pluralities of relationships mediated via high technology which are characterized by competition for the right to define realities and the nature of the self within those multiple realities. In the postmodern world all things are subject to negotiation. In Gergen's terms, the result is "self-multiplication," or the

> ...capacity to be significantly present in more than one place at a time. In the face-to-face community one's capacities to carry on a relationship or

to have social impact were restricted in space and time. Typically one's identity was manifest to those immediately before one's eyes, though books and newspapers made "multiples" of powerful individuals. With the development of radio and film, one's opinions, emotions, facial expressions, mannerisms, styles of relating, and the like were no longer confined to the immediate audience, but were multiplied manifold.... Media—especially radio, television, and the movies—are vitally expanding the range and variety of relationships available to the population [55].

These relationships are said to furnish the individual with an infinite array of vocabularies of the self, such that the individual is increasingly "conjoined" to his or her surroundings via media and comes to "reflect" those surroundings. He or she is accordingly "infused" with partial identities to the extent that "there is the onset of a multi phrenic condition, in which one begins to experience the vertigo of unlimited multiplicity" (49). Gone is the Romantic self (a perspective that attributes to each person the "depth of meaning" found in terms such as passion and creativity) and the Enlightenment, or Modern, self as "one who reasons." In their place we have no self at all:

...Both the romantic and modern beliefs about the self are falling into disuse, and the social arrangements that they support are eroding. This is largely a result of the forces of social saturation. Emerging technologies saturate us with the voices of humankind—both harmonious and alien. As we absorb their varied rhymes and reasons, they become part of us and we of them. Social saturation furnishes us with a multiplicity of incoherent and unrelated languages for the self. For everything we "know to be true" about ourselves, other voices within respond with doubt and even derision. This fragmentation of self-conceptions corresponds to a multiplicity of incoherent and disconnected relationships. These relationships pull us in myriad directions, inviting us to play such a variety of roles that the very concept of an "authentic self" with knowable characteristics recedes from view. The fully saturated self becomes no self at all [6–7].

Can this argument be true? Can we legitimately assert that at the dawn of a new millennium the self is no longer relevant, either to the individual said to possess it or to the broader social order? Has the Internet, with its capacity for the creation of an infinite number of many-to-many social interactions, put the final nail in the coffin of the self? In order to answer these questions we must first work to better understand the history of the self. Only by ascertaining the evolutionary path of what appears to be a most fundamental cornerstone of social life may we predict with any accuracy its future nature and relevance. Accordingly, the remainder of this chapter takes this postmodern stance as its starting point. It presents a brief history of the self in philosophy, political theory and social science. It then evaluates the self in light of media logic, specifically the logic of the Internet. Finally, it reassesses the postmodern argument against the self in light of these factors, in much the same way as previous chapters reassessed claims made about other defining social institutions.

A Brief History of the Self

All theory argues against the existence of the self, while in practice we assume that it exists [Lyons 1978, 123].

Postmodern theorists are not the first to have called into question the nature, meaning and very existence of the self. Since the time of what Van Doren (1991, 29) termed the "Greek Explosion" (beginning in the sixth century B.C.), philosophers, political theorists and social scientists have debated its merits as both concept and entity. Prior to that time, evidence of a self as we currently conceive it is scant. Anderson (1997) notes that, using the works of Homer as primary data on how people of his era understood the world around them,

Some scholars have pointed out that there really isn't a word in the works of Homer that translates neatly into "mind." Thoughts and feelings seem to have happened in and around people, sometimes in locations that can be identified with body parts—such as the lungs and heart—and sometimes they really can't be located anywhere at all.

In the 1970s psychologist Julian Jaynes offered the startling thesis that people of the Homeric era did not possess a personal consciousness that we would recognize as such. He argued that the style of thinking we call consciousness does not blossom spontaneously out of the human brain, but rather is a learned process, the result of a social invention that began to take form only about 3,000 years ago [5–6].

But beginning in earnest in Classical Athens with Socratic philosophy, the idea of the self slowly begins to take hold. For Socrates, the "self" was the soul, but not the same sort of soul embraced by peoples that predated him. That is, the soul in Greek mythology was understood as that which transmigrated from person to person (or from person to animal) but was incapable of remembering what (or where) he or she had been before. Not so with the Socratic soul. Socrates conceived of the self as an "immortal soul," one which is the personal moral agent of the single individual, experiences itself as a conflict between the "baser desires of the body and the higher aspirations of reasoning intelligence," and retains its identity after death. It is, in rough terms, an individual self (Anderson 1997, 9).

Aristotle continued with this new concept of the soul/self by adding to it the idea of the self as a reasoning, "self-aware" entity with an appreciation for its own boundedness and consistency. He added the idea of what Mead would later explain as "mind." The Romans, on the heels of Classical Athens, continued to modify the idea of the self. To Aristotle's reasoning entity they added the concept of "person" as an important element in the legal system:

> In Roman law the word "persona" took on an important meaning, central to the Roman view of self and society: It signified the individual whose family, status, and privileges were officially recognized. The system of family names was firmly laid down by the Senate.... These names established the person as an individual, a self, a free citizen. Personhood seems to have been conceived as an almost-tangible thing, something some people had and some people didn't have. Slaves were denied persona... [Anderson 1997, 12].

With the fall of the Roman Empire and the start of the Middle Ages, "modernist" theorizing on the nature of the self apparently came to a halt. Gone was the individual self/soul, capable of reason (mind) and recognized (to a varying extent) as a legal entity. In its place was an individual largely devoid of personal identity beyond that which was ascribed to him or her by a feudal (caste) system devoid of upward mobility and a religious worldview in which the soul was no longer the "property" of the individual but was instead "a gift from out of a bag of eternity":

> In this tradition the body was the husk and prison of the divine soul, and although they were mutually dependent they were also in conflict, for the crass body weighted the eternal soul with cares and appetites, with flesh and blood from which character was formed, and the soul's reward depended on how well it survived its earthly trial. That trial was essential to the salvation of the soul.... The soul was no more help in lending man a sense of his separate and private being, for being eternal and, as it were, lent by God it was the instrument of his connection to all things. It was often even a particle of a universal soul which, temporarily imprisoned in the body, longed for its true home [Lyons 1978, 19].

With the advent of the Renaissance, the individual self again rises to a position of prominence. Life on earth, and individual experience of that life, become at least as important as the afterlife. The person is again important not merely as an example of the larger struggle between "good and evil," but as an independent, reasoning self. Characterized by the fall of Constantinople, the invention of the printing press, the Reformation and the rise of the nation-state, the Renaissance marks the transition between what we now think of as the medieval and modern worlds. Despite the efforts of philosophers during the "Greek Explosion," it is in the Renaissance that most students of philosophy and political theory locate the birth of the modern self.

Two theorists, Hobbes and Descartes, made particularly important contributions to the Renaissance idea of the self. Descartes is often given credit for the invention of the truly modern self because he locates the individual at the center of the knowable world. The self, seated inside the material brain, is decidedly separate from both the non-material soul (mind) and the preexisting, outside world. For his part, Hobbes declared the very idea of the soul to be a "superstition." Arguing that body and soul are one and the same, he claimed that *the human* is the body *and only* the body. The self simply does not exist. Interestingly, some have suggested that in Hobbes we may find the roots of the postmodern view of the self, leading one ultimately to question the degree to which there is a distinctly postmodern self. We will return to this question later in the chapter.

Despite these contradicting claims about the nature of the self, it remained true that the Renaissance was about the rebirth of individualism. As Lyons has noted,

> At the beginning of the Renaissance, man was everywhere a subject; at the end he was [at least in theory] a citizen.... A correlative of this change was that his own inner life was given a dignity, even an existence, that it had not had previously. At the beginning of the Renaissance, man's place in the world, as described for him by his princes and mediators with God, was perfectly clear. At the end of this period he was often himself responsible for his salvation as well as the material improvement of the world in which he lived [70].

As any number of observers have correctly pointed out, it was the printing press that ultimately made this transition to responsible self possible. Combined with an increased literacy rate, "mass production" of the Bible and other documents made possible the phenomenon of silent, private reading. No longer reliant on interpretations of the keepers of knowledge made available in public readings, it was possible for the individual, while reading alone, to entertain truly private, unique thoughts and opinions. In so doing, the individual undermined the legitimacy of centralized knowledge, or, at a minimum, transferred the legitimacy of "the center" from the Church to the individual.

While the Renaissance served to reestablish the preeminence of the individual self in philosophy and socio-political theory, the two periods of thought that would follow, the Enlightenment and the Romantic Reaction set the stage for debates about the self that continue today. With the self firmly ensconced as the cornerstone of Western thought, debate came to center on the precise "essence" of what that self was about. Enlightenment philosophers, including Locke, Hume and Kant, argued varying conceptions of the self. For Locke, the self

> ...is characterized by activity, by its ability to reappropriate its experiences. Nothing sticks, but everything can be recalled. Through recollection the self continually makes itself anew—not out of nothing but out of itself.... the sense of self is an achievement, an act of appropriation that is never final but must be constantly renewed, reappropriated: not product but process. Otherwise expressed, if the self is not memory but conscious appropriation of memory, then the self is involved in constant labor, constantly reappropriating its memories, reorganizing them, rearranging them to fit new understandings of the self based on new experience [Alford 1991, 135–136].

In order to accomplish this "reappropriation," Locke's self ultimately relies on its experiences with others in the outside world. Through interpretations of what it believes to be others' impressions of it, the self shapes its own definition of itself. While the precise manner in which this reappropriation occurs would be left for G. H. Mead to unravel (an explanation to which we will return momentarily), Locke's self is an important step on the road to what we understand as the modern (and perhaps even the postmodern, if there is any meaningful distinction to be made) self.

Where Locke saw the self as a consistent identity held together by consciousness, by a unity of "narrative history," Hume argued that because the self (which he defined as the mind and its contents) is constantly changing through experience, there really is no such thing as a "permanent identity." Instead, the self is a "bundle of perceptions," rendered meaningful through the use of "categories such as resemblance, succession and causation." In his own way, then, Hume (like Hobbes before him) anticipated the "postmodern" view of the self as ultimately non-existent. Finally, Kant turned the entire Enlightenment discussion of the self on its head, arguing that previous assumptions about "mind" or "consciousness" being derived from—and knower of—the objective external world were incorrect. Instead, "consciousness" (the self) is to a large extent the creator of that outside world, and that in the process of ordering that outside world, of giving it meaning, it in turn orders and gives meaning to the self. It is the self, as a rational transcendental subject, as creator of the world, that explains what we experience as a narrative unity of life.

In response to the Enlightenment conception of self, which, despite the differences among theorists of the period, was oriented around the self as a rational, reasoning, logical knower (interpreter) of the external world, the Romantic self brings its own conception of "soul" back to the self. Philosophers of the Romantic period, perhaps epitomized in the works of Rousseau, rejected the domination of reason and progress through science and posited a self manifest in feelings, in emotion. Taking Kant's notion of the individual as creator of the "external" world, the Romantics argued that it was in the "inner world of the self" that truth may ultimately be found. Each person, under Romantic thought, is accorded a profound sense of uniqueness and worth:

> The real world contains much more than science can disclose. It is the totality of experience, its joys and sorrows, growth and change, paradoxes and fulfillments.... To understand the world we must go to experience as it is lived, not merely to the empiricist's sense perceptions or to the rationalist's clear and distinct ideas. We must explore the dark, hidden areas of the mind and the realms of feeling and imagination; we must discover the inner workings of the human spirit... [Lavine 1984, 203].

In short, for the Romantic philosopher, the self is much more than a "bundle of perceptions" or a self-constructed narrative unity. These facades exist in the modern world, but beneath them there exists a "real self," a unique individual that rebels against the reasoning, socially mandated self. This true self was inherently good, a "deep interior" inhabited by the soul and expressed outwardly as emotion, as passion. And as Lyons (1978) noted, though this conception of self was unique to the Romantic period, it "was treated as though it had always been sleeping in the breasts of men. It was innate, and only had to be revealed through the passions and cultivated by a spontaneous relation to nature" (198).

In summary, over the course of more than 2500 years of human history so briefly analyzed in the preceding pages, the self became the cornerstone of Western thought. Regardless of specific attributes, there could be no doubt that the self was central to the scientific, political, legal and social institutions that are the foundation of modern social order. Endowed with reason, passion and rights, the self was validated as the locus of value, meaning, responsibility—as the locus of social order. Real in some objective sense or not, the self had become real because it was real in its consequences. It was "real enough." Accordingly, rather than debating the existence of the self as philosophers had done, the sociologists who came after them took as their starting point that the self exists, if for no other reason than because people behave *as if* it does. Their task, then, was to explain how the self comes about, its relation to the broader social order, and, conversely, how any change in the process of "self development" may in turn affect that social order.

From its very beginnings, the discipline of Sociology, in both theory and method, has had a vested interest in the self. For Durkheim, the concern with the self was theoretical—he sought to explain the rise of the self, what he termed the "cult of individualism," as an inevitable result of the shift from gemeinschaft to gesellschaft brought on by the division of labor. According to Durkheim, the varied conceptions of "the self" throughout history can be explained by analyzing the basic structures of the society (the "collective conscience") in which those conceptions arose. In a small tribal group (gemeinschaft), social structure is symbolized by concrete and particularistic representations—local gods and spirits. As societies became larger and the division of labor more complex (gesellschaft), symbols of society become more abstract—local gods became one supreme, abstract God:

> ...the conscience collective "comes increasingly to be made up of highly generalised and indeterminate modes of thought and sentiment, which leave room open for an increasing multitude of individual differences" ... mechanical solidarity is increasingly supplanted by a new type of social cohesion [organic solidarity].... The growth of the "cult of the individual" is only possible because of the secularisation of most sectors of social life. It contrasts with the traditional forms of conscience collective in that, while it consists of common beliefs and sentiments, these focus upon the worth and dignity of the individual rather than the collectivity.
>   The sentiment of the supreme worth of the human individual is thus a product of society.... The trend towards increasing individualism is irreversible, since it is the outcome of the profound societal changes brought about by the division of labor [Giddens 1971, 79–80, 116].

In short, in modern industrial societies the only thing everyone has in common is the self. Thus, the self becomes the object of worship (Collins 1988).

For Weber (1946), the issue of the self was one of research methodology. Though he conceived the self as a "composite" of social roles played out across an array of social institutions, he argued that the self could not be understood as merely a social product. Instead, he argued for sociological inquiry founded on "interpretive understanding," in which the ultimate "unit of analysis" is the individual:

> Interpretive sociology considers the individual and his action as the basic unit.... In this approach, the individual is also the upper limit and the sole carrier of meaningful conduct.... In general, for sociology, such concepts as "state," "association," "feudalism," and the like, designate certain categories of human interaction. Hence it is the task of sociology to reduce these concepts to "understandable" action, that is, without exception, to the actions of participating individual men [55].

The individual self, as the interpreter of his or her social world, is for Weber the locus of understanding. If one expects to comprehend social behavior across time and space, one must accept that the individual—as knower and actor—and only the individual, can lead to that understanding.

While Durkheim and Weber, commonly understood as "macro" sociologists, were intrinsically interested in the relation between the individual self and the social order, it was their contemporaries, Cooley and Mead, who explicated how the self comes to exist, how it becomes "real enough," and what that process implies about the social order. In 1902 Cooley defined the self as a social process, and since that time social theorists have tended to agree with that assessment. In keeping with William James' assertions about the self, and in opposition to the Cartesian dualism between the knowing, thinking subject and the external world, Cooley stated that the self, the mind, is social—it can only arise within society and is ultimately inseparable from social consciousness. This is the case because the self is a product of language, and, in turn, that language is a social product. Without the social product of language, there would be no society and certainly no self. Because the self is a social process, the consciousness derived and maintained through continuous social interaction, two important conclusions follow. First, the self is both subject and object, not one or the other. That is, the "I" is self-as-knower (subject), and the "me" is self-as-known (object). Second, each individual has the potential for a plurality of selves, each of which is derived from a particular social group within which that individual interacts.

This conception of self, which Cooley termed the "looking glass self," set the stage for a more thorough analysis by G. H. Mead. According to Mead (1934), the self is the ability to take oneself as an object. The self is not an "entity," but a mental process that arises and develops through social activity, primarily language. The self develops through reflexivity, or the ability to put oneself into others' places and to act as they act. In this way people are able to examine themselves as others would examine them. In order to have a "self," then, the individual must "get outside himself," evaluate himself, and so become an object to himself. This self, this social process, consists of two phases (not "things"), the "I" and the "me." The "I" is the immediate response of an individual to others. It is the unpredictable and creative aspect of the self, and, as such, is the key source of novelty in the social process, and the phase in which we locate our most important values. The "I" is that which we define as our "personality" or "real self." In contrast, the "me" is the organized set of attitudes of others. It is the adoption of the "generalized other," Mead's term for the attitude of the community. It is the "me" which allows the individual to live comfortably within the social world. As Stone (1975) would later point out, the extent to which a person can be understood to have multiple selves depends upon recognizing that participation in multiple social groups (generalized others), leads to multiple "me" phases, or "identities," where identity

> ...is not a substitute word for "self." Instead, when one has identity, he is situated—that is, cast in the shape of a social object by the acknowledgment of his participation or membership in social relations. One's identity is established when others place him as a social object by assigning him the same words of identity that he appropriates for himself or announces. It is in the coincidence of placements and announcements that identity becomes a meaning of the self... [82].

For Mead, it is the existence of the self that differentiates human beings from other animals. By this he means that only the human animal has the capacity to use significant symbols (language), to think, to reflect on their actions, to guide actions consciously and to live within the framework of social organization. The self *is* this capacity, and it is this capacity, and not some supernatural "entity" like the soul, which makes a human a human. A person is an organism with a self, that can perceive itself, has opinions about itself, regulates its actions by reflection, or dialogue with self. The person is an organism capable of internalizing the social act.

The preceding elaboration of the meaning of the self over time was designed to lay the foundation for two key points about self in contemporary society. The first is that the self must be understood on two different but intricately related levels: as a physical process, physical because it occurs through role-taking made possible through acquisition of the symbol system of language; and as a social process, or institution (individualism), in its own right, with its own institutional history. The second is that in order to explain the self as a social process, one must first understand the logic of the symbol system used in the act of that construction.

Consider first the point that the self is both a physical and a social process. Mead's argument serves as the foundation for this claim. The self is a physical process because it is the product of evolution. Anatomically, an animal must possess certain brain and vocal cord features in order for language to even become possible. Without such anatomical features, the animal is limited to what Mead termed "signs" (non-significant gestures). In contrast, the animal that possesses such anatomical features is capable of "significant" symbols, or language, which arouses in the one making the gesture the same kind of response as it does from those to whom the gesture is addressed. So equipped, the human animal is capable, through the use of language, of taking the role of the other, of developing an understanding of the "generalized other," of developing a self:

> The characteristic human response to situations is the inhibition of an immediate response until an act can be constructed that seems to "fit" the situation.... In the development of the species, such inhibition of the individual's act naturally occurred in social situations, since human beings were social animals before they were symbolic. In the course of becoming human, our ancestors were doubtless faced with many circumstances in which individuals had to check their own acts in order to consider the possible results of those acts—not only in terms of environmental response, but also in terms of the reactions of their fellows. Indeed, to function effectively in a group setting ... the individual would have to imagine not merely the response of the environment and of his fellows, but also his own actions in response to alternative possible events.
>
> However it happened, the individual who first used the group's symbolic designation of himself managed to bring within himself the whole group of which he was a part. By naming the others and himself, the individual could represent others, their behavior, his own responses, and their responses to him. Without a symbol for himself, the individual can represent others and their acts; with a symbol, a name, he can represent himself as implicated in their acts, and depict the activities of the group as a whole in his imagination [Hewitt 1984, 70–71].

Understood from this perspective, the self has existed since the dawn of spoken language, regardless of what the philosophers of the day have had to say about it and regardless of its degree of significance in everyday life and the social order. Mead's theory also indicates, and is generally undisputed on this point, that the self is a social process simply because its vehicle, language, is a social product. By definition, the use of language to develop the self and the generalized other implicates the social nature of the process. This being the case, how can we possibly entertain assertions, from the time of Socrates to the postmodern theorists of the new millennium, that the self does not exist? Understanding the self from Mead's perspective, we cannot. Given the fact that language exists and that the use of language is what makes a human a human, it is categorically impossible for the self not to exist. But the self as a social process has a second layer of meaning. It is within this layer that we must locate the philosophical arguments about the "essence" of the self, arguments found in the writings of Renaissance philosophers, Enlightenment theorists, Romantics and, now, postmodernists.

As Meyer (1987) pointed out, the self as we understand it today is a distinctly Western "project." As the cornerstone of modern Western society, the self is

...a creature of public theory, not only private experience; its rules are stored in and regulated by such public theory. There is public political theory, as in the principles of elections, citizenship, and welfare. There is public economic theory, as in the rules of the free markets in labor, land, commodities, and capital. And there are varieties of official religious and cultural theory, enforcing and celebrating appropriate aspects of the doctrine of the self [243].

A distinctive feature of Western collectivities is how they ground themselves in individuals, incorporating and controlling these as the fundamental unit of social organization, rather than families, villages, or castes. But the individual is not incorporated simply as a passive or movable unit—the individual throughout Western history retains a sacred status, and is incorporated as a life [246].

There are certain distinctive commonalities in Western images of the self throughout the modern period. At the core, all the selves are equal, having the same ultimate rights and responsibilities, and all are primordially alike: They exist in the same ultimate moral and physical universes. In practice, they are differentiated and differentially located in social action ... but at bottom, universalistic rules prevail. The rights, powers, and value of the self are central institutions in the modern world [248].

The self has become something far more than the basic ability to take oneself as object. From that elementary capacity, the self has been elevated to its current position in Western society as the locus of all meaning and social order. No sense can be made of any situation, no norms of behavior encoded and enforced, without at least implicit reference to the self as the source of that order. It is in this sense that philosophers since the time of Socrates have debated the meaning, and even the existence, of the self. In Classical Athens the idea of the self began to take hold, but it was commingled with the idea of the soul. In Medieval times this sense of the self seems to have disappeared. While people quite clearly used language and thus had selves in Mead's most basic sense, the self as an institution within an integrated frame of "individualism" did not exist. This is the self that came to stay during the Renaissance. And it is the only meaning of the self that could logically be debated through the Enlightenment, the Romantic Reaction and the "postmodern" era, for Mead's fundamental "self through language" remains indisputable.

While Hume argued that we never encounter the self in experience, Kant that the self is a "transcendental illusion" and Sartre that a key component of the self is "nothingness," the same argument could be made for all social institutions. We never actually encounter the nation-state, the corporation, the church, the university, and on and on. We never encounter conceptualizations or forms, only other people. But that does not make those conceptualizations or forms any less institutionalized or relevant or meaningful. It does not mean that they are not "real in their consequences." Likewise with the self. In modern society the self is far more than the result of biological evolution that made language possible. The self as we now understand it is an institution. It is the linchpin of social order.

Now consider the second point, that in order to explain the self on any level, one must first understand the logic of the symbol system used in the act of that construction. A moment's reflection will reveal why this is the case. As linguists have long noted, language is not simply speech or the written word. It is an institutionalized thought process, a way of ordering the social world. This thought process varies by culture and revolves around a set of rules commonly called grammar. In Western language, especially English, grammatical rules revolve around a subject-verb-object structure that orders the world in terms of cause and effect, of a subject acting on an object to create a specific result. This grammar is particularly relevant here because of what it means for the self. The self is an institution, the meaning, or "essence," of which is debatable and malleable *because* it can be understood, through this logic, as both subject and object. As Bierstedt (1970) notes,

> Everyone who is alive, in any society, has a consciousness of self. The self is what he means, in the English language for example, by the word "I" when he is not thinking of himself. The stipulation of not thinking is important because as soon as one thinks of himself, or of his use of the "I," or even of "I" in quotation marks, the self becomes object rather than subject and the essence of the "I" disappears. The nature of the self, as seen by the self, subjectively and from the inside, is one of the great mysteries to which neither science nor philosophy has anything but partial and inadequate answers. As soon as we say "the nature of the self," as in the preceding sentence, we have already made an object of it, and the self as subject has vanished into a limbo where there is no language and where words are useless. The self as subject is a self that transcends the possibility of explanation [184].

In short, it is precisely because Western language (especially English) operates according to the subject-verb-object logic that the self is simultaneously subject and object. Were it not for the grammar of the language, we would likely have an entirely different understanding of the self, and it is entirely possible that we would have no self at all as understood from the framework of modern "individualism."

More important for our purposes here is that, just as languages operate according to specific logics, or grammars, so do media. As Meyer (1987) went on to note, in modern society, "...people work out selves with a great deal of institutional support. The legal, economic, political, and religious rules prescribing and legitimating personhood have standing. As actors form their own subjective personhood, they are perhaps as much affected by the institutionalized recipes as by any untutored 'experiences'" (242). If one accepts the fundamental premise of media logic that mass media serve as the vehicle by which reality is constructed and interpreted in contemporary society, then one must add media to Meyer's list of social sources for rules about the self. This is true for two reasons. First, from an interactionist perspective that emphasizes the importance of everyday life to the structure of society, it is clear that people (for better or worse) adopt the logics of various media in order to make sense of their immediate circumstances. Second, the institutions embodied in the political, economic and normative orders discussed in previous chapters also adopt media logic to convey what those rules are or ought to be. In a highly modern world society, one seemingly as far removed from Durkheim's gemeinschaft as possible, people use media to sustain the collective conscience.

How is this accomplished? Remember that, regardless of its institutional properties, the self is the ability of an organism to see itself as an object in the environment. Accordingly, that environment (society) will remain integrated in so far as individuals can continue to use common conventional gestures, role-take accurately, rehearse alternatives and see themselves as stable objects of evaluation in situations. However, as society increases in size and level of differentiation, the maintenance of common gestures, the accuracy of role-taking with diverse others, the rehearsal of alternatives in different and often unfamiliar situations, and the ability to see oneself as a consistent object in changing contexts all become problematic. As Hewitt (1984) noted,

> It is possible that in modern, highly differentiated societies, cumulative identity may be difficult to create and sustain. Identity requires a balance between the forces of differentiation and identification. That is, a person's identity rests upon his or her capacity to establish differentiation from others—mainly on the basis of clusters of roles and group membership. But identity also requires identification with a larger social unit—that is, it depends not just on the person's capacity to differentiate himself or herself from others, but also to identify with them, to see all as engaged in a common enterprise or sharing a common destiny of some kind.
>
> Modern life may make this balance difficult to attain, for it is generally better able to provide people with grounds for differentiating themselves from others than for identifying with the society. A complex society offers people many roles on the basis of which they can differentiate themselves, but it makes identification difficult....
>
> This line of reasoning suggests that the self may be an object of special attention, even preoccupation, in complex modern societies. People have

choices of reference others and behavioral standards, and thus come to feel that they can choose who they will be and what rules they will follow. The result is that self-conceptions become problematic rather than taken for granted. The self becomes an object to be constructed rather than one which emerges naturally and smoothly in the course of interaction [131–132].

According to Mead, this potential problem is resolved because large-scale social systems composed of many individuals playing diverse roles will develop numerous subgroups, each of which will reveal its own, somewhat distinctive, "generalized other." In other words, any complex society will evidence multiple generalized others. To the extent that these generalized others are based on an underlying common set of values and beliefs, participation in a variety of them does not lead to social disintegration. In fact, the existence of multiple generalized others that rest on a common moral foundation serves largely to expand the legitimacy of the foundation, thereby enhancing social order and a consistent conceptualization of the self. This is where media come in.

NET(WORK) LOGIC AND THE SELF

Before delving into the specific implications of Net logic for the self, it is instructive to examine the two-pronged relation between the general theory of media logic and the self. First, the modern self is the foundation of media logic. At its very core, media logic assumes an individualized self. Media logic is essentially symbolic interactionist theory writ large, in that mediated communication is argued to be the framework through which reality is socially constructed. In contemporary society much of Mead's self-as-process, its "I" and its "me," are constructed, along with the generalized other(s), through media. As the locus of meaning, it is the self that adopts (or not) the logic of media to understand the surrounding world. It is the self that does the interpreting. And it is the fact of the self that makes all meaning problematic. Selves, in concert, define that which constitutes "entertainment," because there can be no meaningful discussion of "emotions," "larger than life" experience, "non-routine" experience or "vicarious interaction" without situating the self at the center of that discussion. Further, selves are at the center of that which constitutes "ideal-norms." The self as simultaneous subject-object is both the definer of those norms and the entity responsible for (not) conforming to them. The grammar of media logic assumes the self as subject-object, and the perspectives employed assume the self as the locus of the moral order.

Second, the modern individual self is transformed, like all other institutions, via existence in a media culture. Media logic is first and foremost an examination of how institutions are transformed through media. The modern self is implicated in this process because, if media are the primary means by which we "have" and interpret experience, if they are the means by which we make sense of the world around us, it is because they enable us to define the generalized other. They are the ritualized means by which we sustain the collective conscience. By definition, they aid us in the definition and interpretation of the self in relation to that generalized other. Because their logics are audience (self)-oriented and low-ambiguity in terms of perspective, they provide an overarching framework through which the self may be understood. To the extent that the self is presented with multiple and conflicting "vocabularies of self," as postmodernists argue, it is because a defining attribute of the highly modern self, and one that is to be celebrated, is multiplicity. In other words, the modern system of ideal norms through which the self is understood via media posits the self as confronted with conflicting demands that threaten to "pull apart" the unified, true self. As Meyer (1987) noted,

> Much modern research documents the instability found in measures of the self, but this is because researchers define the individual self as that which is not institutionalized or structurally stabilized...
>
> Overall, the modern liberated subjective self should score well on all the modern virtues, but with a good deal of instability over time.
> Although these qualities of the modern actor have been criticized as irrational, narcissistic, and indicative of anxiety, the critics have been insufficiently aware how they directly reflect the proprieties of a highly institutionalized set of rules about the self.
>
> ...the modern subjective self is socially legitimated, but not organized in its content. The modern system, in fact, strips definite and fixed content from the self, leaving it free to find motives, needs, expectations, and perceptions appropriate to the situation. And indeed, engaging in this activity is the central social obligation of the subjective self—to find meaning and satisfaction in the life course situation in which it is located [252–254].

In contemporary society this task is accomplished to a large extent via media. Though a detailed examination of the implications of all media for the self would be interesting, the task of this chapter is to examine only those implications brought through the logic of the Internet. To be successful, inquiry into Net logic must approach the self both directly and indirectly. That is, certain implications about the self may be gleaned through direct inquiry into how it is presented online. This was the strategy employed to assess the status of other social institutions in previous chapters. But because much of the work of constructing social reality makes implicit assumptions about the self, one must also look into the construction of other social institutions. In short, reassessing the status of the nation-state, the corporation, the church, the university and the family from a slightly different angle reveals a surprising amount of information about the importance of the self in contemporary society. It is to such methods of examination that we now turn.

Addressing first the direct evidence of the self online, it becomes evident rather quickly that individuals have figured out how to utilize the logic of the Internet to resurrect (if it ever died in the first place) the Romantic self. Through the application of a specific grammar (syntax, inflection and vocabulary) and perspective, individuals deny the postmodernist's assertion that the "true self," accessible through introspection and Rousseau's "inward path to truth," is dead. In this regard, the Internet is closely related to many non-technological media in its ability to provide each individual the opportunity to present a unique self.

As Altheide and Snow (1979) noted, a medium is any "social or technological procedure or device that is used for the selection, transmission, and reception of information. Every civilization has developed various types of media, transmitted through such social elements as territory, dwelling units, dress and fashion, language, clocks and calendars, dance, and other rituals" (11). These types of media, unlike "mass" technological media (radio, film and television), afford each individual the chance to present a self, and have often been used to convey the "real self." Individuals select (or design) homes, cars and other material goods in order to convey or reflect their true selves. They make "fashion statements," develop subcultural language and "slang," and create dance steps, all in an effort to express feelings of "who they really are." Online, they design personal web pages to that same end, taking advantage of the Net's logic to move beyond the "star"—or "personality"—centered self mandated by mass media. Online, unlimited numbers of ordinary selves become central.

Because the number of personal home pages is, for all practical purposes, infinite, comprehensive examination is impossible. However, exploration of approximately 100 of these pages revealed striking similarities in both ends (the desire to present the "real self") and means (grammar and perspective). All utilized a similar framework of syntax (the organization and scheduling of content), inflection devices (to set the rhythm and tempo of content presentation), vocabulary and perspective to convey information about the social categories and attributes deemed most fundamental to the self, particularly personal values and belief systems.

Turning first to syntax, it perhaps goes without saying that personal pages are centralized. They serve as the locus of all information one requires to understand the "essence" of the self in question. From that central location one can learn more about that particular self by following links to that self in context (family pages, the pages of friends and the pages of additional activities or areas of interest to that self). Further, the majority of personal pages are very current in their content. For most, this means they are updated weekly, but for some it means daily updates. It is not uncommon to come across pages that assume a "journal" format in that they are updated daily with thoughts and the details of day-to-day living. In essence, these pages are public diaries.

But there is a more important aspect of syntax on these pages. They are structured so as to present the self in those contexts deemed most revealing of the true or inner essence. Accordingly, almost all sites examined present the self first as an integrated, consistent unit, through the frame of a "brief bio," and then in relation to four categories: family (including pets), friends, hobbies and "links to cool stuff." These are the categories that people almost universally define as indicative of "who they really are," while categories such as "work" rarely make the cut. How do these individuals capture and present the essence of their selves within this organizational framework? A brief examination of the standard inflection devices used reveals the answer.

Far and away the most prominent inflection device on personal home pages is photography. Supplemented with narrative or descriptive anecdotes, photographs are used to capture and display the essence of the self. In fact, it seems that one cannot have a self (or at least one has minimal chance of conveying its essence to others) without providing such visual information. The physical body is intimately connected with the essence of self. Further, as one would expect, given the understanding of self as social process, the selves portrayed are not removed from the social world, but are ensconced within it. No "stuffy" or "official" portraiture is to be found on these pages. Instead, the documentary style is employed. Photographs are used to position, or frame, the self within those contexts deemed most meaningful, most intimately related to and representative of the "true self." As noted above, the context of the photograph almost universally entails family members, pets and friends engaged in both everyday life activities and special events, such as vacations and birthday parties.

Individuals also make extensive use of the biography and the diary as inflection devices. Clicking on an individual's "about me" section reveals an autobiography in brief, in which he or she has summarized and rendered meaningful (in many cases inevitable) an integrated, unified self. This self, though it has undergone trials and tribulations through the years, has emerged from its life-to-date in what could only be called a highly modernized form. It is defined and described by the person to whom it belongs as individual, as unique and as a continuous essence. Many pages combine the brief bio format with the journal format, thus providing a regularly updated peek into this process of self definition. In reading through the details of someone's daily life, in reading through their thoughts, one is ultimately getting a behind-the-scenes look into how another human being goes about constructing his or her true self. One watches as that individual makes sense of and integrates present with past and potential futures, all in an effort to sustain a continuous identity.

A brief word is also in order regarding several other inflection devices found almost universally on personal home pages. The first is music. Most pages automatically run musical selections while the visitor peruses the information contained therein. These selections are designed to "say something" about the individual who has designed the page; they convey tastes, attitudes, values and, perhaps inadvertently, social class, age and ethnicity related information. The same can be said for the "links to cool stuff" category universally found on personal pages. Unable to capture everything they are "really about" on a single web page, individuals provide additional information about their true selves by linking their pages to others. These pages can include music sites, game-related sites, political and religious sites, hobby-oriented sites and sites representing the physical locations in which those selves live. Finally, individuals select and combine wallpaper, font styles and colors, graphics and "click-able" icons toward the same end. Like NGOs, nation-states, corporations, religious and educational organizations, and families, selves select all such inflection devices in order to accent, to call attention to, who they are.

Vocabulary (the final element of grammar) combines with the ideal-norms perspective on personal home pages to round out the presentation of the Romantic self. The vocabulary is informal and self-oriented, and is designed so that the visitor can get to know the real person. It is welcoming and conversational in nature, inviting the visitor to respond, to open a dialogue, either by signing the guest book (every personal page has one) or by sending private email. It is self-oriented in the sense that it is as much about discovering the real self as it is presenting that self to others. Any number of personal pages state as an objective: "to explore who I really am," "to capture the essence of me," or "to let people see the real me." It is in the act of presenting this self to others that one discovers it. This act of discovery and definition, however, takes place firmly within the confines of the ideal-norms perspective. Recall from earlier chapters that the ideal-norms perspective for solving problems entails "sticking with tradition." Ideal norms refer to "those rules and strategies we all uphold as the best possible way to proceed" (Altheide and Snow 1979, 40). The selves presented in web pages adhere to this perspective in two respects. First, they adhere because they are evaluated and defined relative to their ability to live up to those norms. Second, they adhere because they recognize that it is the self (individualism) that is ultimately the party responsible. Long gone are the days of Homer, when motives and actions were attributed to the gods. Today the modern self recognizes that it is the ultimate source of social order. And the selves presented on these pages, though they may make mistakes from time to time, are ultimately true to the norms. Like the selves hypothesized by Romantics, these selves are inherently good.

As noted above, direct examination of presentation of self online is but one way to assess the importance and future of the self as an institution. But because the self is also implicated in other modern social institutions, reassessing the status of the nation-state, the corporation, the church, the university and the family from the perspective of the self can also reveal a surprising amount of information about the nature and importance of the self in contemporary society.

Turning first to an examination of institutions of the political order, it seems clear that the modern self is alive and well. Though the nation-state in general has been slower in its adoption of Net logic than the NGO, there is evidence to suggest that the "internal workings" of this institution are being altered to secure its continued significance, perhaps even dominance, of the political order. But more important than the fact of these alterations is the direction of their change. That is, the most successful nation-states are those that alter their internal structure and express their institutional mission in order to enhance the modern conception of self-as-citizen. In the most advanced cases, states succeed in their objective of becoming more relevant to the everyday lives of the individual and more meaningful as a source of identity by supporting community building, social integration and participation in the public political process. In other words, they promote nationalism. Each self is treated as a unique, inherently valuable entity whose inputs into the process of policy formation are welcome. They are accorded, if not new rights of participation, new means by which to exercise previously granted rights. And it is this very process of *reciprocal communication*, the fact that people view their selves as endowed with those rights of participation and the fact that they act toward the state as the "actor" obligated to fulfill those rights, that legitimates the modern self in the political order.

The rise of the NGO as a legitimate "actor" in the political order serves to underscore this definition of the modern self. The entire premise of the NGO is centered on the modern self in two interrelated ways. First, these organizations operate on the very modern premise that all humans have selves. These selves are equal and are endowed with fundamental rights and responsibilities. It is the task of the NGO to ensure that the modern self is protected against violations of those rights. Second, the structure of the NGO, its basis in voluntary, reciprocal and horizontal patterns of communication, rests on the modern sense of self. In order to accomplish its goal, the NGO affords selves a new identity—activist. Selves within the NGO are (or can at least define themselves as) more than mere "audience members" engaging in vicarious interaction. They are active participants in a cause. It may well be that this ability to provide a meaningful avenue for self-definition, through the use of Net logic, is the real "source of power" for the NGO. Through sophisticated use of Net grammar and the ideal-norms perspective, the NGO can successfully claim that "each of us can work to make a difference." The success of this claim rests upon two assumptions about the self that are commonly unexamined by postmodernists who argue that the self is dead. The phrase "each of us" implies simultaneously an individual self that is cognizant of its uniqueness and of its centrality to the moral order and a collective conscience (an "us") to which that self belongs. The NGO motto enables the self to accomplish what Hewitt (1984) stated it must—simultaneously *differentiate itself from* and *identify itself with* the collective.

The same argument for the relevance of the self can be made regarding the economic order. Weber's core attributes of "modern rational capitalism"—the existence of free, individual laborers who sell their services on an open market; an absence of status monopolies in production and consumption; the use of a technology organized on the basis of rational principles; and the detachment of production from the household—more accurately reflect the economic order now than they ever have. And the corporation remains the dominant institution operating therefrom. The distinguishing feature of the most successful corporations is that they celebrate the validity of the self via Net logic. It should come as no surprise that customization and community building are the two attributes vital to modern corporate success, as both strategies implicate the modern self at the core. Customization is the recognition of self as a unique, valuable entity. According to Net logic, the individual is no longer part of a "mass." He or she is a unique individual worthy of special attention and endowed with consumer rights. It is the attempt to achieve the first half of Hewitt's equation—differentiation from. Conversely, successful corporate attempts at fostering community online complete the second half of the equation—identification with. Online community is the recognition of self in the Romantic sense—the "real" self in relation to significant others. Online communities, like personal web pages, are designed such that the individual may present his true self and receive validation of that self from significant others.

While the modern self continues to be central to the political and economic orders, it is in the normative order that its presence is most profound. The contemporary religious organization, university and family form are all designed specifically to promote the self as the entity of ultimate worth. Modern religion, as a strategy for addressing the ultimate meaning of human existence, rests not on the eternal soul but on the reasoning, conscious self. In modern times selves are responsible for their own salvation. Long gone is Weber's idea of "predestination" or "calling," in which the individual's fate was determined by forces beyond his control. This is true regardless of whether the form in question is the church or the sect. The most successful religious sites are so because they use the logic of the Internet to promote individual worth and to tie that individual to the larger moral order in which he finds himself. On the most advanced online sites the worshiper and his or her personal problems are acknowledged. It is simultaneously made known to him that he is responsible for his own salvation, but that a community of like-minded selves stands behind him, ready to assist in any way they can.

For its part, the university has long assumed the self as a unique, reflexive entity to be celebrated, promoted and trained for the task of more fully understanding its position in, and importance to, the social order. The entire premise of higher education is the Enlightenment self. This is perhaps even more true of the idea of distance education in general, and the virtual university in particular. The virtual university, recognizing that modern selves play multiple roles, customizes the educational experience to fit the individual's pre-existing set of identities. The promise of the virtual university *is* the modern self—each individual is accorded the respect, rights and privileges that are the foundation of the modern world system. Again, the first element of the equation—differentiation of each self from the other—is fulfilled. Simultaneously, the virtual university promises a community of equal selves. It promises identification with a group of like-minded others, a means by which the self may be integrated into society and guaranteed the ability to live out what Meyer (1987) called the instituted "life course" so characteristic of the modern experience.

Finally, the most pressing social problem to be solved by the family—the satisfaction of emotional and identity-oriented needs of members—revolves around the modern sense of self. Family represents the arena in which the "disconnected" self, celebrated in other areas of life, can be "put back together." Further, the contemporary family structure embodies the modern sense of self in that all members are to be equally valued as unique identities. Husbands and wives are equal partners, and children are to be accorded all of the rights and privileges of that ever-so-modern portion of the instituted life course we call childhood. Accordingly, informational sites on "how to be a family" center on recognizing these basic facts—as do the "ideal type" presentations on family home pages. The "good" family is one that accommodates and celebrates the unique self inherent in all its members and provides an arena in which that real self may be fully expressed.

CONCLUDING COMMENTS: THE SELF AND VIRTUALITY

Anderson (1997) has argued that:

> Every civilization creates its own concept of the self. The modern self-concept defines each of us as an individual, with a distinct identity that remains the same wherever one goes. This idea served its purpose reasonably well, but it rapidly erodes in the postmodern world as different aspects of it are undermined by different currents of thought and action... Anthropologists, historians, artists, and postmodern philosophers keep telling us that the self is constructed—assembled and reassembled in different ways by individuals and societies. The information/communications revolution creates a vast and mysterious electronic landscape of new relationships, roles, identities, networks, and communities, while it undermines that cherished luxury of the modern self–privacy. The globalization of economics and politics sends people scurrying about the planet; pulling up roots; trampling boundaries; letting go of old certainties of place, nationality, social role, and class [xiii–xiv].

As a representation of the general postmodernist assessment, this suggestion that the self is no longer viable is erroneous for at least three reasons. First, it cannot refute Mead's explanation of the self as a linguistic construct. The self is, at base, the ability to take oneself as object. This reflexive ability has existed since the dawn of spoken language, and philosophers of the self (as noted in the opening segment of this chapter) have long argued that the self is a social construction. They may not have used that exact term, but the idea that the self is continually recreated is not a distinctly "postmodern" argument. The self is and has always been possible only in society, only through language. As such, it will continue to exist so long as language exists. The fact that the process by which the self occurs has only been (relatively) recently explicated does not mean that it is only recently true.

Second, the modern self was never defined strictly as a "distinct identity that remains the same wherever one goes." This is true for two reasons. First, the modern world, in contrast to the Medieval world, has supported a number of definitions of the self, most prominently the Enlightenment and Romantic selves. It has encompassed the self as "center of the knowable world," the self as citizen, the self as "inner life," the self as responsible for its own salvation, the self as a continuously renewed reappropriation of experience, the self as a "bundle of perceptions," the "true self" and the "looking glass" self, to name but a few. The core meaning of the modern self, as Meyer (1987, 242–260) noted, is the individual as *fundamental unit* of social organization, as decision-maker. From this foundation one could conceivably build up any of the above arguments about what the self "really is," including that it is "a distinct identity that remains the same wherever one goes." But none of those arguments deviate from the assumption that the individual is the locus of social order. None of those arguments suggest, for example, that the family, the clan, the tribe or the gods are the fundamental unit of social organization.

Further, that particular definition of the self confuses the notion of self with that of identity. As Stone (1975) noted, these two terms are not interchangeable. To have an identity is to be situated within a particular social framework. Modernity consists of the transition from gemeinschaft to gesellschaft, from Durkheim's "mechanical solidarity" to "organic solidarity." This transition is constituted by and constitutive of the modern self as it assumes the individual as the fundamental unit of organization. It is a transition that demands that individuals interact in an increasing number and variety of social situations, each of which necessitates the creation of a particular situated identity. The self is the collection of those identities, not one in particular.

Finally, theorists of the self seem to have a habit of defining the "modern self" in any manner that suits their purposes. At times they emphasize the Enlightenment self. At other times they emphasize the Romantic self. Careful examination reveals that the postmodern argument is ultimately an attack on the perceived loss of the Romantic self. Some have claimed that the recognition of this loss may be found in Riesman's (1955) argument that "modern man" was inner-directed, while "postmodern man" is other-directed. According to this typification, the "inner-directed" person has an "inner source of direction," one that he or she acquired early in life from elders and that directs that individual toward "destined" goals. The rules set by parents (and other authority figures) controlled this individual's behavior and guided him or her along the right path, regardless of the temptations found in the external environment. This "inner directed" person represents the Romantic self in that it assumes each individual to be a unique life, the truth of which may be discovered by following one's inner guide. The "other-directed" individual lacks this internal compass. His or her actions are guided by immediate social surroundings, as he or she "submits to the power of the group" because of an insatiable need for approval by others. He or she is part of the mass of conformists.

The "other directed" individual is one that operates within Gergen's (1991) state of social saturation, a situation in which "…the coherent circles of accord are demolished, and all beliefs thrown into question by one's exposure to multiple points of view" (xi). Generally speaking, this is the postmodern world, in which the "real self" is overrun by technologies, particularly media, that are argued to present so many "incoherent and unrelated languages of the self," so many "mysterious new relationships, roles, identities, networks and communities" that the self is undermined and becomes no self at all (Gergen 1991, 6–7). I argue that this juxtaposition is erroneous on both theoretical and empirical grounds. Theoretically, the distinction posited between "modern" and "postmodern" self is untenable because the only real distinction is who comprises the group within which the individual builds his sense of self and to which he chooses to conform. The self as a social object, as created through the social process of language, by definition means that the self is "other directed." The only question is, who comprises the other? Is it parents? Peer groups? The "nation"? Friends in online chat rooms? There can be no "inner directed" self, no self abstracted from or outside of society.

Empirically, the preliminary evidence from this research indicates that nothing could be further from the truth. Consider the direct evidence of the self available on personal home pages. Taken together, the autobiographical form, the journal, the photographic archiving of the self in myriad meaningful contexts, links to "cool stuff," and musical and graphical selections combine with an organization, vocabulary and ideal norms perspective to present the most complete picture possible of whom one really is. Recognizing that they are picking and choosing from potentially limitless numbers of "vocabularies of the self," which may or may not emphasize place, social role, nationality or class, people still select and integrate those that they feel are representative. The selves presented online are in no way fragmented, "multi phrenic," or dis-integrated. And they certainly do not reflect an "absence of self." To the contrary, they are the epitomes of the Romantic self, and are, perhaps, the most complete conceptualizations of "true self" anyone has yet been able to devise and present.

Now consider the role of the self as presented in other institutional frameworks in light of media logic. From their inception, these problem-solving strategies revolved around the idea of the individual as the fundamental unit of social organization, and this continues to be true. In every instance examined during the course of this research, defining Western institutions continue to elevate the status of the self in the social order. In adopting the logic of the Internet, institutions serve to strengthen Simmel's (1903) definition of the modern self. For Simmel, the modern self consists *simultaneously* of two opposed yet interconnected *forms of individuality*. The first form is that which we commonly term the Enlightenment self. Invented during the Renaissance, this form consisted of

> ...a state of inner and external liberation of the individual from the communal forms of the Middle Ages, forms which had constricted the pattern of his life, his activities, and his fundamental impulses through homogenizing groups. These had, as it were, allowed the boundaries of the individual to become blurred, suppressing the development of personal freedom, of intrinsic uniqueness, and of the sense of responsibility for one's self....
>
> The individualism that sought its realization in this way was based on the notion of the natural equality of individuals, on the conception that all the restrictions just mentioned were artificially produced inequalities and that once these had been banished along with their historical fortuitousness, their injustice, and their burdensomeness, perfected man would emerge. And since he was perfect, perfect in morality, in beauty, and in happiness, he could show no differences. This is why it is man in general, universal man, who occupies the center of interest for this period instead of historically given, particular, and differentiated man. The latter is in principle reduced to the former; in each individual person, man in general lives as his essence... [217–219].

It is this form of the self that makes possible what Hewitt termed "identification with" the generalized other. In Mead's terms, it is the "me" process within the self, the self that takes itself as object and defines itself, or establishes a situated identity, in terms of the generalized other. Simmel's second form of individuality is that which we commonly term the Romantic self today. Simmel suggests that, once the Enlightenment self had firmly established itself as the fundamental unit of social order, once it was sufficiently strong as a concept based on equality and universality, the self

> ...once again sought inequality—but this time an inequality determined only from within. After the individual had been liberated in principle from the rusty chains of guild, hereditary status, and church, the quest for independence continued to the point where individuals who had been rendered independent in this way wanted also to distinguish themselves from *one another* [emphasis added]. What mattered now was no longer that one was a free individual as such, but that one was a particular and irreplaceable individual [222].
>
> ...This ideal image of individualism seems to have nothing at all to do with the earlier notion of "the generally human," with the idea of a uniform human nature that is present in everyone and that only requires freedom for its emergence. Indeed, the second meaning fundamentally contradicts the first. In the first, the value emphasis is on what men have in common; in the second, it is on what separates them [272].

This is the Romantic self, Mead's "I," that part of the self that is unpredictable, given to spontaneity, and the locus of social change. It is the part that declares itself in opposition to society as a unique entity. Though these two aspects of the modern self have often been cast in opposition to one another, Simmel suggests that they are two sides of the same coin. They are interconnected because one cannot be declared without acknowledging the other and because both arise from the "enlargement of the social circle" that occurs when the dominant mode of social organization shifts from mechanical to organic solidarity. Both of these forms of self require a generalized other of considerable size and complexity in order to survive:

> ...As that circle enlarges, so too do the possibilities of developing our inner lives; as its cultural offerings increase, regardless of how objective or abstract they may be, so too do the chances of developing the distinctiveness, the uniqueness, the sufficiency of existence of our inner lives and their intellectual, aesthetic, and practical productivity.
>
> In the fundamental antithesis of these two forms of individualism, there is one point at which they coincide: each of them has a potential for development to the degree that quantitative expansion of the circle that encloses the individual provides the necessary room, impetus, and material [273–274].

This "quantitative expansion of the social circle" is made possible by media. As Altheide (1984) has noted,

> The mass media, as distinctively public phenomena, have implications for, and can directly affect, individuals by adding a dimension of anticipation, focus, and reflection to their conception of self... When we are presented with someone's interpretation and presentation of who we are, what we stand for—in short, with an assertion of some characterological and status-related statement of our self—then self can become problematic, and the raising of self to consciousness is one consequence of media presentations [193].

In this regard, the Internet is no different from so-called mass media. The sense of self is heightened because it is given more possibilities for presentation to others and for situated identities in a variety of social interactions. In contemporary society media serve Hewitt's dual purpose of "differentiation from" and "identification with." The fact that there are more options from which to choose, that the self is a work-in-progress, does not mean it is "decentered" or experienced as "fragmented" or "incomplete." Quite the contrary. It is the fact of its tenuousness that makes it central to modern life. A self's work is never done.

Further, the selves constructed through media are no less integrated than those constructed in face to face interaction. These selves are highly modern in that they represent the necessary unification of Simmel's two forms of individuality, Enlightenment and Romantic. It is because of modern media, not despite them, that the self is more central to the social order than ever before. As Snow (1983) noted, it is because modern media combine the "connotation of rationality" (Enlightenment self) with the legitimated expression of "affective mood response" (Romantic self) that media are accepted as legitimate means by which the social world may be understood.

Alford (1991) has commented, and I agree, that,

> Authors praise the self, blame the self, deconstruct the self, and say it isn't there. The self is the locus of all value, the source of a rapacious individualism that is destroying Western society, and little more than the mirror of its culture. All this and more has been claimed about the self in recent works. Yet few who have claimed any of these things have made a systematic study of the entity they are writing about.
>
> ...One reason academic accounts of the self are frequently so removed from common experience is that the academic is not really concerned with understanding or explaining the self at all. He or she is instead concerned with explaining something else—for example, social inequality. The concept of the self adopted by the academic is chosen strictly with this goal in mind: not what concept best captures the manifold experiences of the self but what concept best allows us to predict or derive something else, perhaps an esteemed value such as community [vii, 12].

Perhaps more so than with any other institution, observers have presumed to understand the implications of media for the self without any empirical investigation. Arguments about media and the self, rather than attempting to investigate what is actually going on, instead offer angst-ridden moral warnings about the impending demise of the self. This is an unfortunate situation because the proliferation of media, the Internet included, does have important implications for the instituted self. With media serving as the strategy by which members of contemporary society construct reality and sustain the collective conscience, it only stands to reason that the nature of social institutions, including the self, will be affected according to the logic by which those media operate. Toss in a new medium, the Internet, and the picture grows even more complex. Combine this with the fact that the modern instituted self is the foundation for so many taken-for-granted assumptions about the nature of that reality, and we have a very muddy picture indeed. Rather than predictions of the imminent demise of the self that fly in the face of ordinary experience, what is needed is empirical research into how Net logic affects the construction of the self. Because other institutions appear to be facing new challenges to their external significance due to the Internet, we might begin with the assumption that the modern self, as the underlying premise of those institutions, faces challenges as well. Suggestions for such research into what those challenges might be include:

1. How "fragmented and unrelated" are the many vocabularies of the self made available via the Internet? That is, to what degree do they deviate from the ideal-norms perspective at the foundation of the social order?

2. Because people behave as if they have selves in the modern sense, they would have to willingly give up their this idea of the self in order for that institution to dissolve. How likely is this?

3. What does the use of the Net to promote the Romantic self portend for this institution? Do the logics of real time chat rooms, discussion forums and home pages imply anything about future evolution along these lines, or about the status of the Enlightenment self?

4. What does the entertainment perspective, as employed in this interaction medium, mean for the future of the self?

5. Based upon research conducted regarding the political order, it seems plausible that the identity of citizen, so integral to the origination of the modern self, is transforming to one of "customer." Is this true? If so, what are the meaningful differences, if any, between these two identities, and what do they mean for the future of the self?

6. It seems that all major forms of interaction (hierarchy, network and market) have their basis in the modern self. If this is the case, what would be the significance of a transition from one form to the other in the political and economic orders, a transition that "strong globalization" theorists argue is so vital to success?

7. What can research into the questions posed regarding the economic and normative orders in chapters four and five tell us about the future of the self? What is the significance, if any, of the changing identity of "customer," "employee," "student," "churchgoer" and "family member" for the institution of the self?

CHAPTER SEVEN

Virtualization and Net Logic: Concluding Remarks

The social history of media is one of so-called "effects." Perhaps more so than any other category of technology, media have been imbued with an autonomy, an agency, that has served to obfuscate their true role in contemporary society. Media in contemporary society are not autonomous agents of social change. Far from it. Media are social institutions. They offer a framework, or lens, through which people interpret the world around them. And, like all institutions, they operate according to a specific logic. "As logic they [media] involve an implicit trust that we can communicate the events of our daily lives through the various formats of media. People take for granted that information can be transmitted, ideas presented, moods of joy and sadness expressed, major decisions made, and business conducted through media... In contemporary society, the logic of media provides the form for shared 'normalized' social life" (Altheide and Snow 1979, 9, 12). Media logic as a form of communication provides for the sustenance of the collective conscience by offering up interpretations of reality and conceptualizations of the generalized other that achieve frame resonance within a broader cultural framework of ideal-norms. Media are strategies for maintaining social order.

As such, if media can be argued to have an "effect," it is not because they are *agents* of change, as all technologies, media included, are expressions of cultural preferences, value systems, beliefs and social norms. Rather, it is because of the logic underlying the interpretations of reality and conceptualizations of the generalized other that they provide. The logic of contemporary media revolves around a modern world view—a rational/practical/scientific framework—that demands the rapid dissemination of accurate, current and dependable information. In the resulting media culture, space, time, physical and geographical place, the physical body and

216

co-presence are rendered irrelevant to the production of reality. The adoption of such a logic to interpret the social world results in the virtualization of that world. Events and ideas experienced through media are real in effect. That is, the individual need not experience this world directly in order to form impressions, make judgments or *act toward* it. With their connotation of rationality, media present a world that is real enough.

To the extent that the Internet can be declared "revolutionary," it is because it alone operates according to a many-to-many (one-to-one) communications logic. Returning for a moment to the argument of Durkheim (1893), modern society is characterized by increases in dynamic density, material density and volume, coupled with the rise of restitutive law. Attempts to understand the implications of the Net for social institutions have placed too much emphasis on purported increases in dynamic density (the *rate of communication* [speed/efficiency] between members of society) and volume (the geographical space or physical boundaries of a society). Changes in material density, the number of individuals in contact with one another (many-to-many), have been either ignored or misunderstood. This oversight prevents a better understanding of the implications of the Internet for the social order because, in media culture, the institutional strategies for maintaining that order operate according to the logic of the dominant medium. In its purported effects on dynamic density and volume, the Internet is no different than other media. As noted in Chapter One, all media have been described as "revolutionary technologies that annihilate time (dynamic density) and space (volume)." When observers have attempted to account for the effects of the Internet on material density, they have perhaps erroneously assumed that this many-to-many framework demands conversion to the network as a social form.

However, evidence from this preliminary research indicates otherwise. To successfully adopt the logic of the Internet does not necessarily demand that the "physical manifestation" of an institution adopt the network form. That is, the many-to-many communication pattern central to Net logic is not synonymous with the "voluntary, reciprocal and horizontal" communication pattern of the network form. Further, the many-to-many pattern does not demand that the communications therein rest on shared beliefs and values. As evidenced throughout this work, the continued success of core social institutions depends not so much on the adoption of the network form as it does on the adoption of a general set of norms of Net logic.

This set of norms, this logic, consists of a general set of grammatical rules coupled with an ideal-norms/entertainment perspective for interpreting social reality. In general, the grammar of the Net includes a syntax that is both centralized in its organization and current (immediate) in its scheduling of information. This syntax conforms to the "connotation of rationality"—the means-ends approach to communication—characteristic of other media. The most successful organizations are those that, though they may be hyper-textually linked to other organizations, serve as *the source*, as the central location, for current information about a particular topic. While links to other organizations assist in the development of an integrated frame of a topic, they are not mandatory for success.

Further, the inflection (rhythm and tempo) of Net grammar is dominated by interaction revolving around visual information. This visual information can include video, photography and the "official-looking" layout of text; and the interaction around it may involve both interaction with other individuals and interaction with the information itself, made possible by the "mouse." The most successful organizations are those that make use of as many of these formats (visual and interaction) as possible, simultaneously providing both a customized experience and a sense of community for the individual.

Finally, the general vocabulary of the Net finds its common denominator in its focus on the modern self. In the political order the vocabulary is that of the self as citizen, as "person with rights." In the economic order this vocabulary manifests itself in terms of self as customer, as "unique, ideal self." In the normative order the vocabulary couches the self in the classic Romantic terms. In every arena actors employ the jargon of Modernity to make sense of their selves and of the world around them. And while the "physical extensions" of the core institutions of Modernity face new challenges brought about by the many-to-many logic of the Internet, the underlying tenets of Modernity—the "psychic phenomena" upon which those institutions are based—are still firmly in place.

This is, perhaps, the most striking conclusion evidenced by this preliminary research. With its capacity for an infinite array of many-to-many interactions, the Internet seems to have an enormous potential to further problematize the construction of meaning, particularly overarching meaning on any scale other than one-to-one. Because the self is also a meaning constructed in interaction, virtualization via the Net expands the situational possibilities through which identity may be legitimately constructed, thus further problematizing the self. As a result, defining the self and the generalized other in a meaningful way becomes one of the key problems of social order in the highly modern world. Yet, despite the enormous potential for social change brought about by the logic of the Internet, individuals persist in upholding the Modern world view in the process of reality construction. As Mead (1964) noted:

> ...Whenever the community is disturbed, we always find this return to the fixed order which is there and which we do not want to have shaken. It is

entirely natural and, in a certain sense, entirely justifiable. We have to have an order of society; and, when what is taking place shakes that order, we have no evidence that we will get another order to take the place of the present one. We cannot afford to let that order to go pieces. We must have it as a basis for our conduct [20].

Accounting for this remarkable stability of the social order in the face of countless claims of "revolution" has been the defining aim of this book. If one were to take at face value the observations made by pundits and based on speculation—the nation-state is dead, the bureaucratic corporation is no longer, the self is non-existent—one would expect to see a society in chaos. This is clearly not the case. The core institutions of the modern political, economic and normative orders are alive and well. And the only way to account for this disparity between theory and the lived world is to acknowledge that the "media effects" framework for understanding the relationship between technology and the social order is fundamentally flawed. With its focus on the "physical extensions" of technology, the media effects framework imbues the technology itself with agency. In the case of the Internet, the focus is on the physical network of computers itself, rather than on the logic by which it operates. This focus on the physical network has resulted in "place based" research methods in which the spatial arrangements and physical features of the network are seen as causative factors of social change. At the micro level of analysis, this assumption manifests itself in research into and theorizing about the nature of "real community." At the macro level, it manifests itself in theorizing about the "network" as a social form.

Left unexamined is the Internet as a strategy for ordering social reality—the Internet as a psychic phenomenon. Unless and until researchers understand the Net as an institution in this regard, we will remain unable to recognize the most important role of all media in contemporary society and thus be unable to answer the ultimate sociological question: How is social order possible?

Bibliography

Albrow, Martin. *The Global Age: State and Society Beyond Modernity*. Stanford, CA: Stanford University Press, 1997.

Alford, C. Fred. *The Self in Social Theory*. New Haven, CT: Yale University Press, 1991.

Altheide, David L. "The Media Self." In *The Existential Self in Society*, ed. Joseph A. Kotarba and Andrea Fontana, 177–195. Chicago: University of Chicago Press, 1984.

_____, and Robert P. Snow. *Media Logic*. Beverly Hills, CA: Sage Publications, 1979.

Anderson, Benedict. *Imagined Communities: Reflections on the Origin and Spread of Nationalism*. London: Verso, 1983.

Anderson, J. A., and T. P. Meyer. *Mediated Communication: A Social Action Perspective*. Newbury Park, CA: Sage Publications, 1988.

Anderson, James, and Liam O'Dowd. "Borders, Border Regions and Territoriality: Contradictory Meanings, Changing Significance." *Regional Studies* 33 (October 1999): 593–604.

Anderson, Walter Truett. *The Future of the Self: Inventing the Postmodern Person*. New York: Penguin Putnam, 1997.

Anzinger, Gunnar. *Worldwide Governments on the World Wide Web*. Electronically available at: *http://www.gksoft.com/govt/en/world.html* 12/30/99 version.

Armstrong, John A. *Nations Before Nationalism*. Chapel Hill, NC: University of North Carolina Press, 1982.

Aron, Raymond. *Main Currents in Sociological Thought II: Durkheim, Pareto and Weber*. Translated by Richard Howard and Helen Weaver. Garden City, NY: Doubleday, 1970.

Becher, Klaus. "Changing Information Requirements in Foreign-Policy Institutions." In *The European Information Network on International Relations and Area Studies 8th Annual Conference Held in Barcelona 2–3 October 1998*, electronically available at: *http://www.cidob.org/einiras/presentations/becher.htm*.

Beck, Ulrich. "Beyond the Nation State." *New Statesman* 12 (December 6, 1999): 25–27.

Becker, Ernest. *The Birth and Death of Meaning*. New York: The Free Press, 1962.

Becker, Howard. "The Quest for Secular Salvation: Social Reform in Relation to the Sociological Impulse." *In Social Thought from Lore to Science,* ed. Howard Becker and Harry Elmer Barnes. 595–98. New York, NY: Dover Publications, 1961.

_____, and Harry Elmer Barnes. *Social Thought from Lore to Science: Volume Two,* 3rd ed. New York: Dover Publications, 1961.

Bell, Colin, and Howard Newby, eds. *The Sociology of Community: A Selection of Readings.* London: Frank Cass, 1974.

Beniger, James R. *The Control Revolution: Technological and Economic Origins of the Information Society.* Cambridge, MA: Harvard University Press, 1986.

Beshers, James M. *Urban Social Structure.* Westport, CT: Greenwood Press, 1981.

Bierstedt, Robert. *The Social Order.* New York: McGraw-Hill Book Company, 1970.

Blumer, Herbert. *Symbolic Interactionism.* Englewood Cliffs, NJ: Prentice-Hall, 1969.

_____. "Industrialization and the Traditional Order." In *From Farm to Factory: The Development of Modern Society,* ed. Paul Mott and Howard M. Kaplan et al. Columbus, OH: Charles Merrill, 1973.

Brecher, Jeremy, John Brown Childs and Jill Cutler, eds. *Global Visions: Beyond the New World Order.* Boston: South End Press, 1993.

Brenner, Neil. "Globalization as Reterritorialization: The Re-Scaling of Urban Governance in the European Union." *Urban Studies* 36 (March 1999): 431–451.

Brissett, Dennis, and Charles Edgley, eds. *Life as Theater: A Dramaturgical Sourcebook.* Chicago: Aldine Publishing, 1975.

Burgess, Ernest W., ed. *The Urban Community.* Chicago: University of Chicago Press, 1926.

Buruma, Ian. "China in Cyberspace." *The New York Review of Books,* 4 November 1999, 9–12.

Byrnes, Nanette, and Paul C. Judge. "Internet Anxiety." *BusinessWeek,* 28 June 1999, 78.

Cairncross, Frances. *The Death of Distance: How the Communications Revolution Will Change our Lives.* Boston: Harvard Business School Press, 1997.

Cappetti, Carla. *Writing Chicago: Modernism, Ethnography and the Novel.* New York: Columbia University Press, 1993.

Castells, Manuel. *The Rise of the Network Society.* Cambridge, MA: Blackwell Publishers, 1996.

_____. *The Power of Identity.* Malden, MA: Blackwell Publishers, 1997.

Ceglowski, Janet. "Has Globalization Created a Borderless World?" In *Business Review,* Federal Reserve Bank of Philadelphia, March/April 1998, 17–27.

Charon, Joel M. *The Meaning of Sociology.* Englewood Cliffs, NJ: Prentice Hall, 1993.

Church, Sue. "Expatriate Keeps in Touch Via the Web." *CMC Magazine,* August 1996, electronically available at: *http://www.december.com/cmc/mag/1996/aug/church.html.*

Collins, Randall. *Theoretical Sociology.* Chicago: Harcourt, Brace Jovanovich, Publishers, 1988.

Cooley, Charles Horton. *Human Nature and the Social Order.* New York: Charles Scribner & Sons, 1902.

_____. *Social Organization: A Study of the Larger Mind*. New York: Charles Scribner & Sons, 1909.

Coser, Lewis. *Masters of Sociological Thought: Ideas in Historical and Social Context*. Chicago: Harcourt, Brace Jovanovich, 1977.

_____, ed. *The Pleasures of Sociology*. New York: Mentor Books, 1980.

Csikszentmihalyi, Mihaly. *Flow: The Psychology of Optimal Experience*. New York: Harper and Row, 1990.

Czitrom, Daniel J. *Media and the American Mind: From Morse to McLuhan*. Chapel Hill, NC: University of North Carolina Press, 1982.

Danitz, Tiffany, and Warren P. Strobel. "Networking Dissent: Cyber-Activists Use the Internet to Promote Democracy in Burma." In *Virtual Diplomacy Project*, November 8, 1999, by the U.S. Institute of Peace (*http://www.usip.org/oc/vd/vdr/vburma_intro.html*).

Davis, Denis K., and Stanley J. Baran. *Mass Communications and Everyday Life: A Perspective on Theory and Effects*. Belmont, CA: Wadsworth, 1981.

DeFleur, Melvin L., and Sandra Ball-Rokeach. *Theories of Mass Communication*. New York: Longman, 1989.

Deibert, Ronald J. *Parchment, Printing and Hypermedia: Communication in World Order Transformation*. New York, NY: Columbia University Press, 1997.

Dertouzos, Michael. *What Will Be: How the New World of Information Will Change Our Lives*. London: Piatkus, 1997.

de Sola Pool, Ithiel. *Technologies Without Boundaries: On Telecommunications in the Global Age*. Cambridge, MA: Harvard University Press, 1990.

Douglas, George H. *The Early Days of Radio Broadcasting*. Jefferson, NC: McFarland, 1987.

Durkheim, Emile. *The Division of Labor in Society*. 1893; reprint, New York: Free Press, 1964.

East Timor Action Network. *U.S. Policy Toward East Timor* and *Press Release: Senate Passes Appropriations Bill Restricting U.S. Military Assistance to Indonesia*. Electronically available at: *http://www.etan.org*, 1999.

Ebo, Bosah. *Cyberghetto or Cybertopia? Race, Class and Gender on the Internet*. New York: Praeger Press, 1998.

Ellul, Jacques. "Preconceived Ideas About Mediated Information." In *Taking Sides: Clashing Views on Controversial Issues in Mass Media and Society*, eds. J. Hanson and A. Alexander, 344–54. Guilford, CN: Dushkin, 1991.

Erickson, Hal. *Religious Radio and Television in the United States, 1921–1991: The Programs and Personalities*. Jefferson, NC: McFarland, 1992.

Falk, Richard. "The Making of Global Citizenship." In Jeremy Brecher et al. *Global Visions: Beyond the New World Order*. Boston: South End Press, 1993.

Ferguson, John. *The Open University from Within*. New York: New York University Press, 1976.

Fisher, David E., and Marshall Jon Fisher. *Tube: The Invention of Television*. New York: Harcourt Brace and Company, 1996.

Flanagan, William G. *Contemporary Urban Sociology*. New York, NY: Cambridge University Press, 1993.

Frankl, Razelle. *Televangelism: The Marketing of Popular Religion*. Carbondale, IL: Southern Illinois University Press, 1987.

Free Burma Coalition. *http://www.freeburmacoalition.org*, 1999.

Gergen, Kenneth. *The Saturated Self: Dilemmas of Identity in Contemporary Life.* New York: Basic Books, 1991.

Gibson, William. *Neuromancer.* New York: Ace Science Fiction Books, 1984.

Giddens, Anthony. *Capitalism and Modern Social Theory: An Analysis of the Writings of Marx, Durkheim and Max Weber.* Cambridge, MA: Cambridge University Press, 1971.

_____. *The Consequences of Modernity.* Stanford, CA: Stanford University Press, 1990.

Goffman, Erving. *The Presentation of Self in Everyday Life.* New York: Doubleday, 1959.

Goldberg, Steven E., and Charles R. Strain, eds. *Technological Change and the Transformation of America.* Carbondale: Southern Illinois University Press, 1987.

Gordon, George N. *The Communications Revolution: A History of Mass Media in the United States.* New York: Hastings House, 1977.

Graham, Gordon. "Power to the Logged-On People." *New Statesman* 12 (November 1999): R4-R5.

Greer, Scott. *The Emerging City: Myth and Reality.* New York: The Free Press, 1962.

Guehenno, Jean-Marie. *The End of the Nation-State.* Translated by Victoria Elliott. Minneapolis: The University of Minnesota Press, 1995.

Harasim, Linda M., ed. *Global Networks: Computers and International Communication.* Cambridge, MA: MIT Press, 1993.

Harvey, David. *The Urbanization of Capital: Studies in the History and Theory of Capitalist Urbanization.* Baltimore, MD: Johns Hopkins University Press, 1985.

Hastings, Adrian. *The Construction of Nationhood: Ethnicity, Religion and Nationalism.* New York: Cambridge University Press, 1997.

Hendry, John. "Cultural Theory and Contemporary Management Organization." *Human Relations* 52 (May 1999): 557–577.

Henslin, James M. *Sociology: A Down-to-Earth Approach,* 2nd ed. Boston: Allyn and Bacon, 1995.

Hertzler, Joyce O. *Social Institutions.* New York: McGraw-Hill, 1929.

Hewitt, John P. *Self and Society: A Symbolic Interactionist Social Psychology.* Boston: Allyn and Bacon, 1984.

Hiltz, Starr R., and Murray Turoff. *The Network Nation: Human Communication via Computer.* Cambridge, MA: MIT Press, 1993.

Hobsbawm, Eric. *Nations and Nationalism Since 1780: Programme, Myth, Reality.* New York: Cambridge University Press, 1990.

_____. *The Age of Revolution.* New York: Vintage Books, 1996.

Holton, R. J. *Cities, Capitalism and Civilization.* Winchester, MA: Allen and Unwin, 1986.

Homans, George. *The Human Group.* New York: Harcourt Brace, 1950.

Hooper, Richard. "New Media in the OU: An International Perspective." In *The Open University Opens,* ed. Jeremy Tunstall, 178–183. Amherst: University of Massachusetts Press, 1974.

International Federation for East Timor. *IFET Statutes.* Electronically available at: *http://etan.org/ifet/statutes.html,* 1999.

Jones, Steven G., ed. *Virtual Culture: Identity and Communication in Cybersociety*. Beverly Hills, CA: Sage Publications, 1997.
_____. *CyberSociety 2.0: Revisiting Computer-Mediated Communication and Community*. Beverly Hills, CA: Sage Publications, 1998.
Karp, David A., Gregory P. Stone and William C. Yoels. *Being Urban: A Social-Psychological View of City Life*. Lexington, MA: D.C. Heath, 1977.
Katznelson, Ira. *Marxism and the City*. New York: Oxford University Press, 1993.
Kay, George F. *The Family in Transition: Its Past, Present and Future Patterns*. New York: John Wiley and Sons, 1972.
Keck, Margaret E., and Kathryn Sikkink. *Activists Across Borders: Advocacy Networks in International Politics*. Ithaca, NY: Cornell University Press, 1998.
Kiesler, Sara, Jane Siegal and Timothy W. McGuire. "Social Psychological Aspects of Computer Mediated Communication." 1984; reprint, *Computerization and Controversy: Value Conflicts and Social Choices,* eds. Charles Dunlop and Rob Kling, 330–49. San Diego, CA: Academic Press, 1991.
King, Anthony D. *Urbanism, Colonialism and the World Economy*. New York: Routledge, 1990.
_____. *Global Cities: Post-Imperialism and the Internationalization of London*. New York: Routledge, 1990.
Langer, Peter. "Sociology: Four Images of Organized Diversity." In *Cities of the Mind: Images and Themes of the City in the Social Sciences*, Lloyd Rodwin and Robert M. Hollister, eds., New York: Plenum Press, 1984.
Laver, Murray. *Computers and Social Change*. New York: Cambridge University Press, 1980.
Lavine, T. Z. *From Socrates to Sartre: The Philosophic Quest*. New York: Bantam Books, 1984.
Law, Sally Ann, and Brent Keltner. "Civic Networks: Social Benefits of Online Communities." In *Universal Access to E-Mail: Feasibility and Societal Implications*, ed. Robert H. Anderson and Tova K. Bikson, et al., 119–150. Santa Monica, CA: Rand, 1995.
Lawley, Elizabeth Lane. *The Sociology of Culture in Computer-Mediated Communication. http://www.well.com/user/hlr/vircom/index.html*, 1994.
Lebow, Irwin. *Information Highways and Byways: From the Telegraph to the 21st Century*. New York: Institute of Electrical and Electronics Engineers, 1995.
Levine, Donald N., ed. *Georg Simmel on Individuality and Social Forms*. Chicago: University of Chicago Press, 1971.
Loader, Brian D. *Cyberspace Divide: Equality, Agency and Policy in the Information Society*. New York: Routledge, 1998.
Lynd, Robert S., and Helen Merrell Lynd. *Middletown: A Study in Modern American Culture*. New York: Harvest Books, 1929.
Lyons, John O. *The Invention of the Self*. Carbondale: Southern Illinois University Press, 1978.
MacDonald, Dwight. "A Theory of Mass Culture." In *Mass Media and Mass Man*, ed. Alan Casty, 12–23. New York: Holt, Rinehart & Winston, 1968.
MacGibbon, Hamish. "The OU Publishing Operation." In *The Open University Opens*, ed. Jeremy Tunstall, 165–169. Amherst: University of Massachusetts Press, 1974.
Macionis, John J. *Sociology*. Englewood Cliffs, NJ: Prentice Hall, 1993.

Malone, Thomas W., and Robert J. Laubacher. "The Dawn of the E-Lance Economy." *Harvard Business Review* 76 (September/October 1998): 144–152.

Martindale, Don. *Institutions, Organizations and Mass Society*. Boston, MA: Houghton Mifflin, 1966.

Marx, Leo. "Does Improved Technology Mean Progress?" In *Technological Change and the Transformation of America*, Steven E. Goldberg and Charles R. Strain, eds., Carbondale: Southern Illinois University Press, 1987.

Matrix Information and Directory Services, Inc., *Internet Survey Reaches 56.2 Million Internet Host Level*. Electronically available at: www3.mids.org/press/amr199907.html, 1999.

Matthews, Diane. "The Origins of Distance Education and Its Uses in the United States." *T.H.E. Journal* 27 (September 1999): 54–67.

McCartney, Scott, and Joan Rigdon. "Society's Subcultures Meet by Modem." *Wall Street Journal*, 8 December 1994, p. B1.

McLuhan, Marshall, and Bruce R. Powers. *The Global Village: Transformations in World Life and Media in the 21st Century*. New York: Oxford University Press, 1989.

_____, and Quentin Fiore. *The Medium Is the Message: An Inventory of Effects*. New York: Random House, 1967.

McQuail, Denis. *Sociology of Mass Communications*. Harmondsworth, Middlesex: Penguin Books, 1972.

_____. *Communication*. New York: Longman, 1984.

_____. *Mass Communication Theory: An Introduction*. Thousand Oaks, CA: Sage Publications, 1994.

Mead, George Herbert. *Mind, Self and Society*. Chicago: University of Chicago Press, 1934.

_____. *On Social Psychology*. Edited and with an Introduction by Anselm Strauss. Chicago: University of Chicago Press, 1964.

Mellor, Roy E. H. *Nation, State and Territory: A Political Geography*. New York: Routledge, 1989.

Meyer, John W. "Self and Life Course: Institutionalization and its Effects." In *Institutional Structure: Constituting State, Society and the Individual*, George M. Thomas, John W. Meyer, et al. Newbury Park, CA: Sage Publications, 1987.

Moore, James F. "The New Corporate Form." In *Creating Wealth in the Era of E-Business*, ed. Don Tapscott, Alex Lowy and David Ticoll. New York: McGraw Hill, 1998, 77–95.

Morgenthau, Hans J., and Kenneth W. Thompson. *Politics Among Nations: The Struggle for Power and Peace*, 6th ed., New York: Alfred A. Knopf, 1985.

Mott, Paul E. and Howard M. Kaplan, et al., eds. *From Farm to Factory: The Development of Modern Society*. Columbus, OH: Charles E. Merrill Co., 1973.

Mowatt, Raoul V. "Web of Faith: Worshipers Worldwide Can Join in Services." *Chicago Tribune*, 24 March 2000, Section 2, p. 1

National Resource Council. Understanding the Digital Economy Conference, *Fostering Research on the Economic and Social Impacts of Information Technology: Report of a Workshop*. Washington, D.C: National Resource Council, 1998.

Nisbet, Robert. *The Sociological Tradition*. 1966; reprint, New Brunswick, NJ: Transaction, 1993.

NUA Internet Surveys. *NUA Analysis*. Electronically available at: *www.nua.ie/surveys/analysis/index.html*, 1999.

Nye, David E. *Narratives and Space: Technology and the Construction of American Culture*. New York: Columbia University Press, 1997.

Ogburn, William F. *On Culture and Social Change*. Chicago: University of Chicago Press, 1964.

Ohmae, Kenichi. *The End of the Nation-State: The Rise of Regional Economies*. New York: Free Press, 1995.

Oldenburg, Ray. *The Great Good Place: Cafes, Coffee Shops, Community Centers, Beauty Parlors, General Stores, Bars, Hangouts, and How They Get You Through the Day*. New York: Paragon House, 1991.

Park, Robert E. "The City: A Spatial Pattern and Moral Order." In *The Urban Community*, Ernest W. Burgess, ed., Chicago: University of Chicago Press, 1926.

_____. "Human Ecology," *American Journal of Sociology* 42 (1936), pp. 1–15.

_____. "Migration and the Marginal Man." In *The Pleasures of Sociology*, Lewis Coser, ed., 241–47. New York: Mentor Books, 1980.

Parsons, Talcott. *The Structure of Social Action, Volume I: Marshall, Pareto and Durkheim*. New York: The Free Press, 1968.

_____. *The Structure of Social Action, Volume II: Max Weber*. New York: The Free Press, 1968.

Peattie, Lisa Redfield, and Edward Robbins. "Anthropological Approaches to the City." In *Cities of the Mind: Images and Themes of the City in the Social Sciences*, Lloyd Rodwin and Robert M. Hollister, eds. New York: Plenum Press, 1984.

Perelman, Michael. *Class Warfare in the Information Age*. New York: St. Martins' Press, 1998.

Pfuhl, Erdwin, and Stuart Henry. *The Deviance Process*. New York: Aldine de Gruyter, 1993.

Poggi, Gianfranco. *The State: Its Nature, Development and Prospects*. Stanford, CA: Stanford University Press, 1990.

Redfield, Robert. *The Folk Culture of the Yucatan*. 1941; reprint, Chicago: University of Chicago Press, 1961.

_____. *Tepoztlan: A Mexican Village. A Study of Folk Life*. 1930; reprint, Chicago: University of Chicago Press, 1973.

Reiss, Albert J., ed. *Louis Wirth on Cities and Social Life*. 1938; reprint, Chicago: University of Chicago Press, 1964.

Reissman, Leonard. *The Urban Process: Cities in Industrial Society*. New York: The Free Press, 1970.

Rheingold, Howard. *The Virtual Community: Homesteading on the Electronic Frontier*. New York: HarperCollins, 1993.

Rhodes, Richard, ed. *Visions of Technology*. New York: Simon and Schuster, 1999.

Riesman, David. *The Lonely Crowd: A Study of the Changing American Character*. New York: Doubleday, 1955.

Ritzer, George. *Contemporary Sociological Theory*, 3rd ed. New York: McGraw-Hill, 1992.

Rodwin, Lloyd, and Robert M. Hollister, eds. *Cities of the Mind: Images and Themes of the City in the Social Sciences*. New York: Plenum Press, 1984.

Rosenberg, Bernard. "Mass Culture Revisited I." In *Mass Culture Revisited*, B. Rosenberg and D. M. White, eds., 3–12. New York: Van Nostrand Reinhold Company, 1971.

Rothkopf, David J. "Cyberpolitik: The Changing Nature of Power in the Information Age." *Journal of International Affairs* 51 (Spring 1998): 325–359.

Saunders, Peter. *Social Theory and the Urban Question*. New York: Holmer and Meier, 1981.

Savage, Mike and Alan Warde. *Urban Sociology, Capitalism and Modernity*. New York: Continuum, 1993.

Schon, Donald A., Bish Sanyal and William J. Mitchell, eds. *High Technology and Low-Income Communities: Prospects for the Positive Use of Advanced Information Technology*. Cambridge, MA: MIT Press, 1999.

Schultze, Quentin J., ed. *American Evangelicals and the Mass Media*. Grand Rapids, MI: Zondervan, 1990.

_____. *Televangelism and American Culture*. Grand Rapids, MI: Baker Book House, 1991.

Schulze, Hagen. *States, Nations and Nationalism: From the Middle Ages to the Present*. Malden, MA: Blackwell, 1996.

Seybold, Patricia. *Customers.com: How to Create a Profitable Business Strategy for the Internet and Beyond*. New York: Random House, 1998.

Simmel, Georg. *The Sociology of Georg Simmel*. Translated and with an Introduction by K. H. Wolff. New York: Free Press, 1950.

_____. "The Metropolis and Mental Life." In *Georg Simmel: On Individuality and Social Forms*, Edited and with an Introduction by Donald Levine. 1903; reprint, Chicago: University of Chicago Press, 1971.

_____. "Freedom and the Individual." In *Georg Simmel: On Individuality and Social Forms,* Edited and with an Introduction by Donald Levine. 1903; reprint, Chicago: University of Chicago Press, 1971.

Singer, Benjamin D. *Social Functions of the Telephone*. Palo Alto, CA: R and E Research Associates, 1981.

Sirjamaki, John. *The Sociology of Cities*. New York: Random House, 1964.

Sjoberg, Gideon. "The Preindustrial City." In *From Farm to Factory: The Development of Modern Society*, Paul Mott and Howard M. Kaplan et al., eds., 5–15. Columbus, OH: Charles E. Merrill, 1973.

Smith, Gordon. "A Future for the Nation-State?" In *The Nation-State: The Formation of Modern Politics*. Leonard Tivey, ed., 197–206. New York: St. Martin's, 1981.

Smith, Marc. "Voices from the WELL: The Logic of the Virtual Commons." Master's Thesis, Department of Sociology, UCLA, 1992.

Snow, Charles C., Raymond E. Miles and Henry J. Coleman, Jr. "Managing 21st Century Network Organizations." *Organizational Dynamics* 20 (Winter 1992): 5.

Snow, Robert P. *Creating Media Culture*. Beverly Hills: Sage Publications, 1983.

Standage, Tom. *The Victorian Internet*. New York: Walker, 1998.

Stearns, Peter N. *The Industrial Revolution in World History,* 2nd ed. Boulder, CO: Westview, 1998.

Stern, Ellen, and Emily Gwathmey. *Once Upon a Telephone: An Illustrated Social History*. New York: Harcourt Brace, 1994.

Stone, Allucquere Roseanne. "Will the Real Body Please Stand Up? Boundary Stories about Virtual Cultures." In *Cyberspace: First Steps*, ed. Michael Benedikt, 81–118. Cambridge, MA: MIT Press, 1991.

Stone, Gregory. "Appearance and the Self." In *Life as Theater: A Dramaturgical Sourcebook*. Dennis Brissett and Charles Edgley, eds., Chicago: Aldine, 1975.

_____, and Harvey Farberman. *Social Psychology Through Symbolic Interaction*. New York: Ginn-Blaisdell, 1970.

Swett, Charles. "Strategic Assessment: The Internet." By the U.S. Department of Defense, Office of the Assistant Secretary of Defense for Special Operations and Low-Intensity Conflict. Electronically available at: *http://www.fas.org/cp/swett.html*, 17 July 1995.

Szacki, Jerzy. *History of Sociological Thought*. Westport, CT: Greenwood Press, 1979.

Tapscott, Don. "E-Businesses Break the Mold." *InternetWeek*, 14 September 1998.

Thomas, George M., and John W. Meyer, et al. *Institutional Structure: Constituting State, Society, and the Individual*. Newbury Park, CA: Sage Publications, 1987.

Thomas, W. I. *The Polish Peasant in Europe and America*. Chicago: University of Chicago Press, 1918–1920.

Thompson, William E. and Joseph V. Hickey. *Society in Focus: An Introduction to Sociology*. New York: HarperCollins, 1994.

Tivey, Leonard, ed. *The Nation-State: The Formation of Modern Politics*. New York: St. Martin's, 1981.

Tonnies, Ferdinand. *Community and Society*. 1887; reprint, New York: Harper and Row, 1957.

Turner, Barry. *Industrialism*. New York: The Longman Group, 1975.

Turner, Jonathan. *The Structure of Sociological Theory*, 6th ed. Detroit: Wadsworth, 1998.

Van der Haag, Ernest. "Of Happiness and Despair We Have No Measure." In *Mass Media and Mass Man*, ed. Alan Casty, 5–11. New York: Holt, Rinehart & Winston, 1968.

Van Doren, Charles. *A History of Knowledge: The Pivotal Events, People, and Achievements of World History*. New York: Ballantine Books, 1991.

Wallerstein, Immanuel. *The Capitalist World-Economy*. New York: Cambridge University Press, 1979.

Walter, Andrew. "Do They Really Rule the World?" *New Political Economy*, 3 (July 1998): 288–292.

Weber, Max. *From Max Weber: Essays in Sociology*. Translated, edited and with an Introduction by H. H. Gerth and C. Wright Mills. New York: Oxford University Press, 1946.

_____. *The City*. Edited and with an Introduction by Don Martindale and Gertrud Neuwirth. New York, NY: Collier Books, 1958.

_____. *The Theory of Social and Economic Organization*. Edited and with an Introduction by Talcott Parsons. New York: Free Press, 1964.

Webster's New Universal Unabridged Dictionary, Deluxe Second Edition. New York: Simon and Schuster, 1983.

Wilder, Clinton. "E-Transformation." *InformationWeek*, 13 September 1999.

Winston, Brian D. *Media, Technology and Society, a History: From the Telegraph to the Internet.* New York: Routledge, 1998.

Wirth, Louis. "Urbanism as a Way of Life." In *Louis Wirth on Cities and Social Life,* ed. Albert J. Reiss, Jr., 1938; reprint, Chicago: University of Chicago Press, 1964.

Zeitlin, Irving M. *Ideology and the Development of Sociological Theory,* 4th ed. Englewood Cliffs, NJ: Prentice Hall, 1990.

Ziegler, Bart, and Jared Sandberg, "On-Line Snits Fomenting Public Storms," *Wall Street Journal,* 22 December 1994.

Index